Progress in IS

Progress in IS encompasses the various areas of Information Systems in theory and practice, presenting cutting-edge advances in the field. It is aimed especially at researchers, doctoral students, and advanced practitioners. The series features both research monographs, edited volumes, and conference proceedings that make substantial contributions to our state of knowledge and handbooks and other edited volumes, in which a team of experts is organized by one or more leading authorities to write individual chapters on various aspects of the topic. Individual volumes in this series are supported by a minimum of two external reviews.

The Series is SCOPUS-indexed.

Dilli Prasad Sharma • Arash Habibi Lashkari •
Mahdi Daghmehchi Firoozjaei •
Samaneh Mahdavifar • Pulei Xiong

Understanding AI in Cybersecurity and Secure AI

Challenges, Strategies and Trends

Springer

Dilli Prasad Sharma
University of Toronto
Toronto, ON, Canada

Arash Habibi Lashkari
York University
Toronto, ON, Canada

Mahdi Daghmehchi Firoozjaei
MacEwan University
Edmonton, AB, Canada

Samaneh Mahdavifar
McGill University
Montreal, Canada

Pulei Xiong
National Research Council of Canada
Ottawa, ON, Canada

ISSN 2196-8705 ISSN 2196-8713 (electronic)
Progress in IS
ISBN 978-3-031-91526-0 ISBN 978-3-031-91524-6 (eBook)
https://doi.org/10.1007/978-3-031-91524-6

This Springer imprint is published by the registered company Springer Nature Switzerland AG
The registered company address is: Gewerbestrasse 11, 6330 Cham, Switzerland

Preface

As part of the Understanding Cybersecurity Series (UCS) knowledge mobilization program, this book explores AI for security and secure AI, covering major vulnerabilities, attack vectors, and security solutions to protect AI systems, making it an essential resource for researchers, industry professionals, and security practitioners.

In 2020, the first team released the initial online article series, *Understanding Canadian Cybersecurity Laws*, which received recognition and was awarded the Gold Medal for Best Blog Column in the Business Division at the 2020 Canadian Online Publishing Awards. Building on this success, the team published the first book, *Understanding Cybersecurity Law and Digital Privacy: A Common Law Perspective*, in 2021 through Springer Nature Switzerland AG.

Continuing the research efforts, the second team launched the second article series in 2021, titled *Understanding Cybersecurity Management for FinTech* (*UCMF*), accompanied by the publication of the related book *Understanding Cybersecurity Management in FinTech: Challenges, Strategies, and Trends*. This book highlights the significance of cybersecurity in financial institutions by showcasing recent cyber breaches, attacks, and financial losses.

Starting in 2022, the third UCS team embarked on the third online series, *Understanding Current Cybersecurity Challenges in Law*, addressing emerging trends and critical legal issues concerning cybersecurity globally. This series, consisting of six parts, explores digital jurisdictional authority and user-generated digital content ownership. The series is complemented by the publication of the third book, *Understanding Cybersecurity Law in Data Sovereignty and Digital Governance: An Overview from a Legal Perspective*, which offers an in-depth understanding of current cybersecurity challenges and their legal implications. Simultaneously, another team also worked on the fourth book, *Understanding Cybersecurity Management in Decentralized Finance: Challenges, Strategies, and Trends*. This book comprehensively reviews cybersecurity in blockchain technologies, analyzing platforms like Ethereum, Binance Smart Chain, Solana, Cardano, Avalanche, and Polygon. It explores cybersecurity issues in smart contracts, and related blogs are currently being published through the IT World Canada website.

Beginning in 2023, the fifth UCS team embarked on the development of the fifth book, *Understanding Cybersecurity on Smartphones: Challenges, Strategies, and Trends*. This book focused on understanding cyber threats and adversaries on smartphones, examining cybersecurity threats, vulnerabilities, and risk management. The book offers practical solutions for securing and protecting smartphones while raising awareness of the importance of smartphone security.

In 2024, the sixth UCS team has focused on understanding the criticality of cybersecurity in healthcare, advocating for robust measures to protect patient data, maintain system integrity, and mitigate evolving cyber threats in a book entitled *Understanding Cybersecurity Management in Healthcare: Challenges, Strategies and Trends*. The book offers practical solutions for securing and protecting healthcare data and the environment for patients, doctors, and hospital IT teams while raising awareness of the importance of healthcare environment security.

The seventh UCS team has dedicated the last 2 years to exploring AI for security and secure AI, addressing the vulnerabilities, attack vectors, and security challenges associated with AI-driven systems. Their work culminates in the book *Understanding AI for Cybersecurity and Secure AI: Challenges, Strategies, and Trends*, which provides an in-depth analysis of threats targeting AI models, adversarial attacks, and robust defense mechanisms. The book serves as a comprehensive guide for researchers, industry professionals, and security practitioners, offering a broad study about the vulnerabilities and threats along with the strategies to enhance AI security while ensuring the safe and ethical deployment of AI technologies.

Toronto, ON, Canada — Dilli Prasad Sharma
Toronto, ON, Canada — Arash Habibi Lashkari
Edmonton, AB, Canada — Mahdi Daghmehchi Firoozjaei
Montreal, Canada — Samaneh Mahdavifar
Ottawa, ON, Canada — Pulei Xiong
Feb 2025

Acknowledgments

Dilli Prasad Sharma
For
My family—my beloved wife, Brinda, and son, Suhan,
And my father, the late Pratiman Sharma, and mother, Gita Devi Sharma,
And my teachers, for your unwavering love, support, and invaluable mentorship.

Arash Habibi Lashkari
For
My family—my beloved wife, Farnaz, and children, Kourosh and Kianna,
And my father, Bahman, mother, Zeynab, and sister, Ziba,
And my teachers and lecturers, for all the lessons you've taught me.

Mahdi Daghmehchi Firoozjaei
For
My family—my beloved wife, Marzi; my beautiful daughters, Mahdis and Meloreen;
And my beloved mother, Leila, thank you for your unconditional love and unwavering support.

Samaneh Mahdavifar
For
My family—my beloved son, Hesam, and my mom and dad,
And my teachers and mentors, thank you for your love, unwavering support, guidance, and patience.

Pulei Xiong
For my family, collaborators, and colleagues, thank you for your unwavering love and support.

Contents

Part I
General

Chapter 1
Why AI and Security?

1.1 Introduction

Artificial intelligence (AI) has dominated our world by incorporating human intelligence and behavior into machines and systems. AI has a pivotal role in automating processes and creating smart and intelligent systems according to today's needs and can be trained to solve specific problems (Sarker, 2022). There are a wide variety of cutting-edge applications of AI in our everyday lives. They have noticeably evolved over the past few years and have made their way in almost every business sector. AI applications include but are not limited to navigation, robotics, healthcare, marketing, agriculture, finance, and transportation (SIMPLILEARN, 2024).

Today, security organizations face many challenges such as sophisticated cyber threats, a continuously growing attack surface, an abundance of data, and increasing infrastructure complexity (IBM, 2024). These factors hinder their capacity to protect data, oversee user access, and promptly identify and address security threats. As a result, traditional ways of attack identification, such as signature-based methods, no longer work. There should be an intelligent way of finding patterns in the underlying threat data and updating the model as a zero-day vulnerability arises, a malware variant evolves, or a phishing email attack happens. We can analyze millions of events using AI, detect attacks, and mitigate threats. One can keep track of the users' behaviors and gradually construct profiles for users and assets in an organization to find deviations from the normal state over a long period. AI encompasses a spectrum of technologies like machine learning, neural networks, deep learning, and expert systems. Using AI-powered solutions, security experts can analyze the captured log files, find attack patterns, extract domain knowledge, and update and retain the intelligence.

In this book, we study the application of AI to cybersecurity and investigate several AI-centric models that have been applied to network security, application security, cloud security, and Internet of Things (IoT)/Operational Technology (OT)

D. P. Sharma et al., *Understanding AI in Cybersecurity and Secure AI*, Progress in IS, https://doi.org/10.1007/978-3-031-91524-6_1

security. We further dive into AI security, which focuses on defending AI infrastructure from cyberattacks. AI security risks encompass multiple aspects, such as data breaches and leaks, susceptible development pipelines, data poisoning, adversarial attacks, and expansion of the attack surface (WIZ, 2024).

1.2 Cyber Threat Landscape

As technology advances, the cyber-attack surface is growing. With more users, we have more smart devices connections, and subsequently, more data is poured into the network traffic. Cyber threats have always had an accumulative trend in that new ones do not replace the attacks in 1 year in the next year. However, the new attacks are combined with the old ones into a broader spectrum of threats. Based on a report RapidScale published in 2022, the origin of most cyber threats is caused by human error. Adversaries exploit human weaknesses and lure them into achieving what they seek (PRNEWSWIRE, 2024). For instance, based on a report by McAfee Lab 2016 threat prediction, "63% of confirmed data breaches involve using weak, default, or stolen passwords, and 26% of miscellaneous human errors involve people mistakenly sending sensitive information to the wrong person!" (Rapidscale, 2024). While the most prevalent cyber threats in 2023 include but are not limited to phishing, ransomware, and extortion hacks, as discussed below:

- **Phishing:** A phishing attack is a cyberattack that employs social engineering to lure Internet users into revealing sensitive information, such as login credentials, credit card numbers, or personal information. In this attack, the malicious actors impersonate legitimate individuals, organizations, or entities and trick the users into clicking on a fraudulent link that is redirected to an adversary's website where she can steal the victim's personal information. Phishing attacks often take the form of fraudulent emails, messages, or websites designed to appear trustworthy.
- **Ransomware:** Ransomware is malicious software (malware) that encrypts a victim's files or locks them out of their computer or network, rendering the data inaccessible. Attackers then demand a ransom from the victim, typically in cryptocurrency, in exchange for a decryption key or to unlock the compromised system. Ransomware attacks can have severe consequences, causing data loss, financial harm, and operational disruptions for individuals, businesses, and organizations. A ransomware attack happens in different stages, including infection, encryption, ransom demand, payment, and decryption (Trellix Threat Labs, 2024).
- **Extortion hacks:** An extortion attack, also known as extortionware or simply extortion, is a type of cyberattack in which malicious actors threaten to reveal sensitive or confidential information, damage data, disrupt services, or carry out other harmful actions unless a specific demand is met. Extortion attacks are a form of cyber extortion where the attacker seeks monetary or non-monetary benefits in exchange for not carrying out their threats. Some common extortion

attacks are ransomware, denial of service attacks, data theft, non-monetary extortion, and physical threats.

1.2.1 Threat Predictions

Now that we are in 2024, we have witnessed significant shifts in the cyber threat landscape over the past year. Throughout 2023, cyberattacks became more sophisticated and targeted, with emerging threats such as AI-powered malware, advanced phishing campaigns, and critical infrastructure attacks dominating headlines. The rise of state-sponsored attacks and the increasing use of ransomware-as-a-service (RaaS) have further exposed vulnerabilities across industries. Social engineering has become more sophisticated and widespread by exploiting human behavior to steal personal information. Nation-states launch cyberattacks with economic, political, and territorial ambitions by executing espionage, warfare, and disinformation through threat activities across Israel, Ukraine, Taiwan, and other regions (Trellix, 2024).

As we step into 2024, it is evident that cyber resilience, zero-trust frameworks, and proactive threat intelligence are no longer optional but essential for safeguarding digital assets. Reflecting on the lessons learned in 2023, organizations must remain vigilant, adaptive, and collaborative to stay ahead in an ever-evolving cybersecurity landscape.

Trellix Advanced Research Center team has predicted the following threats as the leading trends in 2024 (Trellix, 2024):

- **The threat of AI:** One significant security concern would be the underground development of malicious Large Language Models (LLMs) and the security concerns associated with their potential misuse by cyber criminals. Advanced LLMs like GPT-4 are being utilized in phishing campaigns, creating counterfeit web pages, and developing malware, making large-scale attacks more accessible to individuals with limited technical skills. Cybersecurity researchers anticipate accelerating the development and malicious usage of such tools in 2024. The second concern would be related to Script Kiddies, individuals with limited technical expertise who pose a growing threat due to the availability of advanced generative AI tools. There is a potential for unskilled actors to execute sophisticated attacks at scale using unrestricted generative AI that can write malicious code, create deepfake videos, and assist with social engineering schemes. The use of AI-generated voices in scams involving psychological manipulation poses significant risks. The improved quality of AI-generated voices makes it challenging to differentiate between real and fake voices. The accessibility and affordability of AI-voice generation tools empower scammers to automate and amplify their fraudulent activities, targeting victims across diverse linguistic backgrounds. There would be an increase in the use of AI-generated voices in live phone calls to impersonate legitimate entities and enhance the effectiveness of phishing and vishing attacks.

- **Shifting trends in threat actor behavior:** One of the threats predicted in 2024 is Supply Chain Attacks Against Managed File Transfers Solutions. Designing effective Managed File Transfer (MFT) solutions is paramount in securely exchanging sensitive data for businesses. There exist inherent risks associated with MFT systems, including the potential for ransomware attacks due to the valuable information they handle. Recent incidents, such as the Cl0P group exploiting GoAnywhere MFT and the MOVEit breach, underscore the vulnerabilities in these systems. The complexity of MFT integration into business networks adds to security weaknesses. It is advised that organizations review and secure their MFT solutions, implement Data Loss Prevention (DLP) measures, and encrypt sensitive data to mitigate the risk of operational disruptions, reputational damage, and financial losses.
- **Emerging threats and attack methods:**

- Insider threats are employees, contractors, or partners who have legitimate access to an organization's critical assets and can intentionally or unintentionally harm the organization's resources, personnel, facilities, information, networks, and systems (CISA, 2024). Based on Trellix 2024 Threat Predictions published in Oct. 2023, insider threats have increased by 47% over the last two years, imposing a significant loss of $15.38 million to contain these threats over organizations. Therefore, it is essential for organizations to identify, detect, and mitigate these threats to retain their stakeholders' satisfaction. Another emerging threat is related to the rising usage of QR codes by the public everywhere. QR code-based phishing attacks are on the rise due to the trust people place in QR codes, which cybercriminals exploit to distribute malware or lead victims to fake websites. QR codes are easy to create and are widely used in daily activities, therefore, they have become an attractive tool for cybercriminals to exploit in conducting phishing attacks. Edge devices such as firewalls, routers, and switches are prone to be targeted by Advanced Persistent Threats (APT) due to their inherent vulnerabilities and lack of intrusion detection capabilities. The number of connected devices over the Internet has increased substantially, making edge devices a crucial but vulnerable component of the digital infrastructure. Another target that threat actors are lured into is new attack vectors, such as Python scripts in Microsoft Excel which are alternatives to old Macros. Although Microsoft claims security measures, potential vulnerabilities or misconfigurations might exist which could be exploited by threat actors. Signed vulnerable drivers pose significant threats by allowing attackers to achieve kernel-level privilege escalation. Despite some mitigation efforts, such as the Vulnerable Driver Blocklist by Microsoft (Microsoft, 2024), these attacks remain simple to execute and are likely to increase in 2024, impacting security systems widely.

1.2.2 *The Cyber Attacker's Motivation*

Normally, cyber attackers have a wide range of motivations for conducting attacks. There could be political reasons behind a cyber-attack campaign or a script kiddie wanting to show off their coding talents. Usually, the main motivation behind cyber-attacks is to earn money by stealing personal information or blackmailing users to hide some secret information.

Some common motivations for cyberattacks include (SOPHOS, 2024):

- **Financial gain:** Many cybercriminals are primarily motivated by financial incentives. They may engage in activities such as stealing credit card information, perpetrating fraud, or conducting ransomware attacks to extort money from victims.
- **Espionage:** State-sponsored cyber attackers, or APTs, aim to steal sensitive government, military, or corporate information for political, economic, or military purposes. Their motivation is often tied to espionage or gaining a competitive advantage.
- **Hacktivism:** Some individuals or groups use cyberattacks to promote a political or social agenda. They may deface websites, leak sensitive information, or disrupt services to draw attention to their cause.
- **Revenge:** In some cases, individuals may launch cyberattacks as revenge against a specific person or organization. This can be motivated by personal grievances or vendettas.
- **Intellectual property theft:** Competing companies or nations may seek to steal intellectual property, research, or proprietary information for economic or technological advantage.
- **Challenge:** Some hackers are motivated by the thrill of outsmarting security systems or the challenge of breaking into highly secure networks. They may not have specific malicious intent but are driven by curiosity or a desire to prove their skills.
- **Cyber warfare:** Nation-states may engage in cyber warfare to disrupt critical infrastructure, sabotage military operations, or gain strategic advantages in conflicts.

Understanding these motivations is crucial for devising effective defense mechanisms and implementing mitigation strategies accordingly to contain the risk in an organization.

1.3 What Is AI?

AI refers to the simulation of human intelligence in machines, enabling them to perform tasks that typically require human intelligence, such as visual perception, speech recognition, decision-making, and language translation. AI is a broad-spectrum encompassing machine learning and deep learning models and uses software-coded heuristics (INVESTOPEDIA, 2024).

Machine Learning (ML) is a subset of AI that concentrates on developing algorithms and statistical models that allow computers to perform tasks without being explicitly programmed. In other words, ML algorithms learn from data, identifying patterns and making decisions based on that data. ML techniques are categorized into three groups: supervised learning, unsupervised learning, and reinforcement learning.

Deep Learning (DL) is a subset of machine learning that involves neural networks with multiple layers. These deep neural networks with huge parametric space can learn from extensive amounts of data layer-wise, automatically extracting high-level features, and making complex decisions. DL has achieved remarkable success in various tasks, such as image recognition, speech recognition, natural language processing, and game playing.

Overall, AI is the overarching concept of creating intelligent systems, machine learning is a technique within AI that enables machines to learn from data, and deep learning is a subset of computational models that uses deep neural networks to learn complex numerical patterns in input data like image, text, or voice (ZENDESK, 2024).

1.4 Traditional Approach to Cybersecurity

Before the adoption of AI, cybersecurity companies largely relied on traditional approaches such as rule-based systems and signature-based detection methods to detect known threats like phishing emails, network intrusions, and malware infections. These methods could not identify zero-day vulnerabilities and deal with complex cyber threats. With massive data and security logs, human analysts could not manually audit logs and find suspicious activities. They could not provide real-time responses and react to sophisticated cyber-attacks. As a result, a dire need was felt to utilize an automated cyber threat detection system, which is more proactive and dynamically being matured as a new malware or a zero-day attack emerges (ANALYTICSVIDHYA, 2024).

1.5 AI-Centric Cybersecurity

AI transformed many cybersecurity applications different from traditional approaches in various significant aspects as follows (Kaur et al., 2023):

1. **Dynamic adaptation:** Unlike static rule-based systems and signature-based methods, AI models could be dynamically updated as new data streams and experience are generated continuously. Therefore, this adaptability allows AI to stay ahead of emerging cyber threats.

2. **Automation and efficiency:** AI-powered cybersecurity solutions reduce the need for manual intervention by automating tasks such as threat analysis, detection, and response. This automation improves efficiency and realizes real-time responses to cyber incidents.
3. **Scalability:** AI can efficiently handle large volumes of data, making it scalable to the extensive amounts of information generated in modern networks. Traditional methods cannot scale well to large amounts of cybersecurity data. For example, in rule-based methods, human experts should revise or regenerate the rules to respond to rapid data change, leading to delays in threat detection and response.
4. **Detection of unknown threats:** AI utilizes machine learning or deep learning algorithms to detect anomalies or zero-day threats. Traditional approaches primarily rely on known signatures or patterns and may overlook unknown threats.
5. **Behavioral analysis:** AI systems excel in behavioral analysis, identifying suspicious activities or deviations from normal behavior across users and systems. This capability works by user profiling and enables the detection of insider threats and sophisticated attacks that evade traditional detection methods.
6. **Proactive defense:** AI enables proactive defense strategies by predicting potential threats based on historical data and trends. Traditional approaches often focus on reactive measures and respond after an attack, resulting in system downtime and a huge monetary loss on the network.

1.6 Applications of AI to Cybersecurity

Recently, numerous state-of-the-art machine learning and deep learning algorithms have been applied to detect or classify malware threats, detect network intrusions, specify phishing attacks, and identify software vulnerabilities (Mahdavifar, 2021). AI could be applied to a broad category of cybersecurity applications including but not limited to network security, application security, cloud security, and Internet of Things (IoT)/Operational Technology (OT) security. These algorithms could range from generic ML models like linear regression to sophisticated Generative AI models, such as BERT or GPT-4.

The ML model we use to identify threats highly depends on the input data, ranging from structured files to images of binary files, assembly code, malware-analysis logs, and network packet files. If we have tabular data as the input, based on the value types, i.e., numerical and categorical, we could use decision trees, random forest, linear regression, Naive Bayes, or SVM. If we have image or textual data as the input, we could use deep learning methods such as the Convolutional neural network (CNN), Recurrent Neural Network (RNN), and Auto Encoders (AE). Furthermore, based on the size of the input and the data complexity, we could employ transformer-based models such as GPT, BERT, GPT-2, RoBERTa, DistilBERT, XLNet, BART, GPT-3, LUKE (HUGGINGFACE, 2024).

The essence of the cybersecurity problem we want to solve and the distribution of the samples in each class determines whether to use a model with a non-linear decision boundary or a linear one. A non-linear decision boundary in machine learning refers to a classification boundary that is not a straight line (for two-dimensional data) or a hyperplane (for higher-dimensional data). Instead, it can take complex shapes, such as curves, circles, or any other irregular shape, to separate different data classes.

Time performance and scalability of the ML-based model are other factors that determine which model to use. If we are limited with time-constrained applications, we need to use more lightweight models with a smaller number of parameters that are scalable to large, diverse samples. Using high computational resources either on-premises or on the cloud can boost model run time. Furthermore, the possibility of updating and retraining the model periodically as new attacks emerge is another vital aspect to consider when selecting the ML model.

Accessibility to labeled samples is an important factor to consider when categorizing AI-based models in the cybersecurity area. We need to use supervised learning methods if the security data is labeled. If we have a few labeled samples and many unlabeled samples, we could exploit the power of semi-supervised models. Finally, if we do not access labeled data, we need to use unsupervised learning methods, which is the case for most real-world applications. Validating the labeling process is a time-consuming, complicated task that usually requires human experts and is deemed a barrier in training highly efficient ML-based models in cybersecurity applications. Data labeling is a subtask in the preprocessing stage, which is the most crucial step in data science. When it comes to cyber security data, labeling would be a more daunting task since there are a lot of variables and dynamics evolving based on the behaviors of the adversaries, so a previous malicious input may no longer be malicious, and normal behavior is abnormal due to multiple unknown factors in zero-day attacks. Reinforcement learning is another type of unsupervised method that takes advantage of an agent to explore a cybersecurity environment and take actions to maximize some notions of cumulative reward. In this way, the agent can learn through trial and error and rewards and punishment, which are the results of a feedback system to an optimization function (Kaelbling et al., 1996).

Finally, the model's desired interpretability (CHRISTOPHM, 2024) level is important in choosing the appropriate technique to solve the cybersecurity problem. Some ML models, such as linear regression, logistic regression, decision trees, and rule-based learning, are inherently interpretable. Inherent interpretable models are self-explanatory models incorporating interpretability into the model structure (Mahdavifar, 2021).

After choosing a set of models, we must conduct a thorough experimental analysis to evaluate the models and compare the results to determine which approach works best for a specific problem.

1.7 Secure AI

With the unprecedented rise in the application of AI in our everyday lives, security and privacy concerns of AI models become of paramount importance. Adversaries conduct multiple attacks from the perspective of data and models, including data poisoning, membership inference, model inversion, model evasion (adversarial), and model theft, to name a few (OWASP, 2024). These potential vulnerabilities and challenges can undermine ML models' performance, security, and reliability (TOWARDSDATASCIENCE, 2024).

In a data poisoning attack, an adversary injects malicious data into training datasets to manipulate model behavior, leading to incorrect predictions or biases. To compromise user privacy and data confidentiality, membership Inference refers to an attack where adversaries exploit model responses to infer whether specific data points were used during training. In model Inversion attacks, using reverse engineering techniques, attackers attempt to extract sensitive information from a model which might compromise user privacy and data confidentiality. In model evasion, the most common attack during inference, the input is crafted in a way that seems normal to humans but can fool the ML model into a misprediction. Finally, any unauthorized access to or replication of proprietary ML models, which leads to intellectual property theft or misuse of proprietary algorithms, is called model theft.

We require a comprehensive approach to address these threats and risks, including robust model validation, monitoring for adversarial behavior, implementing privacy-preserving techniques, and ensuring transparency and accountability in model development and deployment processes. On top of that, by applying software engineering practices to our AI workflow, such as software testing, providing patches, and quality assurance, we can make sure our AI systems are reliable, more accurate, and easier to maintain. This book will introduce common AI security risks and provide insights on designing, developing, and evaluating secure and privacy-preserving AI systems.

1.8 Summary

AI revolutionizes cybersecurity by offering dynamic adaptation, automation, scalability, advanced threat detection capabilities, behavioral analysis, and proactive defense strategies, which traditional methods often lack. AI-powered solutions expedite threat detection and mitigation, minimize reverse engineering and forensics, and protect users' identity and data.

Choosing the appropriate AI-based model to solve cybersecurity problems depends on the nature of the dataset, computational resources, efficiency and scalability requirements, and desired model interpretability. Experimentation and model evaluation are crucial to determine which approach works best for a cybersecurity problem. Addressing the security and privacy concerns in AI applications is critical due to their increasing prevalence in everyday life. Various types of attacks exist targeting both data and models, such as data poisoning, membership inference, model inversion, and model evasion. To mitigate these risks, the application of software engineering practices such as testing, patching, and quality assurance is recommended.

References

ANALYTICSVIDHYA. *AI in cybersecurity: What you need to know*. Accessed Mar 2024., https://www.analyticsvidhya.com/blog/2023/02/ai-in-cyber-security/

CHRISTOPHM. *Chapter 5: Interpretable models*. Accessed Apr 2024., https://christophm.github.io/interpretable-ml-book/simple.html

CISA. *Defining insider threats*. Accessed Jan 2024., https://www.cisa.gov/topics/physical-security/insider-threat-mitigation/defining-insider-threats

HUGGINGFACE. *The transformer model family*. Accessed May 2024., https://huggingface.co/docs/transformers/en/model_summary

IBM. *AI to accelerate your security defenses*. Accessed Jan 2024, https://www.ibm.com/ai-cybersecurity

INVESTOPEDIA. *Artificial Intelligence (AI): What it is and how it is used*. Accessed Feb 2024., https://www.investopedia.com/terms/a/artificial-intelligence-ai.asp

Kaelbling, L. P., Littman, M. L., & Moore, A. W. (1996). Reinforcement learning: A survey. *Journal of Artificial Intelligence Research, 4*, 237–285.

Kaur, R., Gabrijelčič, D., & Klobučar, T. (2023). Artificial intelligence for cybersecurity: Literature review and future research directions. *Information Fusion*, 101804.

Mahdavifar, S. (2021). *Explainable deep learning for detecting cyber threats*.

Microsoft. *Microsoft recommended driver block rules*. Accessed Feb 2024., https://learn.microsoft.com/en-us/windows/security/application-security/application-control/windows-defender-application-control/design/microsoft-recommended-driver-block-rules

OWASP. *OWASP AI security and privacy guide*. Accessed Apr 2024., https://owasp.org/www-project-ai-security-and-privacy-guide/

PRNEWSWIRE. *Verizon's 2016 data breach investigations report finds cybercriminals are exploiting human nature*. Accessed Jan 2024, https://www.prnewswire.com/news-releases/verizons-2016-data-breach-investigations-report-finds-cybercriminals-are-exploiting-human-nature-300258134.html

Rapidscale. *The cyber threat landscape*. Accessed Jan 2024., https://rapidscale.net/resources/blog/managed-cloud-services/cybr-threat-landscape

Sarker, I. H. (2022). AI-based modeling: Techniques, applications and research issues towards automation, intelligent and smart systems. *SN Computer Science, 3*(2), 158.

SIMPLILEARN. *18 Cutting-edge artificial intelligence applications in 2024*. Accessed Jan 2024, https://www.simplilearn.com/tutorials/artificial-intelligence-tutorial/artificial-intelligence-applications

SOPHOS. *Threat actors*. Accessed Feb 2024., https://www.sophos.com/en-us/cybersecurity-explained/threat-actors#:~:text=Some%20common%20motivations%20for%20threat,or%20use%20for%20fraudulent%20activities

TOWARDSDATASCIENCE. *How to attack machine learning (Evasion, poisoning, inference, trojans, backdoors)*. Accessed Apr 2024., https://towardsdatascience.com/how-to-attack-machine-learning-evasion-poisoning-inference-trojans-backdoors-a7cb5832595c

Trellix. *Trellix 2024 threat predictions*. Accessed Jan 2024., https://www.trellix.com/about/newsroom/stories/research/trellix-2024-threat-predictions/

Trellix Threat Labs. *The threat report*. Accessed Jan 2024., https://www.trellix.com/en-us/advanced-research-center/threat-reports/jul-2022.html

WIZ. *AI security explained: How to secure AI*. Accessed Jan 2024., https://www.wiz.io/academy/ai-security

ZENDESK. *Deep learning vs. machine learning*. Accessed Feb 2024., https://www.zendesk.com/blog/machine-learning-and-deep-learning/

Chapter 2
Understanding AI and ML

2.1 Introduction

For many years, scientists have looked for intelligent systems to automate daily tasks, identify patterns in images, understand speech, diagnose diseases, improve crop quality, and develop self-driving cars. Ultimately, this vision was realized by employing AI with many practical applications and multiple research topics. AI has revolutionized almost every aspect of our lives today, from improving traffic management and students' learning curves, language translation, and fraud detection in financial transactions to online grocery shopping and gaming.

The main focus of each AI task is to describe problems in mathematical rules and models. AI has gained satisfactory success in tackling intellectually complicated problems for human beings. However, researchers found it challenging for AI to solve problems that seem easy and intuitive for human beings but are challenging to formalize by mathematical equations (Goodfellow et al., 2016). To tackle these intuitive problems, computers must understand the world and gather knowledge from experience. In this case, it will not be necessary to formalize and retain all the concepts in advance; rather, it will be necessary to learn complicated concepts from the simpler ones through hierarchical structures.

Some AI-based models rely on a knowledge base to hard-code learning about the world in formal languages (Akerkar & Sajja, 2009). These systems have proven to suffer from inconsistencies in the rule inferencing process. Therefore, to achieve a better learning experience, an AI-based system should be able to extract knowledge from the raw data, which is known as machine learning. The efficiency of ML models highly depends on how we represent the data as the input to these models. These pieces of data, so-called features, are of various types, namely numerical, categorical, or arrays. If we can feed the machine-learning model with the right set of features, we can solve many AI-based problems. But in the real world, crafting input

D. P. Sharma et al., *Understanding AI in Cybersecurity and Secure AI*, Progress in IS, https://doi.org/10.1007/978-3-031-91524-6_2

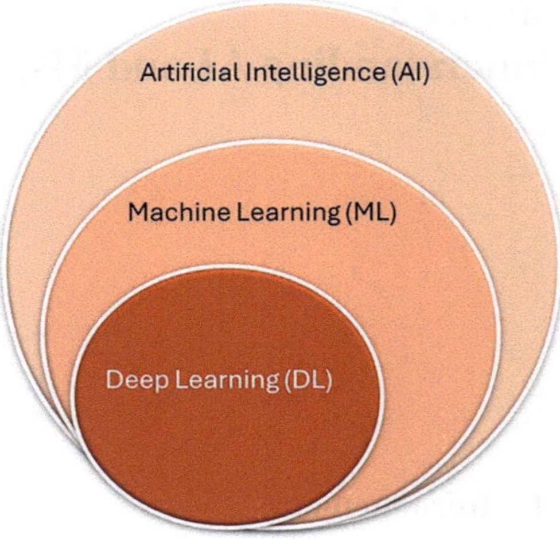

Fig. 2.1 Relationship of AI, ML, and DL

features for the ML model input is not straightforward. It is a time-consuming and manually intensive process.

Many image processing and voice recognition applications require complicated feature engineering procedures to extract meaningful features. One solution for this problem is to use deep-learning algorithms to map the input representation of data to another representation. Deep learning is a class of machine learning that generates concepts from more straightforward concepts using multiple hierarchical layers. It creates abstract representations based on less abstract ones by modeling a mathematical function composed of many more straightforward functions (LeCun et al., 2015).

Figure 2.1 shows the association of AI, ML, and DL which are interconnected fields and built upon each other. AI is the broadest concept, referring to the simulation of human intelligence in machines to perform tasks such as reasoning, problem-solving, and learning. ML is a subset of AI, focused on algorithms that allow machines to learn from data and improve over time without explicit programming. DL, in turn, is a subset of ML, involving neural networks with many layers that can model complex patterns and representations in large datasets. In essence, all DL is ML, and all ML is AI, but not all AI involves ML or DL.

This chapter explores various types of machine learning (ML) models and their applications in cybersecurity. It provides a concise historical overview of deep learning, highlighting the evolution of deep neural network architectures and their role in addressing complex cybersecurity challenges. Additionally, it examines how different deep learning techniques have been leveraged to enhance threat detection, intrusion prevention, and anomaly detection in modern security systems.

2.2 Overview of ML Models

In this subsection, we will describe different types of ML models and then we explain fundamental ML algorithms as the building blocks for the most practical learning algorithms (Burkov, 2019).

2.2.1 Supervised Learning

Supervised machine learning is a type of machine learning where you train a model on labeled data. In labeled data, you have input-output pairs, where you know what the correct output should be for given inputs (Cunningham et al., 2008). Let $\{(x_i, y_i)\}_{i=1}^{n}$ be a dataset where x_i is a feature vector, y_i is the label for x_i, n is the number of samples in the dataset. Each feature vector x_i contains m features and each feature is denoted as $x_i^{(j)}$. Label y_i can either be an element part of the set of classes $\{1, 2, \ldots, C\}$, a real number, a vector, or even a matrix. For example, in the diabetes prediction dataset, each sample x represents a patient and the data includes features such as age, gender, hypertension, heart disease, smoking history, blood glucose level, and Body Mass Index (BMI). Labels belong to the set $\{0, 1, 2\}$ where 0 is for no diabetes or only during pregnancy, 1 is for prediabetes, and 2 is for diabetes (KAGGLE, 2024).

The goal of a supervised learning algorithm is to use a dataset to construct a model. This model is designed to take a feature vector x as input and produces an output that facilitates inferring the label associated with this feature vector. For example, if we use a dataset containing information about individuals, the resulting model might accept a feature vector representing a person and generate an output indicating the probability that the individual has Diabetes.

There are two main types of supervised learning, classification and regression. In classification tasks, the model learns to classify input data into predefined categories, for example, classifying patients based on various symptoms into two categories of diabetes or non-diabetes. In regression tasks, the model learns to predict continuous values. For example, predicting house prices based on features like size, number of bedrooms, and neighborhood.

During the training process, the model adjusts its parameters to minimize the loss function which differentiates between its predictions and the actual labels in the training data. Once trained, the model can be used to make predictions on new, unseen data.

2.2.2 Unsupervised Learning

An unsupervised learning algorithm is a type of machine learning algorithm used to discover structures, patterns, and hidden relationships in data without the use of labels (Hastie et al., 2009). Unsupervised learning algorithms work with data that has no labels, unlike supervised learning, where the model is trained on a dataset that includes input-output pairs. The goal of unsupervised learning is to gain insights and explore the underlying structure of the data.

Given $\{x_i\}_{i=1}^{n}$ as a set of unlabeled samples, the goal of the unsupervised learning algorithm is to take a feature vector x as input and produce an output in the form of either a feature vector or a real number based on which we decide how to tackle a problem. For example, in dimensionality reduction, the model outputs a feature vector with fewer features than the input vector x. In clustering, the model assigns a cluster ID to each feature vector in the dataset. In outlier detection, the output is a real number that signifies how much xx deviates from the norm.

2.2.3 Semi-Supervised Learning

A semi-supervised learning algorithm is a type of machine learning algorithm that falls between supervised and unsupervised learning (Zhu, 2005). It uses both labeled and unlabeled data for training. Typically, a small amount of labeled data and a large amount of unlabeled data are used. Semi-supervised learning aims to leverage the abundant unlabeled data to improve learning accuracy when labeled data is inadequate or expensive to acquire. The goal of a semi-supervised learning algorithm is to employ many unlabeled samples to help the learning algorithm generate a higher-quality model.

2.2.4 Reinforcement Learning

A Reinforcement Learning (RL) algorithm is a type of machine learning algorithm used to train agents to make a sequence of decisions by interacting with an environment (Wiering & Van Otterlo, 2012). The agent learns to achieve a goal by taking action and receiving feedback in the form of rewards or penalties. The goal of the agent is to learn a policy that maximizes the cumulative reward over time. In a reinforcement learning algorithm, we aim to learn a policy. A policy is a function f that takes a feature vector of a state as input and produces an optimal action to perform in that state. An action is considered optimal if it maximizes the expected average reward.

2.3 Fundamental Algorithms

In this section, we introduce five fundamental ML algorithms that have been effective and are being used as building blocks for other well-known learning algorithms (Burkov, 2019). Figure 2.2 shows the generic steps of machine learning model training and prediction. In the training phase, models learn patterns from historical data. This process involves optimizing model parameters to minimize errors and improve accuracy. The trained models are deployed for prediction with new data samples to produce output such as classification or regression.

2.3.1 Linear Regression

Linear regression is a foundational statistical method used for predicting a continuous target variable based on one or more predictor variables. It is a basic but still powerful statistical method that assumes a linear relationship between the input features and the target variable. The general equation for linear regression can be expressed as:

$$y = \beta_0 + \beta_1 x_1 + \beta_2 x_2 + \ldots + \beta_n x_n + \epsilon,$$

where,

- y is a target variable (dependent variable).
- $x_1, x_2, \ldots, x_n$ are input features (independent variables)
- β_0 is an intercept, which is the value of y when all x-values are zero.
- $\beta_1, \beta_2, \ldots, \beta_n$ are Coefficients that represent the weights of the respective features $x_1, x_2, \ldots, x_n$.
- ϵ is an error term.

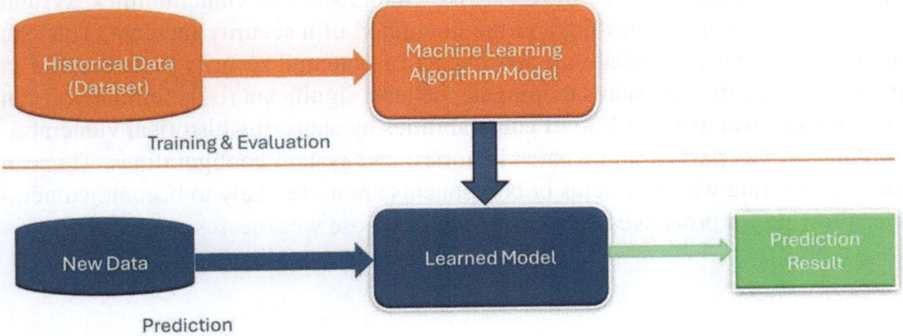

Fig. 2.2 Model training and prediction in machine learning

The unknown parameters $\beta_0, \beta_1, \beta_2, \ldots, \beta_n$ are estimated by minimizing the residual sum of squares (RSS), which is given below

$$RSS = \sum_{\{i=1\}}^{m} (y_i - \hat{y}_i)^2$$

Linear regression is foundational in both statistics and machine learning and serves as a starting point for understanding more complex predictive modeling techniques. There are some assumptions in linear regression, which are as follows:

- **Linearity:** The relationship between the independent variables (predictors) and the dependent variable (target) is linear. This means the change in the target variable is proportional to the change in any predictor variable.
- **Normality of errors:** The residuals or errors (differences between observed and predicted values) are assumed to follow a normal distribution and independent. This is essential for hypothesis testing and constructing confidence intervals.
- **Homoscedasticity**: The variance of residuals is constant across all levels of the predictors. This means that the spread of errors does not increase or decrease systematically with the predicted values.
- **No multicollinearity:** Predictor variables are not highly correlated with one another. High correlation among predictors can make it difficult to determine the unique contribution of each predictor to the target variable.

In cybersecurity, linear regression is used for several tasks including anomaly detection, risk assessment, and predicting vulnerabilities. In anomaly detection, linear regression can model normal behaviors of network traffic patterns or user activities by creating a baseline using historical data. Once this baseline is established, the model can predict expected behaviors and flag deviations as potential anomalies, which may indicate security threats like intrusions, malware, or unauthorized access attempts.

Figure 2.3 shows the linear regression where X-axis represents input points (blue solid circles) and Y-axis value is an output, red solid line is an estimated regression equation or fitted curve (linear). Linear regression can help quantify risks by modeling the relationship between different risk factors such as vulnerabilities, system configurations, network traffic, and the likelihood of a security incident. This can help in assessing the probability and impact of potential security breaches and in prioritizing security measures to mitigate the most significant risks. Similarly, it can help identify patterns that lead to vulnerabilities by analyzing historical vulnerability data such as past exploits, patch histories, and system configurations. This can aid in predicting which systems or components are more likely to become vulnerable, allowing for proactive measures to address those weaknesses.

Fig. 2.3 Linear regression

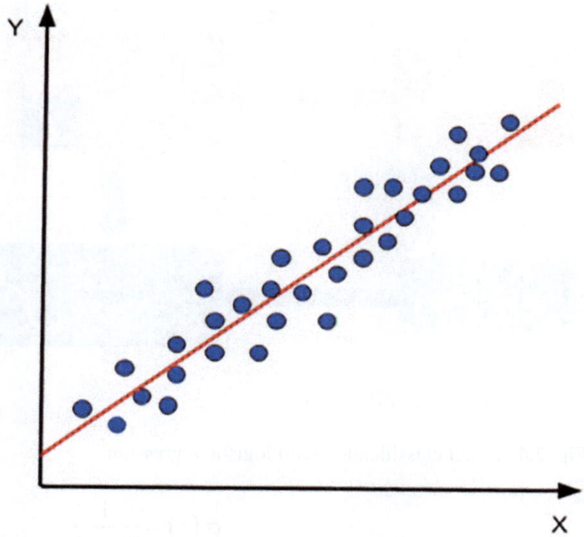

2.3.2 *Logistic Regression*

Logistic Regression is a statistical model primarily used for binary classification tasks. Despite its name, it is a classification algorithm rather than a regression method. The goal of logistic regression is to estimate the probability that a given input belongs to one of two classes. The model is based on the equation:

$$p(X) = \frac{1}{1 + e^{-(\beta_0 + \beta_1 x_1 + \ldots + \beta_n x_n)}}$$

where p(y = 1|X) is the probability of class 1, and the function e^{-z} is the exponential function of the linear combination of the inputs ($z = \beta_0 + \beta_1 x_1 + \ldots + \beta_n x_n$). It can be written with a simple expression in terms of weights, and intercept (bias) with the following general notations:

$$z = w.x + b,$$

where:

- *w* is the weight of the feature(s),
- *x* is input features,
- *b* is bias (intercept).

The value of z is transferred into a probability value between 0 and 1 using the sigmoid function, which is defined as follows defined as:

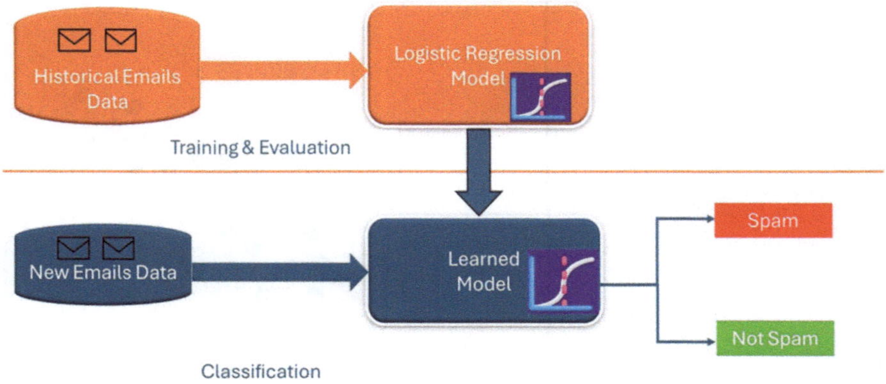

Fig. 2.4 Email classification with logistic regression

$$\sigma(z) = \frac{1}{1+e^{-z}}$$

The output of the sigmoid function is a probability (value between 0 and 1). By setting a threshold (e.g., 0.5), the probability can be converted into binary class labels. Logistic regression uses log-loss or binary cross-entropy loss to measure the difference between predicted probabilities and actual labels. To minimize this loss, it employs optimization techniques such as gradient descent by iteratively adjusting the weights (w) and bias (b) to improve accuracy. Figure 2.4 illustrates how the logistic regression model works for a binary classification.

Logistic regression is widely used in cybersecurity for binary classification tasks such as identifying whether a network packet is malicious or benign, or classifying email as spam or not. It is particularly effective in threat detection systems like intrusion detection and malware classification, where the goal is to classify events into one of two categories (e.g., normal vs. anomalous).

2.3.3 *Decision Tree*

A decision tree is a supervised machine-learning algorithm used for both classification and regression tasks. It works by splitting the data into subsets based on feature values, forming a tree-like structure where each internal node represents a decision based on a feature, branches represent the outcome of that decision, and leaf nodes represent the final prediction. It builds a model by splitting data into subsets based on the values of input features. It operates by recursively splitting data at each node based on a feature and a threshold value. This process is aimed at maximizing the separation between target classes in classification tasks or minimizing prediction error in regression tasks. At each step, the algorithm evaluates all possible splits by examining the values of the features and selects the one that optimizes a specific criterion. The goal is to partition the feature space in such a way that the data in each subset is as homogenous as possible. The decision tree splits based on the feature that maximizes the information gain. The decision-making process is represented by:

$$split = argarg\ Gain\left(X_j\right)$$

In a classification task, measures such as Gini Impurity or Entropy are used for these criteria. These measures determine how well a potential split reduces uncertainty or "impurity" in the resulting subsets. A good split will produce groups of data points that are as homogeneous as possible in terms of the target variable.

In regression tasks, the splitting criterion is typically Mean Squared Error (MSE), which calculates the average squared difference between actual and predicted values. By minimizing MSE, the algorithm ensures that splits result in subsets with more accurate predictions for the dependent variable. The recursive splitting continues until a stopping condition is met, such as reaching a maximum tree depth, having a minimum number of samples in a node, or when further splitting does not significantly improve the model's performance.

Like logistic regression, decision trees are also useful in intrusion detection systems (IDS) for classifying network traffic or identifying potential threats based on observed behaviors. The decision tree's transparency allows analysts to understand why certain traffic patterns are flagged as malicious. They are also employed in malware detection, where the tree can help classify, files based on features like file size, file execution behavior, and metadata.

2.3.4 Support Vector Machine

Support Vector Machine (SVM) is a supervised learning algorithm used for classification and regression tasks. It works by finding the optimal hyperplane that separates the data into different classes. The objective is to maximize the margin between the support vectors (data points closest to the hyperplane) while maintaining a decision boundary. The model parameters of the SVM models are optimized with the following:

$$\frac{1}{2}|w|^2 \quad \text{subject to} \quad y_i\left(w \cdot x_i + b\right) \geq 1, \forall i$$

where:

- w is the weight vector,
- b is the bias term,
- x_i represents the input features,
- y_i is the class label for the data point.

SVM is a commonly used supervised method in many cybersecurity applications specifically in detecting malware, identifying phishing websites, and classifying network traffic as either normal or anomalous. It is particularly useful when the dataset is highly dimensional. The kernel trick allows SVM to classify non-linearly separable data by mapping it into higher-dimensional spaces.

2.3.5 k-Nearest Neighbors

k-Nearest Neighbors (k-NN) is a simple, non-parametric algorithm used for classification and regression. The algorithm classifies a data point based on the majority class of its k nearest neighbors. The prediction is based on the distance between the point and its neighbors in the feature space. The prediction rule can be written as:

$$\hat{y} = \text{argarg} \sum_{i=1}^{k} I(y_i - y_j)$$

where:

- I is the indicator function, which returns 1 if the condition is true,
- y_i are the labels of the nearest neighbors.

The k-NN models are commonly used in anomaly detection for identifying unusual network behavior or classifying malicious network traffic. It is also used in detecting botnets, where it compares the activity of a device to that of known malicious or benign devices in the network.

2.4 Neural Networks and Deep Learning

Deep learning is a subset of machine learning that uses multi-layered artificial neural networks to model complex patterns and representations in data.

2.4.1 A Brief History

The origins of deep learning can be traced back to the mid-twentieth century when artificial intelligence (AI) and neural networks were first conceived. In the 1950s, Alan Turing and John McCarthy laid the groundwork for AI research, contributing to early neural network models (HOLLOWAY, n.d.). One of the first attempts to implement a neural network was the Perceptron (Rosenblatt, 1958). Perceptron introduced the concept of a neural network capable of binary classification, making it a foundational model in the development of AI. Despite early enthusiasm, neural networks faced challenges, especially due to the limitations of computational power and the inability to address non-linear problems, which led to a temporary decline in the field. It wasn't until the 1980s that significant progress was made, largely due to the work of Geoffrey Hinton and colleagues. Hinton, along with David Rumelhart and Ronald Williams, popularized the backpropagation algorithm, which enabled the efficient training of multi-layer neural networks, overcoming some of the earlier challenges (Rumelhart et al., 1986). However, deep learning still faced issues like the vanishing gradient problem, which hampered the training of very deep networks for decades. The development of restricted Boltzmann machines and deep belief networks by Hinton and others helped reignite interest in deep neural networks (Hinton et al., 2006)

The real breakthrough for deep learning came in the early 2010s, powered by Convolutional Neural Networks (CNNs) and advancements in computational power. In 2012, AlexNet, a deep CNN trained on the ImageNet dataset, won the ImageNet Large Scale Visual Recognition Challenge, outperforming previous methods and showcasing the vast potential of deep learning for image classification tasks (Krizhevsky et al., 2017). This achievement was a game-changer and significantly accelerated the adoption of deep learning across various domains. Hinton continued to play a critical role in advancing deep learning, particularly in shaping the development of CNNs and deep architectures for a wide range of applications. The rise of GPUs for faster computation and the availability of large-scale datasets further fueled the deep learning revolution. Today, deep learning models are central to many AI applications, including natural language processing, computer vision, and reinforcement learning.

2.4.2 *Overview of Neural Networks*

A neural network consists of layers of nodes (neurons), where each neuron computes a weighted sum of its inputs, applies an activation function, and passes the result to the next layer. The process of learning in deep learning involves adjusting the weights of the neurons through optimization techniques, typically using gradient descent.

The basic equation for a single-layer neural network is given by:

$$y = f\left(\sum_{i=1}^{n} w_i x_i + b\right)$$

where:

- x_i are the input features,
- w_i are the weights,
- b is the bias,
- f is the activation function (e.g., sigmoid, ReLU, or taha).

In a multi-layer neural network, the output of each layer becomes the input to the next layer, and the network is trained by minimizing the loss function.

Activation functions introduce non-linearity into the model, allowing neural networks to approximate complex functions. Common activation functions include sigmoid, ReLU, Taha, SoftMax, etc. are the common activation functions.

Sigmoid Function
The sigmoid activation function maps input values to a range between 0 and 1. It is commonly used in binary classification problems due to its probabilistic interpretation. The sigmoid is smooth and differentiable, making it suitable for gradient-based optimization. However, it suffers from the vanishing gradient problem for inputs with large magnitudes, as gradients approach zero, which can hinder learning in deep networks.

$$\sigma(x) = \frac{1}{1+e^{-x}}$$

ReLU (Rectified Linear Unit)
ReLU is one of the most widely used activation functions in deep learning. It is computationally efficient and introduces sparsity in the network by setting negative input values to zero. ReLU function outputs the input directly if it is positive; otherwise, it outputs zero. It is defined as follows.

$$ReLU(x) = \max(0,x)$$

ReLU helps mitigate the vanishing gradient problem and enables faster training of deep networks. However, it can lead to the dying ReLU problem, where neurons output zero for all inputs, effectively becoming inactive. Variants like Leaky ReLU address this issue by allowing small negative outputs.

Leaky ReLU
Leaky ReLU modifies the ReLU function by allowing a small, non-zero gradient for negative input values. This is defined as

$$f(x) = \{x, x > 0\, \alpha x, \text{otherwise}$$

where α is a small positive constant. It addresses the dying ReLU problem and ensures that no neurons become permanently inactive. It retains the benefits of ReLU while allowing for learning on negative inputs, making it effective in deeper networks where activation sparsity needs to be managed.

Tanh (Hyperbolic Tangent)
Tanh activation function maps inputs to a range between −1 and 1. It is zero-centered, which can help during optimization by reducing biases in weight updates. It is defined as follows:

$$\tanh(x) = \frac{e^{x} - e^{-x}}{e^{x} + e^{-x}}$$

Like the sigmoid function, tanh suffers from the vanishing gradient problem for large inputs, making it less effective in deeper networks.

SoftMax Function

Softmax is commonly used in the output layer of classification networks, especially for multi-class problems. It converts raw scores (logits) into probabilities by applying the formula

$$\sigma(x_i) = \frac{e^{x}i}{\sum_{j=1}^{K} e^{x}j},$$

where, x_i represents the score for class i. The outputs sum to 1, making them interpretable as class probabilities. SoftMax is essential for tasks requiring a probabilistic interpretation of outputs, but it can be sensitive to large input values, leading to numerical instability. Proper regularization and preprocessing are often needed when using SoftMax.

2.4.3 *Deep Neural Networks*

A deep neural network (DNN) consists of multiple hidden layers between the input and output layers. The number of layers and neurons in each layer defines the depth and complexity of the network. Figure 2.5 depicts a generic structure of the DNNs. Each layer transforms the input data nonlinearly, allowing the network to learn hierarchical features. The forward pass in a deep neural network can be described as:

$$a^{(l)} = f^{(l)}\left(W^{(l)}a^{(l-1)} + b^{(l)}\right)$$

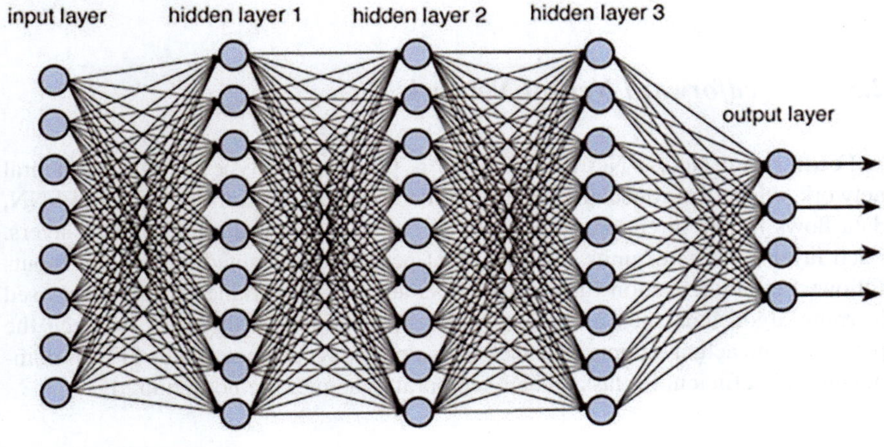

Fig. 2.5 A general structure of a deep neural network

where:

- $a^{(l)}$ is the output (activation) of the lth layer,
- $W^{(l)}$ is the weight matrix of the lth layer,
- $b^{(l)}$} is the bias vector of the lth layer,
- $f^{(l)}$ is the activation function of the lth layer,

Training deep learning models typically involves using backpropagation to compute gradients of the loss function for the weights and biases and updating them using gradient descent or its variants. The gradient descent update rule is given by:

$$W^{(l)} \leftarrow W^{(l)} - \mu \frac{\partial L}{\partial W(l)}$$

where:

- μ is the learning rate,
- $\frac{\partial L}{\partial W(l)}$ is the gradient of the loss function L with respect to the weights $W^{(l.)}$

2.5 Deep Learning Models

There are numerous deep-learning-based models at the forefront of modern AI research. Some of the most common and foundational models include Feedforward Neural Networks (FFNNs), Convolutional Neural Networks (CNNs), Recurrent Neural Networks (RNNs), Autoencoders, and Transfer Learning. Each technique is suited for specific tasks. For example, FFNNs are used for general-purpose learning, CNNs excel in image processing, RNNs are designed for sequence learning, autoencoders are effective for unsupervised learning, and transfer learning enables leveraging pre-trained models for new tasks. This section presents a brief discussion of the concept, characteristics, structure, and applications of these models.

2.5.1 *Feedforward Neural Network*

A Feedforward Neural Network (FFNN) is the simplest type of artificial neural network, where the connections between the nodes do not form a cycle. In FFNN, data flows in one direction, from input to output, passing through hidden layers. Each layer consists of units (neurons) that perform a weighted sum of the inputs followed by an activation function. FFNNs are typically trained using supervised learning algorithms such as gradient descent to minimize the error between the predicted and actual outputs. The lack of cycles and recurrence makes FFNNs computationally efficient for tasks where temporal dynamics are not required.

The architecture of a Feedforward Neural Network generally consists of three layers: the input layer, one or more hidden layers, and the output layer. The input layer receives the data, which is then processed by hidden layers where computations happen based on weights and biases. The output layer produces the result, which could be a class label for classification tasks or a continuous value for regression. The network's layers are fully connected, meaning each neuron in a layer is connected to every neuron in the adjacent layer. Training involves adjusting the weights using backpropagation, where the error from the output is propagated backward to update weights iteratively.

FFNNs are widely applied in cybersecurity for tasks such as intrusion detection, malware analysis, and phishing email detection. In intrusion detection systems (IDS), FFNNs are trained to classify network traffic as normal or malicious based on features such as packet size, protocol, and connection patterns (Rosay et al., 2020).

2.5.2 *Convolutional Neural Networks*

Convolutional Neural Networks (CNNs) are specialized neural networks designed for processing structured grid-like data, such as images. They are similar to ordinary neural networks but have several key distinctions that optimize their performance for visual data such as images, videos, etc. CNNs leverage the spatial and hierarchical structure of images, whereas the regular neural networks do not account for any spatial structure, treating all input features as independent.

CNNs are a class of deep learning models specifically designed for processing structured grid-like data, such as images and time series. Figure 2.6 shows the general CNNs model such as CNNs consisting of layers such as convolutional, pooling, and fully connected layers that work together to extract hierarchical features from

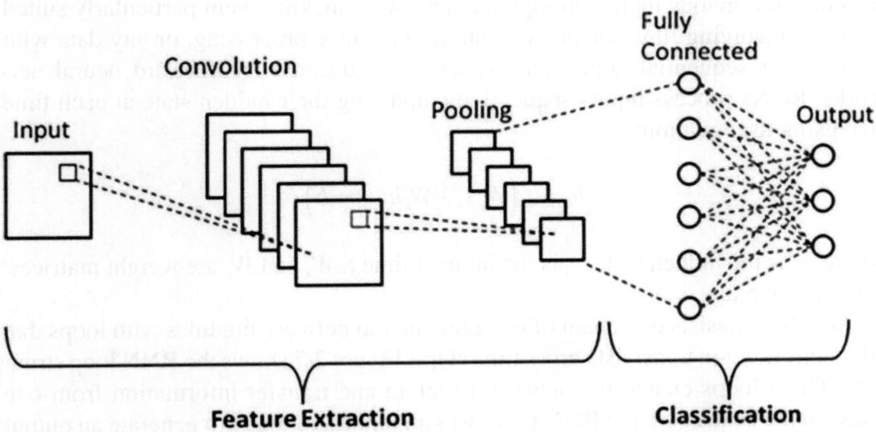

Fig. 2.6 shows the general structure of a convolutional neural network

the input. The convolutional layers apply learnable filters to local regions of the input data, enabling the detection of patterns like edges, shapes, and textures. Pooling layers reduce the spatial dimensions of the feature maps, making computations efficient and introducing invariance to minor transformations. Finally, fully connected layers at the end of the network aggregate these features to make predictions, often for tasks like classification or regression. CNNs excel in handling high-dimensional data due to their ability to reduce the number of learnable parameters while retaining critical information. This makes them versatile and highly effective for complex tasks in computer vision, natural language processing, and beyond.

Initially, CNNs were developed for image processing tasks, but their utility has expanded to fields like natural language processing, audio recognition, and cybersecurity. In cybersecurity, Deep learning models including CNNs play a vital role in addressing complex challenges by automating threat detection and response (Vinayakumar et al., 2017). For instance, in malware classification, traditional methods rely on manual feature engineering to identify malicious patterns in files or executables. CNNs, however, can directly learn these patterns from raw binary files or visual representations of malware. CNNs can convert malware binaries into grayscale images and classify them based on learned visual patterns, eliminating the need for extensive manual intervention (Nataraj et al., 2011)

2.5.3 Recurrent Neural Networks and LSTM

An artificial neural network with a sequential information structure is known as a Recurrent Neural Network (RNN). They are referred to as recurrent because they execute the same function on each sequence element, with the outcome depending on prior calculations. RNNs are designed to handle sequential data by incorporating connections that form directed cycles. These cycles enable RNNs to maintain a memory of previous inputs through hidden states, making them particularly suited for tasks involving time-series data, natural language processing, or any data with temporal or sequential dependencies. Unlike traditional feedforward neural networks, RNNs process inputs sequentially, updating their hidden state at each time step using the equation:

$$h_t = f\left(W_x x_t + W_h h_{\{t-1\}} + b\right)$$

where, h_t is the hidden state, x_t is the input at time t, W_x and W_h are weight matrices, and b is the bias.

An RNN consists of a chain of repeating neural network modules with loops that allow information to persist across time steps. Figure 2.7 shows the RNN loop structure. These loops enable the network to retain and transfer information from one phase to the next. A simple RNN processes an input x_t at time t to generate an output h_t, with the loop facilitating the flow of information between network states.

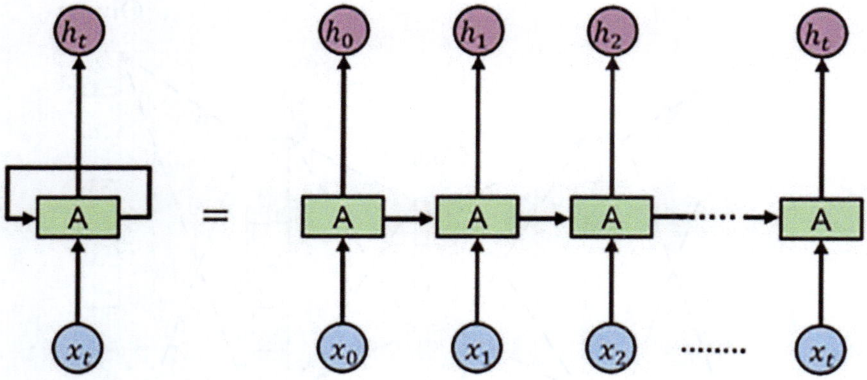

Fig. 2.7 A simple RNN loop structure

However, traditional RNNs often struggle with maintaining long-term dependencies, which LSTMs are explicitly designed to overcome.

Long Short-Term Memory (LSTM) networks are a specialized type of Recurrent Neural Network (RNN) designed to learn and retain long-term dependencies in sequential data (Hochreiter & Schmidhuber, 1997) LSTM networks have demonstrated exceptional performance across a wide range of problems and are extensively used in various applications. Unlike traditional RNNs, which struggle with the vanishing gradient problem during training. LSTMs are specifically engineered to address this issue enabling them to capture long-term relationships in data effectively.

RNNs-based models including LSTM are increasingly used in cybersecurity to model sequential patterns in data such as system logs, network traffic, and user behavior. For example, RNNs are employed in anomaly-based intrusion detection systems (IDS) to analyze network traffic over time and identify suspicious activities (Ullah & Mahmoud, 2022)

2.5.4 Autoencoders

An autoencoder is a specialized type of neural network primarily designed to learn a compressed, meaningful representation of input data and then reconstruct it in such a way that the output is as close as possible to the original input (Bank et al., 2023). Figure 2.8 depicts the general architecture of autoencoder models. This architecture is typically composed of two main parts: encoder and decoder. The encoder compresses the input data into a lower-dimensional latent space (codes), while the decoder attempts to reconstruct the original input from this compressed form. The aim is to minimize the reconstruction error ensuring that the decoded output is as similar as possible to the input.

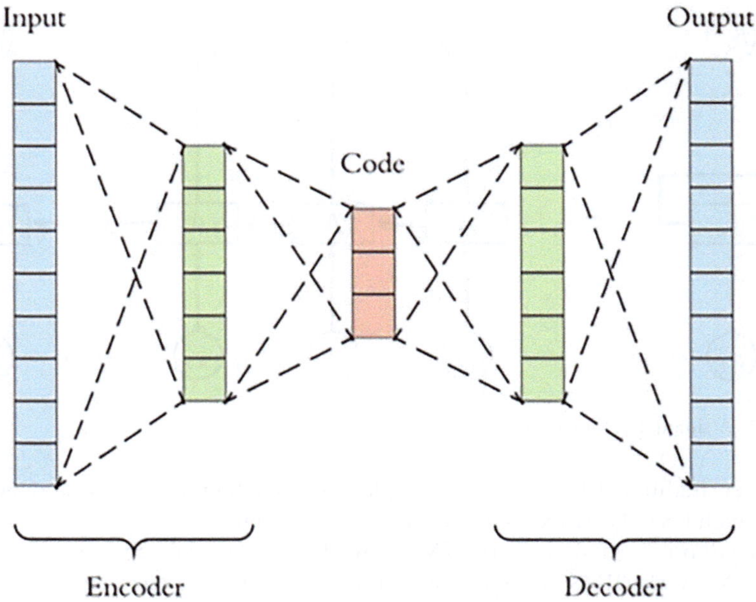

Fig. 2.8 A generic autoencoder model structure

Autoencoders have become an essential tool in unsupervised learning, particularly for tasks involving dimensionality reduction, feature learning, and anomaly detection. Their ability to learn from unlabeled data makes them suitable for various real-world applications. Common types of autoencoders include:

- **Vanilla autoencoders (AEs):** these autoencoders are very simple and commonly used for reconstruction tasks.
- **Variational autoencoders (VAEs):** VAEs incorporate probabilistic modeling to generate new data samples.
- **Denoising autoencoders (DAEs):** These autoencoders are trained to reconstruct data with noise for improving robustness.

Autoencoders are versatile and can be used in various fields. In cybersecurity, autoencoders are effective in detecting anomalies or intrusions by learning the normal behavior of a system or network traffic.

2.5.5 Transfer Learning

Transfer learning is a powerful technique in machine learning where a model trained on one task is repurposed for another related task. This approach is particularly advantageous when the target task has limited labeled data, as the knowledge gained from the source task can be transferred to improve the performance of the model on the target task. Transfer learning leverages pre-trained models, where the lower layers capture generic features such as textures in images or word embeddings in text, and the upper layers are fine-tuned for the new task. This methodology significantly reduces the need for extensive computational resources and time, while also improving model generalization on the target domain.

In computer vision, pre-trained Convolutional Neural Networks (CNNs) like VGGNet, ResNet, and Inception serve as foundational models. These networks are trained on large datasets such as ImageNet, which contains millions of labeled images (Szegedy et al., 2015, 2017). For example, a ResNet model pre-trained on ImageNet can be fine-tuned for specific tasks like medical image analysis or autonomous driving by retraining the upper layers on a smaller, domain-specific dataset. Similarly, in natural language processing (NLP), transformer-based models like BERT (Bidirectional Encoder Representations from Transformers) and GPT (Generative Pre-trained Transformer) have revolutionized the field (Devlin, 2018; Yenduri et al., 2024). These models are pre-trained on vast amounts of text data to understand context and relationships between words, and they can be fine-tuned for tasks such as sentiment analysis, translation, or question answering, with relatively small task-specific datasets.

In cybersecurity, transfer learning is employed to detect anomalies or threats using pre-trained models that are fine-tuned for tasks like malware classification or intrusion detection. For example, pre-trained CNNs can analyze visual representations of malware, while BERT can be adapted for phishing detection by analyzing email content and user messages (Songailaitė et al., 2023).

2.6 Summary

In this chapter, we explored the foundational concepts of AI and ML, starting with an introduction to their importance and applications. The chapter provided an overview of various machine learning models, categorizing them into supervised, unsupervised, semi-supervised, and reinforcement learning. Each machine learning type was discussed in detail, highlighting their unique approaches to problem-solving based on (un) labeled data, data patterns, or environmental interaction.

The chapter then delved into fundamental ML algorithms such as linear regression, logistic regression, decision trees, support vector machines, and k-nearest neighbors, explaining their roles and applications in cybersecurity. We explored the core concepts behind neural networks and their evolution, with an emphasis on deep neural networks (DNNs) and their transformative impact on AI.

Lastly, we discussed deep learning models in detail including Feedforward Neural Networks (FFNNs), Convolutional Neural Networks (CNNs), Recurrent Neural Networks (RNNs) and Long Short-Term Memory (LSTM) networks, Autoencoders, and Transfer Learning. Each model's specific use cases were outlined, showcasing their importance in handling complex data types such as images, sequences, and unsupervised data, and how Transfer Learning has enabled more efficient use of pre-trained models for new tasks. We also briefly discussed their applications in cybersecurity problems including anomaly detection, intrusion detection, malware detection, etc. After studying this chapter, readers can answer the following questions:

- What are the primary differences between supervised, unsupervised, semi-supervised, and reinforcement learning?
- Explain the concept of overfitting and how it can affect a machine learning model's performance.
- How does linear regression differ from logistic regression in terms of its application and use cases?
- What is a decision tree, and how does it make predictions based on input data?
- Describe how Support Vector Machines (SVM) work and their main strengths in classification tasks.
- What are the key advantages of using k-Nearest Neighbors (k-NN) for classification tasks?
- What is the architecture of a simple neural network, and how do neurons work together to solve problems?
- How do Convolutional Neural Networks (CNNs) differ from traditional neural networks, especially in image processing?
- What role do Long Short-Term Memory (LSTM) networks play in processing sequential data?
- How does Transfer Learning work, and why is it useful for tasks where data is limited or expensive to acquire?
- These questions should help reinforce your understanding of the chapter and ensure you have a solid grasp of the key concepts in AI and ML.

References

Akerkar, R., & Sajja, P. (2009). *Knowledge-based systems*. Jones & Bartlett Publishers.

Bank, D., Koenigstein, N., & Giryes, R. (2023). Autoencoders. In *Machine learning for data science handbook: data mining and knowledge discovery handbook* (pp. 353–374).

Burkov, A. (2019). *The hundred-page machine learning book* (Vol. 1). Andriy Burkov.

Cunningham, P., Cord, M., & Delany, S. J. (2008). Supervised learning. In *Machine learning techniques for multimedia: case studies on organization and retrieval* (pp. 21–49). Springer.

Devlin, J. (2018). Bert: Pre-training of deep bidirectional transformers for language understanding. *arXiv preprint* arXiv:1810.04805.

Goodfellow, I., Bengio, Y., & Courville, A. (2016). *Deep learning*. MIT Press.

Hastie, T., et al. (2009). Unsupervised learning. In *The elements of statistical learning: Data mining, inference, and prediction* (pp. 485–585). Springer.

Hinton, G. E., Osindero, S., & Teh, Y. (2006). A fast learning algorithm for deep belief nets. *Neural Computation, 18*(7), 1527–1554. https://doi.org/10.1162/neco.2006.18.7.1527

Hochreiter, S., & Schmidhuber, J. (1997). Long short-term memory. *Neural Computation, 9*(8), 1735–1780.

HOLLOWAY. (n.d.). *A brief history of AI — Making things think: How AI and deep learning power the products we use.* https://www.holloway.com/g/making-things-think/sections/a-brief-history-of-ai

KAGGLE. Diabetes Health Indicators Dataset, Accessed May 2024., https://www.kaggle.com/datasets/alexteboul/diabetes-health-indicators-dataset

Krizhevsky, A., Sutskever, I., & Hinton, G. E. (2017). ImageNet classification with deep convolutional neural networks. *Communications of the ACM, 60*(6), 84–90. https://doi.org/10.1145/3065386

LeCun, Y., Bengio, Y., & Hinton, G. (2015). Deep learning. *Nature, 521*(7553), 436–444.

Nataraj, L., Karthikeyan, S., Jacob, G., & Manjunath, B. S. (2011). Malware images: visualization and automatic classification. In *Proceedings of the 8th international symposium on visualization for cyber security* (pp. 1–7).

Rosay, A., Carlier, F., & Leroux, P. (2020). Feed-forward neural network for network intrusion detection. In *2020 IEEE 91st Vehicular Technology Conference (VTC2020-Spring), Antwerp, Belgium* (pp. 1–6). https://doi.org/10.1109/VTC2020-Spring48590.2020.9129472

Rosenblatt, F. (1958). The perceptron: A probabilistic model for information storage and organization in the brain. *Psychological Review, 65*(6), 386–408. https://doi.org/10.1037/h0042519

Rumelhart, D., Hinton, G., & Williams, R. (1986). Learning representations by back-propagating errors. *Nature, 323*, 533–536. https://doi.org/10.1038/323533a0

Songailaitė, M., Kankevičiūtė, E., Zhyhun, B., & Mandravickaitė, J. (2023). BERT-based models for phishing detection. In *CEUR Workshop proceedings: IVUS 2023: Proceedings of the 28th international conference on Information Society and University Studies, Kaunas, Lithuania, May 12, 2023* (Vol. 3575, pp. 34–44). CEUR-WS.

Szegedy, C., Liu, W., Jia, Y., Sermanet, P., Reed, S., Anguelov, D., Erhan, D., Vanhoucke, V., & Rabinovich, A. (2015). Going deeper with convolutions. In *Proceedings of the IEEE conference on computer vision and pattern recognition* (pp. 1–9). IEEE.

Szegedy, C., Ioffe, S., Vanhoucke, V., & Alemi, A. (2017). Inception-v4, inception-resnet and the impact of residual connections on learning. *Proceedings of the AAAI Conference on Artificial Intelligence, 31*(1).

Ullah, I., & Mahmoud, Q. H. (2022). Design and development of RNN anomaly detection model for IoT networks. *IEEE Access, 10*, 62722–62750. https://doi.org/10.1109/ACCESS.2022.3176317

Vinayakumar, R., Soman, K. P., & Poornachandran, P. (2017). Applying convolutional neural network for network intrusion detection. In *2017 International Conference on Advances in Computing, Communications and Informatics (ICACCI), Udupi, India* (pp. 1222–1228). https://doi.org/10.1109/ICACCI.2017.8126009

Wiering, M. A., & Van Otterlo, M. (2012). Reinforcement learning. *Adaptation, Learning, and Optimization, 12*(3), 729.

Yenduri, G., et al. (2024). GPT (Generative Pre-Trained Transformer)—A comprehensive review on enabling technologies, potential applications, emerging challenges, and future directions. *IEEE Access, 12*, 54608–54649. https://doi.org/10.1109/ACCESS.2024.3389497

Zhu, X. J. (2005). *Semi-supervised learning literature survey.*

Part II
AI in Security

Chapter 3
AI in Security

3.1 Introduction

With the rapid advancements in Artificial Intelligence (AI), its applications in cybersecurity have become increasingly prominent. AI-driven solutions are now integral to modern threat detection, network security, and anomaly characterization, offering enhanced precision, automation, and real-time response capabilities. However, AI serves as a double-edged sword in cybersecurity, with the same advancements that strengthen security research also being exploited by cyber adversaries. Attackers are utilizing AI-generated attacks, creating sophisticated and evasive threats that challenge traditional security defenses.

This sub-chapter explores the general structure of AI and examines how both security researchers and attackers incorporate AI into their work. It discusses the core principles of AI models, their applications in cybersecurity, and the dual role AI plays in both defensive and offensive strategies. By understanding how AI is deployed on both sides, we can better assess its strengths, weaknesses, and the ongoing battle between AI-driven security solutions and AI-enhanced cyber threats.

3.2 General Framework of AI in Security

In the rapidly evolving landscape of cybersecurity, AI has emerged as a critical tool for detecting, analyzing, and mitigating threats. However, there is no universal, one-size-fits-all AI framework that can comprehensively address the diverse challenges faced by the industry. Cybersecurity encompasses a broad spectrum of domains, ranging from network intrusion detection and malware analysis to fraud prevention and endpoint security. Each area presents unique threats, attack vectors, and data

D. P. Sharma et al., *Understanding AI in Cybersecurity and Secure AI*, Progress in IS, https://doi.org/10.1007/978-3-031-91524-6_3

types, requiring tailored AI approaches to effectively respond to specific security needs (Mahdavifar & Ghorbani, 2019).

The dynamic nature of cyber threats further complicates the development of a general AI framework. Attackers continually adapt their methods, leveraging new vulnerabilities and exploiting emerging technologies, which demands that AI solutions remain flexible, adaptive, and scalable. An AI model trained for phishing detection, for instance, may not be effective for ransomware identification or anomaly detection in industrial control systems. This fragmentation highlights the necessity for AI frameworks that can be modular, context-aware, and interoperable across various cybersecurity domains.

Moreover, data availability, quality, and diversity play a pivotal role in shaping AI's effectiveness in security. AI systems thrive on large, high-quality datasets; however, cybersecurity datasets are often scarce, imbalanced, or anonymized, posing challenges to training robust models. The complexity is further amplified by the need for real-time analysis, low-latency responses, and privacy-preserving techniques in sensitive environments.

A general AI framework for cybersecurity must therefore focus on:

- Flexibility: Ability to integrate with various security tools and platforms.
- Continuous Learning: Models that evolve with emerging threats.
- Explainability and Trust: Transparent decision-making to foster trust and reduce false positives.
- Collaboration: Sharing threat intelligence across networks and organizations to build collective resilience.

By recognizing the diverse and evolving nature of cyber threats, the pursuit of a general AI framework lies not in creating a single monolithic solution, but in developing interconnected, adaptive, and specialized models capable of addressing distinct aspects of the security ecosystem (KEARNEY, n.d.; MEDIUM, 2025, n.d.). However, generally, we can define the following generalized tasks when using AI for cybersecurity (OREILLY, 2024) (Fig. 3.1):

- Data collection: AI models require much data to be trained effectively. In cybersecurity, this data can come from multiple sources such as network traffic, system or application logs, memory snapshots, website domains, emails, binary files and others.
- Data analysis: Once the data is collected, it needs to be analyzed based on the type of input feed. If we have binary or APK files, we need to analyze them statically or dynamically. If the input feed is in the binary file format, we must disassemble them using reverse engineering tools such as IDA Pro or Ghidra. If we deal with traffic data, we must select all or part of the payload (depending on the network layer we want to scrutinize) or the header if the traffic is encrypted.
- Pre-processing: Pre-processing consists of different stages, including data cleaning, data transformation, labeling, or feature selection. For example, normalization is one of the steps of data transformation. In the feature selection stage, we remove one of the highly correlated features because they might increase the

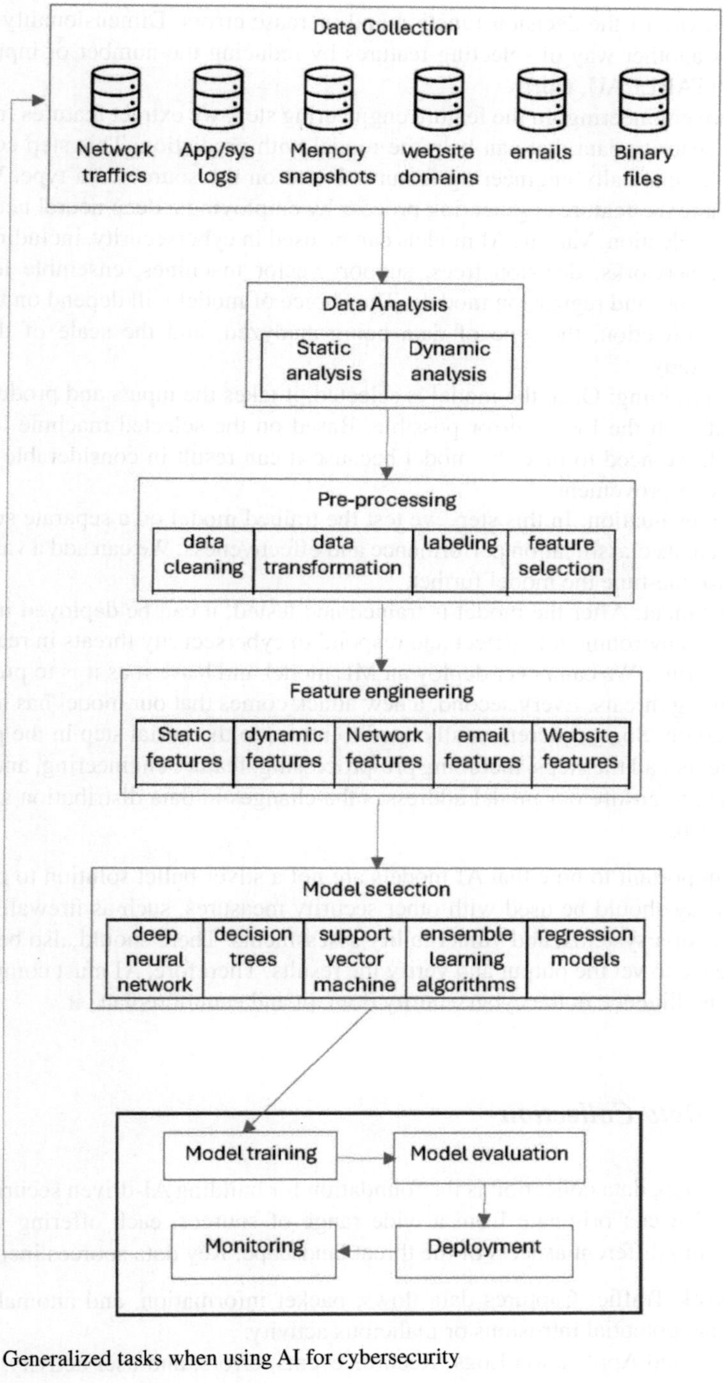

Fig. 3.1 Generalized tasks when using AI for cybersecurity

complexity of the decision function and increase errors. Dimensionality reduction is another way of selecting features by reducing the number of input variables (TABLEAU, n.d.).

- Feature engineering: In the feature engineering step, we extract features from the input security data that can help the model with prediction. This step could be done by manually engineering features based on the source data type. We can automate the feature engineering process by employing a deep neural network.
- Model selection: Various AI models can be used in cybersecurity, including deep neural networks, decision trees, support vector machines, ensemble learning algorithms, and regression models. The choice of model will depend on the specific application, the type of data being analyzed, and the scale of the data under study.
- Model training: Once the model is selected, it takes the inputs and produces the output with the lowest error possible. Based on the selected machine learning model, we need to tune the model because it can result in considerable performance improvement.
- Model evaluation: In this step, we test the trained model on a separate subset to evaluate its classification performance and effectiveness. We can add a validation step to fine-tune the model further.
- Deployment: After the model is trained and tested, it can be deployed in a production environment to detect and respond to cybersecurity threats in real time.
- Monitoring: We can never deploy an ML model and leave it as it is to predict all incoming threats. Every second, a new attack comes that our model has not been trained on. So, we incrementally need to return to the initial step in the pipeline and revisit all the steps, including pre-processing, feature engineering, and model design, to ensure our model addresses the changes in data distribution and concept drift.

It is important to note that AI models are not a silver bullet solution to cybersecurity. They should be used with other security measures, such as firewalls, intrusion detection systems, and vulnerability assessments. There should also be human intelligence to vet the output and verify the results. Therefore, AI must complement human intelligence in the cybersecurity domain and cannot replace it.

3.2.1 Data Collection

As a first step, data collection is the foundation for building AI-driven security solutions, and it can originate from a wide range of sources, each offering valuable insights into different aspects of the threat landscape. Key data sources include:

- Network Traffic: Captures data flows, packet information, and anomalies that indicate potential intrusions or malicious activity.
- System and Application Logs: Records events, errors, and user activity, providing visibility into system behavior and potential breaches.

- Memory Snapshots: Offers insight into the state of running processes, aiding in malware detection and forensic analysis.
- Website Domains and URLs: Used to identify phishing sites, domain generation algorithms (DGA), and malicious web addresses.
- Emails: Analyzed for phishing attempts, malicious attachments, and suspicious links.
- Binary Files and Executables: Scanned for malware signatures, behavioral patterns, and vulnerabilities.
- Smartphone Package Kit (APK/IPA) Files: Assessed to detect mobile malware, permissions abuse, and code tampering.
- CVE (Common Vulnerabilities and Exposures): Details known vulnerabilities, allowing AI models to recognize and mitigate exploits.
- CWE (Common Weakness Enumeration): Highlights software weaknesses that could lead to security vulnerabilities.
- CAPEC (Common Attack Pattern Enumeration and Classification): Describes common attack patterns to anticipate and defend against emerging threats.
- Threat Intelligence Feeds: Provides real-time data on evolving threats, IP blacklists, and attack campaigns.

By aggregating and analyzing data from these diverse and distributed sources, AI frameworks can build a comprehensive security posture, improving threat detection, response, and prevention across multiple attack surfaces. This multi-faceted data-driven approach is essential for developing **robust and adaptive AI models** capable of addressing the dynamic nature of cyber threats.

3.2.1.1 Structured vs. Unstructured Data

In cybersecurity applications, we typically encounter two primary forms of data:

- **Structured data:** This type comprises flattened feature vectors, often illustrated by elements like API call frequencies. Generated through comprehensive preprocessing, they offer a holistic understanding of the entire dataset.
- **Unstructured data:** This category encompasses sequences such as deep packet captures, malware log recordings, and binary code patterns. These sequences are detailed and unrefined, with significant dependency on their individual components. Drawing clear interpretations from merging elements of these sequences is difficult, unlike the more linear sequences seen in textual or DNA data.

3.2.1.2 Data-Centric AI for Security

Understanding the input data and ensuring its quality guarantees the success of an AI-based security model (ANALYTICSINDIAMAG, n.d.). Preparing a clean security dataset with minimum noisy data, high variance, and consistent labeling is one of cybersecurity AI-based models' most challenging tasks. A data-centric perspective for deploying an efficient ML model in cybersecurity allows us to create high-quality security datasets. It would be an invaluable weapon in our arsenal for solving security problems.

3.2.2 Data Analysis

Data analysis in cybersecurity is a critical step following data collection. It involves examining security data to extract insights, detect threats, and support decision-making. The analysis techniques can be broadly categorized into static analysis and dynamic analysis, depending on whether the data is analyzed without execution or in a live environment.

The process often begins with the examination of security files, such as APK or binary files. This examination can be approached in two predominant ways:

Static Analysis

- For static analysis, an APK file is first unzipped, revealing key components like the Android manifest (*.XML) and classes (.dex). The .dex files are then disassembled to generate Dalvik VM assembly code, while *.XML files are parsed to extract metadata, such as the package name, permissions, and linked libraries. For binary files, e.g., Windows executables, the process differs slightly. These binaries are often compressed using tools like UPX or ASPack Shell and require unpacking before analysis. Once unpacked, they are disassembled using reverse engineering tools such as IDA Pro or Ghidra to examine their structure and behavior.

Dynamic Analysis

- In dynamic analysis, the APK or binary file is executed in a controlled environment, such as an emulator, sandbox, or directly on hardware (smartphone or PC). During execution, various data points, such as network traffic, API calls, and system call traces are captured to analyze runtime behavior. To ensure accurate results, the application's natural operational environment must be mirrored as closely as possible. This often involves interacting with the application, either manually or via automated tools like Monkey, which simulates user behavior.

By combining static and dynamic analysis, cybersecurity professionals can gain a comprehensive understanding of potential threats, vulnerabilities, and anomalous behaviors in software and systems.

3.2.3 Pre-Processing

In the pre-processing stage, the extracted features undergo several modifications. Initially, data is cleaned by filtering outliers, eliminating duplicates, and rectifying missing values, often via imputation methods. Subsequently, features undergo a transformation, which might involve normalization or even conversion into RGB color images. The processed data, whether as images, sequences, or tables (tabular data), is further refined into a final feature vector. Given the potential volume of this vector, it's often condensed using techniques like Principal Component Analysis (PCA) for more efficient input into the machine learning model. It is also essential to identify and address highly correlated features at this stage, as they can adversely affect the robustness of the subsequent classifier.

3.2.4 Feature Engineering

Feature engineering is a crucial step in applying AI to cybersecurity problems, as it transforms raw security data into meaningful features that improve model performance. The extraction of features depends on the nature of the data being analyzed—whether it's sequential, image-based, or structured. In most cases, the data is structured, forming a matrix that is suitable for machine learning models. Static features are typically extracted after static analysis, which involves decoding resources. These features can take various forms, including API calls, strings, URL-based attributes, opcode sequences, and file-related traits like permissions. On the other hand, dynamic features are derived from logs or packet capture files (e.g.,. PCAP files) recorded during application execution. These features capture behaviors such as API call patterns, system call sequences, and network traffic. For network traffic, dedicated components are used to extract key features from. PCAP files, which can reveal important attack patterns. In cases involving email datasets, features might include bag-of-words, structural attributes, link details, and specifics about individual email elements. For websites, the features can be diverse, ranging from URL details and source code insights to security aspects and content presentation. When dealing with sequential data, like website text or network traffic logs, embeddings are often created and utilized in language models to further analyze patterns and anomalies. This helps capture contextual meaning, making the analysis more effective in detecting sophisticated threats.

3.2.5 Model Selection

The ML model we select directly depends on the data type, the correlation between statistical variables, the scalability and performance requirements, the size of the dataset, and the level of explainability demanded. For example, if we have too much highly correlated data, we would prefer to use deep neural network data to extract interesting patterns in the data. Otherwise, we would choose SVM or logistic regression if the decision function is highly linear. For nominal features, decision trees and random forest work might be the best option, and if the variables are independent, we will select Naive Bayes (TOWARDSDATASCIENCE, n.d.).

3.2.6 Model Training

During the model training phase, the data is typically divided into two sets: one for training and the other for testing. About 70%–80% of the data is allocated for training, while the remaining 20%–30% is reserved for testing. We then configure the model's hyperparameters and initiate training using the training dataset. Particularly for AI models like deep learning systems, careful adjustment of these hyperparameters is essential, as they can significantly influence the final results.

3.2.7 Model Evaluation

Once the AI model has been trained and stabilized over multiple iterations, it's saved for evaluation. We then test the model using the testing dataset to assess its classification accuracy. In some cases, a separate validation set might be used for fine-tuning, with the most effective model being retained. Additional testing, either on the data or the model itself, may also be conducted to ensure the model is ready for deployment.

3.2.8 Deployment

Once ready, the model is integrated into the target security application, be it for detecting network attacks, malware, or phishing sites. It can be deployed across various settings, and users typically interact with it via APIs embedded in software applications. ML engineers must ensure optimal resource allocation, considering GPU/CPU and memory needs. They also need to strategize how security data streams into the model. Proper training should be provided to users to leverage the model's full potential.

3.2.9 Monitoring

AI models cannot remain static. They need regular updates and retraining to stay abreast of emerging threats. There are inherent biases in cybersecurity data, such as spatial and temporal biases (Pendlebury et al., 2019), which can impede the model's robustness against evolving threats. Spatial bias, for instance, can skew the distribution between benign and malicious data, differing from real-world scenarios. Temporal bias can arise when training and testing data sets don't align timewise. As new threats surface, the feature set might need refining or expanding, necessitating frequent model retraining. Incremental machine learning offers a practical approach to continual model training during the monitoring phase.

3.3 AI-Driven Security Models

AI is a dual-edged sword in cybersecurity, with both defenders and adversaries leveraging its capabilities to achieve their objectives. On one side, cybercriminals and malicious actors utilize AI to automate attacks, evade detection, generate sophisticated malware, and exploit vulnerabilities at an unprecedented scale. On the other side, security researchers and professionals harness AI to develop advanced intrusion detection systems, automated threat intelligence, anomaly detection, and proactive defense mechanisms. This section will explore both aspects in detail, first examining how attackers exploit AI to enhance cyber threats, and then shifting to the defensive side, showcasing how AI-driven security solutions are designed to counter these evolving attacks. Understanding this interplay is crucial for developing resilient, adaptive, and intelligent cybersecurity strategies that stay ahead of adversarial AI techniques.

3.3.1 AI-Driven Cyberattacks

AI-driven cyberattacks utilize AI and ML methods to automate, accelerate, and enhance various phases of an attack. These attacks can identify vulnerabilities, deploy campaigns along specific attack vectors, establish backdoors in systems, tamper with or exfiltrate data, and disrupt operations (Guembea, et al., 2022; Stanham, 2025). The adaptive nature of AI allows such attacks to evolve and bypass detection, making them increasingly difficult to counter. The rise of large language models (LLMs) with enhanced capabilities such as interacting with external tools, reading and analyzing documents, and even recursively calling themselves has sparked significant impact on cybersecurity (Fang et al., 2024). The potential for LLMs to act autonomously as agents introduces both opportunities and risks in the cybersecurity landscape. Weaponized AI as malicious AI algorithms degrade the performance and disrupt the normal functions of the AI systems and provide technological edge attack scenarios in both cyberspace and physical spaces (Yamin et al., 2021). Data misclassification, synthetic data generation and data analysis are new types of cyberattacks powered by AI. However, AI technology can be applied to various other attack scenarios. Figure 3.2 shows the taxonomy of AI driven cyberattacks which broadly classify AI driven cyberattacks into following five broad categories.

AI-Powered Attacks In this attack, an attacker utilizes AI and ML algorithms to automate and enhance various phases of cyberattacks. These attacks utilize AI/ML

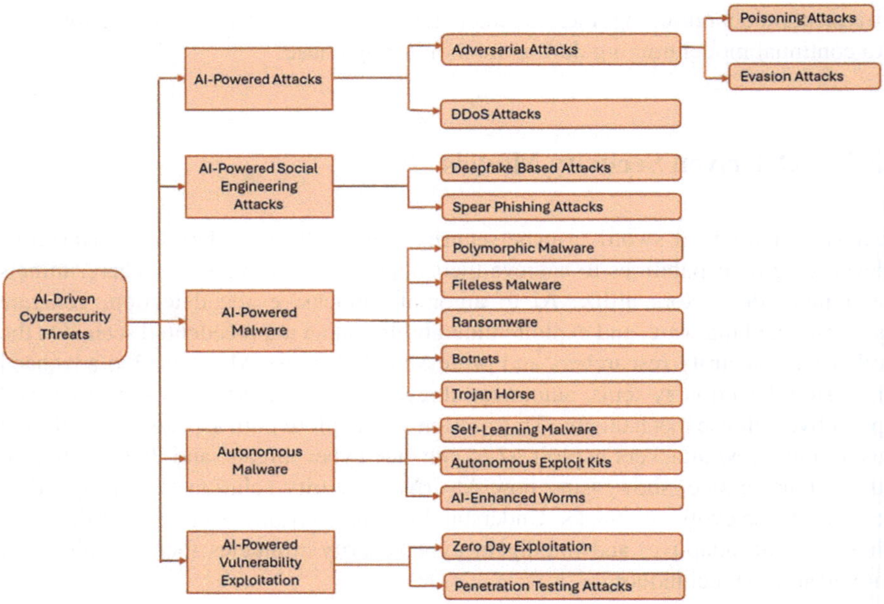

Fig. 3.2 AI-driven cybersecurity threats taxonomy

to identify vulnerabilities, adapt to defenses, and improve success rates. Two prominent types of attacks under this category are adversarial attacks and DDoS attacks are under this class.

- In adversarial attacks, attackers manipulate the inputs to AI systems to deceive or compromise their decision-making. AI methods are used to craft adversarial examples or to learn about a target model's weaknesses. Poisoning attacks, and evasion attacks are two common adversarial threats to AI systems.
- Poisoning attacks target the training phase of machine learning models, aiming to corrupt the model's learning process by injecting malicious or misleading data into the training dataset. For example, an AI-powered poisoning attack can target a facial recognition system used for security authentication in airports or banking services. An attacker inserts manipulated images into the system's training dataset—such as subtly altered images of individuals with imperceptible pixel modifications. These malicious images mislead the model into learning incorrect facial patterns, allowing unauthorized individuals to bypass security by being misclassified as trusted users. Over time, the model becomes compromised, making it easier for attackers to evade detection and gain unauthorized access to restricted areas or sensitive accounts.
- Evasion attacks occur during the inference phase where attackers manipulate input data to fool the model into making incorrect predictions or classifications. For example, an evasion attack can target an email spam filtering system that relies on machine learning to classify emails as spam or legitimate messages. An

attacker manipulates the structure of spam emails by slightly modifying key words, sentence structures, or embedding spam content in image attachments instead of text. By doing so, the attacker avoids detection, as the altered emails no longer match the patterns the spam filter has learned. Over time, the attacker refines the strategy using AI-powered techniques, ensuring that a higher percentage of spam emails successfully reach users' inboxes while bypassing traditional filtering mechanisms.

– AI-powered DDoS attacks use machine learning algorithms to optimize attack strategies and making them more effective at overwhelming a target's resources. In this attack, AI enables learning of normal traffic patterns to blend malicious traffic more effectively and avoid detection and optimize the coordination of massive botnets to execute large-scale DDoS attacks. For example, An attacker leverages AI-driven botnets to launch a highly adaptive DDoS attack against an online banking platform. The AI model first analyzes normal traffic patterns of legitimate users, learning the typical request rates, access times, and behavior of real customers. Using this intelligence, the attacker orchestrates a botnet composed of thousands of compromised IoT devices and cloud-based virtual machines. By the way, instead of flooding the target with obvious high-volume traffic spikes, the AI-powered botnet mimics real user behavior, generating requests that appear legitimate while slowly exhausting the system's resources. The attack dynamically adjusts in real-time, modifying request intervals and payload sizes to evade traditional DDoS detection mechanisms. As a result, the bank's servers become overwhelmed, leading to service disruptions, slowdowns, or complete outages, preventing legitimate customers from accessing their accounts.

AI-Powered Social Engineering Attacks Social engineering attacks manipulate individuals into revealing sensitive information, such as credentials or personal details, through psychological tactics. AI enhances social engineering attacks by crafting highly personalized and convincing messages (Schmitt & Flechais, 2024).

– Deepfake-based attacks and spear phishing emails are two common categories under these types of attacks. For example, a cybercriminal uses deepfake technology to impersonate the CEO of a multinational company in a video call. The attacker first collects publicly available video and audio clips of the CEO from conferences, interviews, and social media. Using advanced AI deepfake tools, they generate a highly realistic video that mimics the CEO's voice, facial expressions, and speech patterns. The attacker then contacts the company's finance department via video call, appearing as the CEO, and urgently instructs the CFO to transfer $5 million to a "confidential acquisition deal." Since the deepfake perfectly replicates the CEO, the CFO does not suspect fraud and authorizes the transaction before verifying the request.
– Attackers leverage generative AI models for analyzing vast amounts of data to mimic individual writing styles, creating phishing emails or messages and other forms of social engineering that looks legitimate ones (Muraleedhara, 2024). This makes it difficult for users to distinguish between real and fraudulent com-

munications, increasing the likelihood of falling victim to the scam. For example, a cybercriminal uses a generative AI model to analyze publicly available emails, LinkedIn posts, and social media interactions of a senior executive at a financial firm. The AI model learns the executive's writing style, tone, and typical phrases, allowing the attacker to generate a highly convincing phishing email. The attacker then sends an email to the company's HR department, impersonating the executive. The email requests an urgent update on payroll details and includes a malicious link disguised as an internal company portal. Since the email closely matches the executive's actual communication style, HR personnel do not suspect fraud and click the link, unknowingly entering their credentials on a fake login page controlled by the attacker.

AI also enables hackers to automate and scale these attacks, speeding up the exploitation process and allowing for more widespread attacks. Deepfake attacks use AI to manipulate audio, video, and images to impersonate individuals and create convincing fake content. Attackers use publicly available media such as social media photos, videos, and phone calls to generate realistic content to deceive or manipulate public opinion.

AI-Powered Malware AI-powered malware can autonomously modify its code, making it more challenging for security systems to identify and neutralize threats. Polymorphic malware, fileless malware, ransomware, botnets, and trojan horse are the common cyberattacks they used AI methods for making their malicious activity more effective. For instance, AI algorithms can be used to create polymorphic malware that changes its signature to avoid signature-based detection systems. Similarly, AI-powered ransomware attacks enable hackers to automate the entire attack process from identifying network vulnerabilities to exploiting them and encrypting company data. Once the files are encrypted, then attackers demand a ransom payment in exchange for the decryption key, streamlining and accelerating the attack. In this case, AI enables attackers to scale operations, optimize ransom demands, and adapt dynamically to security defenses.

Autonomous Malware Autonomous malware refers to a new generation of malicious software that incorporates self-learning capabilities. Unlike traditional malware, which is manually crafted and programmed with specific instructions, autonomous malware can adapt to its environment, learn from its interactions, and make decisions on its own to evade detection or increase its impact (Bolen, 2024).

- Self-learning malwares operate without direct human control, making decisions in real-time to optimize its impact. These malwares can be different types such as self-learning malware, autonomous exploit kits and enhanced worms. Self-learning malware can adapt and improve over time by learning from its environment. A new strain of self-learning ransomware, called "AdaptiveCrypt," spreads through phishing emails and malicious downloads. Unlike traditional ransomware, AdaptiveCrypt uses AI-driven decision-making to analyze the infected system in real-time. Once inside a network, the malware monitors user behavior,

system defenses, and file access patterns. It delays encryption until it identifies high-value targets, such as financial records or confidential corporate documents. If it detects security scans or sandbox environments, it alters its behavior to avoid detection, waiting for a more vulnerable moment to activate. Over time, AdaptiveCrypt learns the best attack vectors by analyzing multiple infected systems. It automatically refines its encryption techniques, ransom note strategies, and communication methods to increase success rates. Additionally, it can mutate its code dynamically, making it harder for traditional antivirus programs to detect and mitigate. By continuously evolving based on real-world interactions, self-learning malware like AdaptiveCrypt poses a growing threat to cybersecurity, requiring more advanced AI-driven defense mechanisms to combat it.
- Autonomous exploit kits can automatically identify and exploit vulnerabilities in systems without human intervention. For example, BlackMamba is an AI-powered autonomous exploit kit that automatically identifies vulnerabilities and generates polymorphic malware in real-time. It utilizes machine learning models to evade detection by modifying its attack patterns dynamically. This enables it to bypass traditional security defenses and execute targeted cyberattacks without human intervention.
- AI-enhanced worms are self-replicating and self-propagating malware that use AI to adapt and spread. For example, WormGPT is an AI-powered autonomous exploit kit designed for automated cyberattacks. It can identify system vulnerabilities, generate exploit code, and execute attacks without human intervention. WormGPT adapts to different security environments, enabling cybercriminals to launch sophisticated zero-day exploits and ransomware campaigns at scale.

AI-Powered Vulnerability Exploitation AI tools can be used to automatically detect and exploit vulnerabilities in software and networks. Automatic vulnerability discovery and zero day exploitation are common examples of AI-driven vulnerability exploitation attacks. In automatic vulnerability discovery, AI or ML models can be trained to recognize patterns in code that suggest vulnerabilities such as buffer overflows, race conditions, or logic errors and discover new attack surfaces. By automating the process of vulnerability discovery, AI enables attackers to find zero-day flaws faster and more efficiently.

- A zero-day exploitation attack leverages AI to automatically identify and exploit unknown vulnerabilities in software or systems before developers can patch them, enabling stealthy and highly effective cyberattacks. For example, DeepExploit is an AI-powered automated penetration testing tool that utilizes machine learning to detect and exploit zero-day vulnerabilities in software and networks. It autonomously scans, identifies weaknesses, and launches targeted exploits without human intervention. Unlike traditional vulnerability scanners, DeepExploit continuously learns and adapts its attack strategies, making it more effective at breaching systems and discovering previously unknown security flaws.
- An **AI-based penetration testing attack** utilizes machine learning and automation to simulate real-world cyberattacks, rapidly identifying vulnerabilities in

networks, applications, and systems with minimal human intervention. For example, MITRE CALDERA, leverages machine learning to simulate real-world cyberattacks, autonomously probing networks, adapting attack strategies in real-time, and identifying security weaknesses that human testers might overlook.

3.3.2 AI-Driven Security Solutions

This rest of this section, AI in Security, will explore AI-driven cybersecurity solutions across various domains, detailing how artificial intelligence and machine learning enhance network security, software security, cloud security, and IoT/OT security. Each chapter focuses on a specific cybersecurity area, demonstrating how AI-based methodologies improve threat detection, risk mitigation, and proactive defense mechanisms. Additionally, we will analyze how adversaries are leveraging AI for cyberattacks, making it imperative to develop robust, adaptive, and intelligent security solutions.

- Chapter 4 will focus on AI for Network Security, covering traditional network protection strategies such as signature-based, anomaly-based, policy-based, and reputation-based detection. It then explores AI/ML-based protection mechanisms, examining how supervised, semi-supervised, unsupervised, and reinforced learning models improve intrusion detection and prevention systems. The discussion extends to the future of AI in network security, outlining key challenges and advancements in intelligent traffic analysis, automated response mechanisms, and adversarial resilience.
- Chapter 5 shifts the focus to AI for Software Security, detailing AI-driven approaches for securing applications against cyber threats. It highlights smartphone and web application vulnerabilities, including injection attacks, cryptographic failures, and authentication weaknesses. Furthermore, it delves into AI-based user authentication, biometric security, anomaly detection, and malware analysis, showcasing how AI enhances vulnerability assessment and patch management to reduce security risks.
- Chapter 6 explores AI for Cloud Security, discussing security and privacy challenges such as misconfigurations, unauthorized access, malware injections, and insider threats. AI solutions such as predictive analysis, proactive defense, behavioral authentication, security automation, and cloud compliance will be examined, demonstrating how AI strengthens threat hunting and incident response in cloud environments.
- Finally, Chapter 7 addresses AI for IoT and OT Security, emphasizing security concerns across IoT layers, Industrial IoT (IIoT), and Operational Technology (OT) networks. The chapter introduces AI-based OT security, AI-driven IoT protection, and the emerging risks of AI-powered attacks on IoT systems. It also outlines future trends in AI-driven IoT security, providing insights into adaptive

security frameworks, self-healing systems, and AI-powered real-time threat mitigation.

Each chapter will systematically explore how AI is transforming cybersecurity, highlighting both opportunities and challenges in its adoption. By analyzing AI-driven solutions and adversarial threats, this section aims to provide a comprehensive understanding of AI's dual role in cybersecurity and the evolving landscape of AI-powered defense strategies.

3.4 Summary

This chapter outlined a comprehensive framework for integrating AI into a cybersecurity strategy, covering data collection, analysis, preprocessing, feature extraction, model selection, training, evaluation, and deployment. The process does not end at deployment, as continuous monitoring and updates are crucial to maintaining effectiveness. While AI significantly enhances cybersecurity, it must work alongside other security measures and human expertise for a well-rounded defense.

A key aspect explored is AI's dual-edged role in cybersecurity, benefiting both defenders and adversaries. Cybercriminals leverage AI to automate attacks, evade detection, and generate advanced malware, while security professionals use AI to develop intrusion detection systems, threat intelligence, and proactive defense mechanisms. Understanding this dynamic is essential to building adaptive, intelligent cybersecurity strategies that stay ahead of adversarial AI techniques.

References

Mahdavifar, S., & Ghorbani, A. A. (2019). Application of deep learning to cybersecurity: A survey. *Neurocomputing, 347*, 149–176.

MEDIUM. (2025). *AI security frameworks and guidelines, Michael Hannecke*. Accessed February 2025, https://medium.com/bluetuple-ai/outsmarting-the-smart-guys-a-list-of-ai-security-frameworks-and-guidelines-5d126569a2fa

KEARNEY. (n.d.). *Securing AI systems with a comprehensive framework*. https://www.kearney.com/service/digital-analytics/article/securing-ai-systems-with-a-comprehensive-framework

MEDIUM. (n.d.). *AI security frameworks in-depth — Part 2, Sita Lakshmi Sangameswaran*. https://medium.com/google-cloud/ai-security-frameworks-in-depth-ca7494c030aa

OREILLY. *Building machine learning pipelines by Hannes Hapke, Catherine Nelson*. Accessed April 2024, https://www.oreilly.com/library/view/building-machine-learning/9781492053187/ch01.html

ANALYTICSINDIAMAG. (n.d.). *Big data to good data: Andrew Ng urges ML community to be more data-centric and less model-centric*. https://analyticsindiamag.com/big-data-to-good-data-andrew-ng-urges-ml-community-to-be-more-data-centric-and-less-model-centric/?utm_campaign=Events%20and%20Community&utm_content=161083931&utm_medium=social&utm_source=linkedin&hss_channel=lcp-18246783

TABLEAU. (n.d.). *Guide to data cleaning: Definition, benefits, components, and how to clean your data*. https://www.tableau.com/learn/articles/what-is-data-cleaning

TOWARDSDATASCIENCE. (n.d.). *Considerations when choosing a machine learning model.* https://towardsdatascience.com/considerations-when-choosing-a-machine-learning-model-aa31f52c27f3

Pendlebury, F., et al. (2019). TESSERACT: Eliminating experimental bias in malware classification across space and time. In *Proceedings of the 28th USENIX security symposium*. USENIX Association.

Guembea, B., Azetab, A., Misra, S., Osamora, V. C., Fernandez-Sanz, L., & Pospelova, A. V. (2022). The emerging threat of AI-driven cyber attacks: A review. *Applied Artificial Intelligence*. https://doi.org/10.1080/08839514.2022.2037254

Stanham, L. (16 de January 16 de 2025). *AI-powered cyberattacks*. Obtenido de Crowdstrike: https://www.crowdstrike.com/en-us/cybersecurity-101/cyberattacks/ai-powered-cyberattacks

Fang, R., Bindu, R., Gupta, A., Zhan, Q., & Kang, D. (2024). LLM agents can autonomously hack websites. *arXiv preprint* arXiv:2402.06664. Obtenido de https://arxiv.org/abs/2402.06664

Yamin, M. M., Ullah, M., Ullah, H., & Katt, B. (2021). Weaponized AI for cyber attacks. *Journal of Information Security and Applications*. https://doi.org/10.1016/j.jisa.2020.102722

Schmitt, M., & Flechais, I. (2024). Digital deception: Generative artificial intelligence in social engineering and phishing. *Artificial Intelligence Review, 57*. https://doi.org/10.1007/s10462-024-10973-2

Muraleedhara, P. (23 de April de 2024). *The need for AI-powered cybersecurity to tackle AI-driven cyberattacks*. Obtenido de ISACA: https://www.isaca.org/resources/news-and-trends/isaca-now-blog/2024/the-need-for-ai-powered-cybersecurity-to-tackle-ai-driven-cyberattacks

Bolen, S. (21 de November de 2024). *AI: The new frontier of zero-day exploits*. Obtenido de Medium: https://medium.com/@scottbolen/ai-the-new-frontier-of-zero-day-exploits-750dde0a69ac

Chapter 4
AI for Network Security

4.1 Introduction

Nowadays, communication network architectures continually evolve to integrate a diverse range of devices with unique requirements for different network parameters. This has resulted in sophisticated challenges for network security. Network security is a broad and complex field, but it can be distilled into several main principles that serve as the foundation for protecting data, systems, and networks from various threats. These principles include confidentiality, integrity, and availability.

Since the early 1980s, when the first generation of network security protection technologies were introduced, they have evolved through several stages and phases. In general speaking, the network security protection evolution can be classified into nine stages, as follows (LaPorte, 2023):

- Stage 1: Firewall.

  A firewall is a network security device which acts as a first line of defense in network security to monitor incoming and outgoing network traffic. Based on a defined set of security rules, the firewall decides whether to allow or block specific traffic. In fact, a network firewall establishes a barrier between secured and controlled internal networks that can be trusted and untrusted outside networks, such as the Internet. The firewall can be hardware, software, software-as-a service (SaaS), public cloud, or private cloud (virtual). The first generation of firewall was the packet filtering firewall and was developed by Digital Equipment Cooperation (DEC) in the year of 1988. It was not aimed to detect a virus or any network threats, it was only used to protect the network against unwanted packets from certain source IP addresses (Liang & Kim, 2022).
- Stage 2: Unified Threat Management (UTM):

  UTM provides multiple security features or services combined into a single device. It provides a wide range of security services such as rule matching packet filtering, stateful inspection, deep packet inspection, intrusion detection (or pre-

D. P. Sharma et al., *Understanding AI in Cybersecurity and Secure AI*, Progress in IS, https://doi.org/10.1007/978-3-031-91524-6_4

vention) system, application, circuit gateway, and etc. UTM reduces the complexity of maintaining multiple firewalls for different purposes, and it is easy to deploy and install (Liang & Kim, 2022). As the network capacity increases to 40 Gbps and beyond, it becomes important to tune network analysis tools (e.g., Snort[1] and Suricata[2]) to provide lossless detection to the network. By developing UTM capabilities, they are able to handle higher traffic speeds. For instance, Crystal Eye UTM appliances[3] are multi-core systems that enable multi-threaded applications to use the underlying hardware for high performance (Jakimoski & Singhai, 2019).

- Stage 3: Intrusion Detection System (IDS):
  IDS products search for suspicious behavior or signs of a potential compromise by analyzing the packets that move across the network and the traffic patterns to identify any anomalies. The main purpose of an IDS is to detect various types of malicious network communications and computer systems usage for prevention. An IDS conducts the process of identifying malicious cyber-attack behavior on a network while monitoring and evaluating the daily activities in a network or computer system to detect security risks or threats such as denial-of-service (DoS). It also helps to discover, determine and identify unauthorized system behavior such as unauthorized access, or modification and destruction. Detecting various types of cyber-attacks and anomalies in a network and to build an effective IDS that performs an essential role in today's network security is needed to facilitate a system's security (Sarker et al., 2020).
- Stage 4: Intrusion Prevention System (IPS).
  An IPS monitors network traffic for potential threats and automatically takes actions (e.g., blocking/removing malicious traffic, or enforcing security policies). Basically, it has the same threat detection and reporting functions as an IDS plus automated threat prevention abilities, which is why IPSs are sometimes called "intrusion detection and prevention systems" (IDPS). IPS solutions can be software applications installed on endpoints; dedicated hardware devices connected to the network or delivered as cloud services. Because IPSs must be able to block malicious activity in real time, they're always placed "inline" on the network, meaning traffic passes directly through the IPS before reaching its destination (IBM Documentation, 2023a).
- Stage 5: NetFlow.
  NetFlow is a Cisco IOS technology that provides statistics on packets flowing through the router. It is the standard for acquiring IP operational data from IP networks (both IPv4 and IPv6 flows). NetFlow provides data to enable network and security monitoring, network planning, traffic analysis, and IP accounting. NetFlow is a proprietary accounting technology and monitors traffic flows through a network device (e.g., switch or router), and interprets the client, server,

[1] https://www.snort.org/

[2] https://suricata.io/

[3] https://redpiranha.net/crystal-eye-xdr-appliances

protocol, and port that is used. It also counts the number of bytes and packets and sends that data to a NetFlow collector (Cisco docs, 2023).

- Stage 6: Network Forensic Technology (NFT).
  Network forensics technology tools focus primarily on surveillance and analysis of network traffic to track, avoid, and diagnose security incidents. Network forensic acts as a tool to identify and detect the network loopholes and prevent further failures by detecting the root cause of the issue or exposing the attacker's intentions. There are two categories of network forensic based on data processing mode, namely proactive and reactive network forensic. Proactive Network Forensic is used for real-time investigation of the incident by supplying the device with automation while reducing user interaction. In real-time, although it provides more accurate and precise data and offers early detection of network attacks, it increases overhead processing and storage. Reactive Network Forensic is used to investigate an attack after it has occurred and is a postmortem method. To ascertain the root cause of the attack, correlate the attacker to the attack, mitigate the impact of the attack, and investigate the malicious incident with reduced processing, it examines network vulnerabilities by detecting, storing, gathering, and analyzing digital evidence collected from the network (Waseem et al., 2021).
- Stage 7: Network Analysis and Visibility (NAV).
  Network Analysis and Visibility (NAV) solutions (a.k.a., network traffic analysis (NTA) or network detection and response (NDR) solutions) are essential for creating a robust and effective zero trust architecture. In a zero-trust network we assume that networks are inherently untrusted and thus require visibility into and analysis of internal network traffic. NTA software monitors network traffic and provides expanded visibility into network activity and communications. These tools are used to document and analyze network resource utilization and performance, constantly tracking granular details related to network communications (IBM Documentation, 2023b). NAV allows companies to ingest telemetry data from endpoint detection and response (EDR) solutions, extended detection and response (XDR) solutions and other sources, the report notes. With this information, the NAV solution can provide EDR, XDR, or security orchestration, automation, and response (SOAR) tools with the information needed to respond to identified cyberthreats (ExtraHop, 2021).
- Stage 8: Security Information and Event Management (SIEM).
  SIEM is a set of tools and services offering a comprehensive security protection for an organization. In general, SIEMs have the capacity to collect, aggregate, store, and correlate events generated by a managed infrastructure. They constitute the central platform of modern security operations centers as they gather events from multiple sensors (IDSs/IPs, anti-virus, firewalls, etc.), correlate these events, and deliver synthetic views of the alerts for threat handling and security reporting. Although these security protection devices and applications can work independently from each other, without them all working together, the SIEM will not function properly (González-Granadillo et al., 2021). For instance, IBM

QRadar[4] SIEM is a network security management platform that provides situational awareness and compliance support. QRadar SIEM can analyze millions of events in near real time by using thousands of prebuilt use cases, User Behavior Analytics, Network Behavior Analytics, application vulnerability data, and X-Force Threat Intelligence[5] to deliver high-fidelity alerts (IBM, n.d.).

- Stage 9: Network Detection and Response (NDR).
  Network detection and response (NDR) is a category of cybersecurity technologies that use non-signature-based methods—such as AI, ML, and behavioral analytics—to detect suspicious or malicious activity on the network and respond to cyber threats. Instead of scanning for specific known signatures, NDR solutions monitor and analyze network traffic and activity in real time to identify any suspicious activity, outside or inside the network, that could indicate a known or unknown cyber threat. NDR solutions do this by modeling baseline network behavior and detecting suspicious and potentially malicious activity. To model baseline network behavior, NDR solutions ingest raw network activity data and metadata from dedicated sensors and application agents throughout the network, and from network infrastructure like firewalls and routers. NDR tools then apply behavioral analytics, AI and machine learning to the data to generate a baseline model of normal network behavior and activity. For detecting suspicious and malicious activity, NDR monitors the network continuously, and uses the same analytics and AI capabilities to identify deviations from baseline behavior in real time. Examples might include a user accessing sensitive data outside of work hours, an endpoint device communicating with an unknown external server, or a port receiving unusual data packets (IBM Documentation, 2023c).

This chapter explores network protection solutions that safeguard modern networks from cyber threats, malware, and unauthorized intrusions. It begins by discussing different threat detection methods used in IDSs and IPSs, including signature-based, anomaly-based, policy-based, and reputation-based detection. Each approach has its strengths and limitations, with signature-based methods excelling in identifying known threats, while anomaly-based and AI-driven systems are more effective at detecting novel attacks.

The chapter further delves into AI and ML-based security solutions, explaining how supervised, semi-supervised, unsupervised, and reinforcement learning techniques are applied to detect and respond to network anomalies, cyber intrusions, and evolving threats. AI-powered systems continuously learn from network traffic patterns, malicious behaviors, and threat intelligence feeds, enabling real-time threat detection and automated response mechanisms. The chapter also discusses the future of AI in network security, emphasizing how AI-driven solutions will evolve toward autonomous cybersecurity systems capable of predicting and mitigating threats without human intervention.

---

[4] https://www.ibm.com/ca-en/products/qradar-siem

[5] https://www.ibm.com/ca-en/reports/threat-intelligence

Despite the advantages of AI-powered network security, the chapter highlights challenges and risks, including the need for high-quality training data, adversarial machine ML attacks, and AI-driven cyber threats. Cybercriminals are increasingly leveraging AI-based attack techniques, such as DeepLocker and adversarial AI, to evade detection and launch more sophisticated cyberattacks. The chapter concludes by stressing the importance of continuous advancements in AI security models to counteract AI-driven cyber threats and enhance network resilience against evolving attacks.

4.2 Network Protection Solutions

The advent of cloud-based services, and the popularity of outsourcing, edge computing, State sponsored cyber-attacks, sophisticated hackers, and a rapidly growing assortment of malicious software makes the need for adequate network security techniques. Network protection is implemented by analyzing the network traffic (inband or outbound) to detect malicious or unwanted actions. Network traffic data can be flow based or packet based. Flow-based and packet-based data can be analyzed to detect malicious action and intrusion. Packet-based data represents the entire packet payload besides the header, while flow-based data represents the aggregated information of related packets of network traffic in the form of flow. A flow-based record typically contains the IP network addresses of the hosts, network ports, network protocol, amount of data, and the time when the flow occurred, while packet-based data records contain the raw data packet information themselves. The flow-based model captures traffic flow data from the traffic passing inward and outward via the router ports, and then it is sent to a live database to tabulate and generate input data for the models (Andreas et al., 2020).

Basically, main methods of detecting threats that intrusion detection systems use to alert network administrators of signs of a threat are shown in Fig. 4.1.

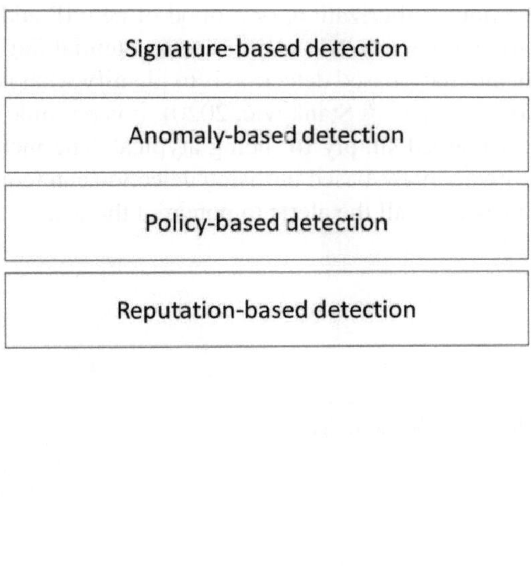

Fig. 4.1 Threat detection methods used by IDSs

4.2.1 *Signature-Based Detection*

Signature-based detection is typically best used for identifying known threats. Many traditional threat detection tools, e.g., antivirus software, early intrusion detection and prevention systems (IDPSs), and some types of firewalls, identify and prevent threats by looking for unique indicators of compromise (IOCs), or signatures. These signatures are determined as patterns and clues to reveal unwilling events. Basically, it operates by using a pre-programmed list of known threats and their IOCs. An IOC might be a specific behavior that generally precedes a malicious network attack, file hashes, malicious domains, known byte sequences, or even the content of email subject headings. As a signature-based IDS monitors the packets traversing the network, it compares these packets to the database of known IOCs or attack signatures to flag any suspicious behavior. As a basic requirement, the signature database needs to be updated constantly. Snort[6] is a well-known and the most popular signature-based solution. Snort is an open-source security software product that looks at network traffic in real time and logs packets to perform detailed analysis used to facilitate security and authentication efforts (Hussain & Sharma, 2019; Sommestad et al., 2022).

4.2.2 *Anomaly-Based Detection*

Anomaly-based detection systems can detect suspicious behavior that is unknown. Instead of searching for known threats, an anomaly-based detection system utilizes techniques to recognize a normalized baseline. The baseline represents how the system normally behaves, and then all network activity is compared to that baseline. Rather than searching for known IOCs, anomaly-based IDS simply identifies any out-of-the-ordinary behavior to trigger alerts. With an anomaly-based IDS, anything that does not align with the existing normalized baseline—such as a user trying to log in outside of standard business hours, new devices being added to a network without authorization, or a flood of new IP addresses trying to establish a connection with a network—will raise a potential flag for concern. The biggest challenge in anomaly-based detection is to identify what is considered normal network behavior (Danijela & Stanković, 2020). It is possible that many non-malicious behaviors get flagged simply for being atypical. The increased likelihood for false positives with anomaly-based intrusion detection can require additional time and resources to investigate all the alerts to potential threats.

[6] https://www.snort.org/

4.2.3 *Policy-Based Detection*

A network security policy defines the rules for the access and usage of the network and the traffic that flows through it. It identifies a boundary or the perimeter of the network, where the policies can be enforced to protect the network resources and guard against the threats. The network that resides within the security parameter is referred to as a trusted network (Handa, 2009). Policy decisions are generated based on the attributes extracted from network traffic. The attributes are extracted by real-time traffic monitoring modules of every connection traversing the gateway. Generally, network attributes are those attributes which give information on the network parameters of traffic like source and destination IP address, protocol, Server Name Indication (SNI) of the external user, etc. In addition to network attributes, the module also extracts flow attributes that provide information on traffic flow like time, packet size, or count of packets (Alzahrani, 2013).

Based on the predefined security policies, upon detecting a violation, an action is enforced. The enforcement actions may include "Allow Connection," "Block Connection," "Mandatory Inspection," or "Optional Inspection."

4.2.4 *Reputation-Based Protection*

In reputation-based security systems, the reputation of the malicious files, IP addresses, domain names, or software producers/distributors are analyzed to make decisions to protect the network/system. Reputation-based security is a security mechanism that classifies a file or its sender as safe or unsafe based on its inherently garnered reputation. This makes it possible to identify and predict file safety based on its overall use and reputation over a wide community of users. It is primarily used in anti-virus, anti-malware, and information security (IS) software. Typically, reputation-based security is implemented on executable files, batch files, and other file formats that are subject to carrying unsafe code. It works by collecting and tracking several attributes of a file, such as age, source, signature, and overall usage statistics across thousands of users consuming that file. To rate the reputation, the data is analyzed within a reputation engine using algorithms and statistical analysis. The reputation-based system is extremely effective in detecting polymorphic malware on download (Jacobs et al., n.d.).

4.3 AI/ML-Based Protection Solutions

While new technologies such as big data and cloud computing continue to emerge, hackers' offensive methods are also constantly developing. With the rapid growth of data volume and increasing access to the Internet, hackers are committed to find "lethal points" of the network and launch attacks on the network at any time. The original IDSs/IPSs have been unable to adapt to the characteristics of the network. However, the high-speed flow of data is also conducive to finding traces left by hacking activities and has become important evidence for taking security precautions in advance (Zhang et al., 2022). Integrating AI into IDSs/IPSs will remove the human element from the machinations and will result in a system that can dynamically react to new attack patterns in real-time based on past experiences. A system, as described, would be able to detect attack patterns based on relevant data, past attacks, provide its knowledge base with real-time updates, and be more accurate at recognizing potential threats than a human or human-updated knowledge base system (Rozendaal & Mailewa, n.d.). It can be trained to categorize traffic flow to detect abnormal flow based on classification, statistics, clustering, and information theory (Zhang et al., 2022).

AI/ML-based solutions are utilized in numerous security applications, e.g., IDSs/IPSs, fraud detection, impersonation attacks, eavesdropping, spam detectors, and scammers. Generally, these solutions work by analyzing huge amounts of data generated by network traffic, host processes, and users to detect suspicious activities using efficient algorithms. This trend envisages that AI/ML-based security applications will become part of the commonly used security techniques. The benefits of AI/ML-based models have been demonstrated over traditional heuristics solutions in identifying complex network traffic patterns for a wide range of network security problems (Jacobs et al., n.d.). AI and ML can take part in providing intelligence at the edges and can be utilized for self-learning security solutions. The edge data centers are exposed to various security attacks. Also, in some cases, the same edge device within the network can be assigned to multiple applications, and that device can be used by various entities that would likely impose security threats (Porambage et al., 2019).

4.3.1 Supervised Learning

Supervised learning, as the name suggests, is learning that entails the application being monitored and corrected for most of the decisions made. Rashidi et al. (Rashidi et al., 2019) demonstrated that by using supervised ML, an application would be capable of learning from training data and the rules of the tasks and the parameters. Supervised learning, in turn, aids the application in further understanding based on standards based on data type or label. Supervised learning also entails labeling the application's data to learn better and execute its queue processes. Röning and Siirtola (Siirtola & Röning, 2019) explained that other approaches could be used regarding supervised machine learning, such as a combination of user-independent and personal models to aid in the recognition process. The variety of user-independent and individual models aids in reducing user interference over time through continuous application learning.

Supervised learning highly depends on user input, which still puts the work's weight on the administrators (Jahan & Afshar Alam, 2017). Labeling of data is necessary with supervised data. It aids the application in understanding what needs to be done to accomplish tasks based on the labels attached to the data. IDS and IPS are perfect examples of supervised ML utilized within a network. Though supervised learning may produce excellent results at times, it is prone to having inaccurate results or not being entirely up to date if administrators do not update and label data promptly (Morgan, 2021).

4.3.2 Semi-Supervised Learning

Semi-supervised learning is the second approach that is utilized in AI/ML, which entails labeling most of the data and allowing the AI/ML application to handle the rest on its own. Semi-supervised learning encompasses the use of both labeled and unlabeled data and is capable of understanding and executing while being partially supervised (Jahan & Afshar Alam, 2017). Semi-supervised learning is much more efficient and allows the application to learn while depending on some user-labeled data. Based on this approach, the application will be capable of learning and responding more and, for defined situations, utilize labeled data (Morgan, 2021).

4.3.3 Unsupervised Learning

Unsupervised learning is the final approach that does not rely on labeled data but executes all data provided by the user, labeled or unlabeled. Unsupervised learning is used primarily for unlabeled data and identifies various inputs and similarities (Jahan & Afshar Alam, 2017). Unsupervised learning is where an AI/ML application is fully capable of analyzing and processing all the data presented to it. The significant difference between supervised and unsupervised learning is the type of data and depth the data contains. Supervised learning data is mainly for labeled data, while unsupervised learning is for unlabeled and more massive data sets (Karthiga et al., 2019). Both supervised and unsupervised learning methods are primarily used in AI, with one main difference being the depth of the data. Rashidi et al. (Rashidi et al., 2019) explained that the significant difference between supervised and unsupervised learning is the type of data and the depth the data contains. Supervised learning data is mainly used for labeled data, while unsupervised is used for unlabeled and more massive data sets (Morgan, 2021).

4.3.4 Reinforced Learning

Another approach used in AI/ML is reinforced learning, which combines both supervised and unsupervised ML. Reinforced learning combines supervised and unsupervised learning and receives feedback from an administrator after each action

(Jahan & Afshar Alam, 2017). Having this in place aids the AI/ML application to fully comprehend whether the action taken was correct or not and have the administrator in place to correct what is wrong. For AI to defend against threats, there needs to be a fully developed baseline for the application to utilize and learn from entirely. Once the application grasps a complete understanding of the tasks at hand, in the future, these applications will be capable of making their own decisions based on trends in the traffic (Zeadally et al., 2020). The application of AI/ML has been applied to cybersecurity through numerous means. Having data from the internal network is enough to understand the network's vulnerabilities but having the data from external sources also aids the AI application to understand what they need to prepare for that the network has not experienced (Chen et al., 2019). As explained earlier, AI/ML based IDSs/IPSs, data is being labeled using signatures that help detect attacks within the network (Mosteanu, 2020).

Having the ability to observe events occurring within the network and adjust security posture based on data followed by the AI/ML application is the end goal. Visner (Visner, 2016) emphasized the necessity of technology to achieve this by outlining how regularly occurring attacks adjust to technologies as they are produced. The adjustment of attacks by attackers creates a unique problem on the horizon, including AI/ML possibilities soon (Morgan, 2021).

4.4 Future of AI in Network Security

The end-to-end automation of future networks demands proactive threat discovery, application of mitigation intelligent techniques, and ensuring the achievement of self-sustaining networks (Siriwardhana et al., 2021). It would be achieved based on AI/ML solutions. AI/ML-based solutions use algorithms and learning techniques to identify potential vulnerabilities and weaknesses in a network. They detect and analyze malicious threats and suspicious activities more quickly and accurately than traditional solutions. Moreover, AI/ML-based solutions can also detect patterns in cybersecurity threats and provide insights into potential attack vectors. Since AI gets smarter over time, the next generations of AI/ML-based network security solutions can gradually increase network security to a more effective and sophisticated level than its name might imply.

Future AI-based network security solutions will be independent of human control. The next step would be to build algorithms capable of providing expert knowledge rather than needing humans to identify the patterns discovered by clustering techniques (Veiga, 2018). Using machine learning and deep learning techniques, they monitor and understand the network behavior of an organization over time to identify the normal and abnormal patterns presented on the network in different conditions. Then, classify them and learn the sources of those conditions before determining whether any deviations from typical traffic or security incidents occurred. When it has finished processing the traffic, it reacts to them. AI-driven solutions lead to intelligent computing in network security to analyze and predict potential cyber-attacks (Sarker et al., 2021). The key properties of AI that will change future network security solutions are prediction, detection, and response. Data-driven methods, e.g., machine learning, deep learning, or data mining techniques, are used to understand the raw security data as the first step to build an intelligent security model for predicting future incidents. Predictive analysis is incredibly difficult and complex to implement. It requires analyzing massive datasets to identify consistent patterns and build predictive models using multiple variables, such as user behavior, network traffic, or threat intelligence feeds. Businesses that use AI for prediction can use the technology to automatically analyze their assets and network topology, pinpoint significant weaknesses, and constantly strengthen their network defenses against any potential catastrophic assaults (Chin, 2023).

To continuously identify unusual traffic, AI-based cybersecurity solutions use behavioral analysis. This is one of AI's distinctive features, enabled by ML/DL. For instance, an Intrusion Detection Tree (IntruDTree) is an ML-based security model that first considers the ranking of security features according to their importance and then builds a tree-based generalized intrusion detection model based on the selected important features (Sarker et al., 2020). Upon detecting a malicious activity, an AI-based response system effectively blocks it with no human interface between the detection and response systems. This entails building new defense mechanisms in real-time and automating the development of a virtual patch for threat identification.

4.5 Challenges and Issues

Despite the benefits of AI/ML for network security, there are some challenges with AI technologies. A large amount of data is required for training AI/ML systems to be able to effectively detect and respond to suspicious activity. As such, organizations need to ensure they have access to sufficient amounts of high-quality data for their AI/ML systems to perform optimally. Another challenge is ensuring that AI-based solutions are properly integrated into security protocols. Furthermore, AI/ML-based security solutions might be vulnerable to a new type of sophisticated attack known as adversarial ML. In many security domains, the attacker can effectively control the information of the input to the ML algorithms to equivocate classifiers designed to distinguish them. Furthermore, the training data set utilized to construct classifiers can be disturbed by adding standard samples to the abnormal sample class and/or vice versa. It is essential to develop strong security measurements for any system, network, or organization. However, it is important to understand the different security threats and how they work together to break the security measures.

Network cyber threats are becoming more sophisticated and ubiquitous due to AI-driven techniques used by attackers. Cybercriminals are inevitably adopting AI-based techniques to evade cyberspace and cause greater damage without being noticed (Guembe et al., 2022). Highly targeted and evasive attacks in benign carrier applications, such as DeepLocker,[7] an AI-powered malware, have demonstrated the intentional use of AI for harmful purposes (Kaloudi & Li, 2020). These AI-driven attacks are highly adaptive, allowing them to blend into their environment and modify their behavior based on specific conditions within the infected system. Adversarial attacks, which exploit weaknesses in AI models, further exacerbate this threat and are explained in detail in Chap. 10.

4.6 Summary

This chapter reviewed network security protection solutions and their evolutions to new techniques and AI-based solutions. It discussed the capabilities of AI-based solutions to improve network security protection. AI can analyze vast network traffic data in real-time to detect anomalies and potential threats. ML models can identify patterns indicative of malware, phishing attempts, or other cyber threats faster than traditional methods. Continuous improvement and fine-tuning of AI models are needed to reduce the rate of false positives and negatives, improving detection accuracy over time. Finally, the chapter discusses the future of AI-based network solutions and the potential challenges. AI has the potential to significantly enhance network security by providing advanced threat detection, rapid incident response, and proactive defense measures. However, it also introduces challenges related to complexity, cost, the need for continuous maintenance and updates, and adversarial misuse or abuse.

References

Ali Mousa G. Alzahrani. (2013). *Efficient enforcement of security policies in distributed systems.*

Andreas, B., Dilruksha, J., McCandless, E., Chakrabarty, S., & Youssef, O. (2020). Flow-based and packet-based intrusion detection using BLSTM. *SMU Data Science Review, 3*(3), 8.

Chen, C. -M., Wen, D. -W. M., Fang, J. -J., Lai, G. -H., & Liu, Y. -H. (2019). A study on security trend based on news analysis. In *2019 IEEE 10th International Conference on Awareness Science and Technology (iCAST), Morioka, Japan* (pp. 1–4). https://doi.org/10.1109/ICAwST.2019.8923373

Chin, K. (2023). *The impact of AI on cybersecurity: predictions for the future.* https://www.upguard.com/blog/the-impact-of-ai-on-cybersecurity

Cisco docs. *NetFlow* (accessed in 2023), https://www.cisco.com/c/dam/en/us/td/docs/routers/asr920/configuration/guide/netmgmt/fnf-xe-3e-asr920-book.html

Danijela, P., & Stanković, M. (2020). Detection of anomalies in the computer network behaviour. *European Journal of Formal Sciences and Engineering, 5*(2), 78–88.

ExtraHop. (2021). *Forrester: Network analysis and visibility are essential.* https://www.extrahop.com/company/blog/2023/forrester-network-analysis-and-visibility-are-essential/

[7] https://github.com/CyberWarefare/DeepLocker

González-Granadillo, G., González-Zarzosa, S., & Diaz, R. (2021). Security information and event management (SIEM): Analysis, trends, and usage in critical infrastructures. *Sensors, 21*, 4759. https://doi.org/10.3390/s21144759

Guembe, B., Azeta, A., Misra, S., Osamor, V. C., Fernandez-Sanz, L., & Pospelova, V. (2022). The emerging threat of AI-driven cyber attacks: A review. *Applied Artificial Intelligence, 36*(1), 2037254.

Handa, A. (2009). Chapter 3: Basics of IP networks. In A. Handa (Ed.), *System engineering for IMS networks* (pp. 35–43., ISBN 9780750683883). https://doi.org/10.1016/B978-0-7506-8388-3.00003-4

Hussain, A., & Sharma, P. K. (2019). Efficient working of signature based intrusion detection technique in computer networks. *International Journal of Scientific Research in Computer Science, Engineering and Information Technology, 12*(10), 60–64.

IBM. (n.d.). *Advanced threat detection with IBM security QRadar SIEM*. https://www.ibm.com/products/qradar-siem/advanced-threat-detection

IBM Documentation. *What is an intrusion prevention system (IPS)?* (accessed in 2023a), https://www.ibm.com/topics/intrusion-prevention-system

IBM Documentation. (2023b). *Grid® report for network traffic analysis (NTA)*. https://www.ibm.com/downloads/cas/7ZLYW2DO

IBM Documentation. *What is NDR (network detection and response)?* (accessed in 2023c). https://www.ibm.com/topics/ndr. [7-1] Brook Andreas, Jayaweera Dilruksha, Eric McCandless, Shaibal Chakrabarty, and Omar Youssef, Flow-based and packet-based intrusion detection using BLSTM. SMU Data Science Review, 2020, vol. 3, no 3, p. 8.

Jacobs, A. S., Beltiukov, R., Willinger, W., Ferreira, R. A., Gupta, A., & Granville, L. Z. (n.d.). AI/ML for network security: The emperor has no clothes. In *Proceedings of the 2022 ACM SIGSAC conference on computer and communications security* (pp. 1537, 2022–1551).

Jahan, A., & Afshar Alam, M. (2017). Intrusion detection systems based on artificial intelligence. *International Journal of Advanced Research in Computer Science, 8*(5).

Jakimoski, K., & Singhai, N. V. (2019). Improvement of hardware firewall's data rates by optimizing suricata performances. In *2019 27th telecommunications forum (TELFOR)* (pp. 1–4). IEEE.

Kaloudi, N., & Li, J. (2020). The AI-based cyber threat landscape: A survey. *ACM Computing Surveys (CSUR), 53*(1), 1–34.

Karthiga, R., Keerthiga, B., & Preethi, S. R. (2019). Analysis on machine learning techniques. *I-Manager's Journal on Computer Science, 7*(3), 46–50. https://doi.org/10.26634/jcom.7.3.16739

LaPorte, B. *The evolution of network security systems: How they've changed in response to ever-greater threats* (accessed in 2023), https://ordr.net/blog/evolution-of-network-security-systems/

Liang, J., & Kim, Y. (2022). Evolution of firewalls: Toward securer network using next generation firewall. In *2022 IEEE 12th annual computing and communication workshop and conference (CCWC)* (pp. 0752–0759). IEEE.

Morgan, R. A. (2021). *Exploring the feasibility of developing a customized IDS/IPS security control for computer network security*. PhD diss., Colorado Technical University.

Mosteanu, N. R. (2020). Artificial intelligence and cyber security–A shield against cyber attack as a risk business management tool–case of European countries. *Quality-Access to Success, 21*(175).

Porambage, P., Kumar, T., Liyanage, M., Partala, J., Lovén, L., Ylianttila, M., & Seppänen, T. (2019). *Sec-EdgeAI: AI for edge security vs security for edge AI*. The 1st 6G Wireless Summit, 2019.

Rashidi, H. H., Tran, N. K., Betts, E. V., Howell, L. P., & Green, R. (2019). Artificial intelligence and machine learning in pathology: The present landscape of supervised methods. *Academic Pathology*, 6. https://doi.org/10.1177/2374289519873088

Rozendaal, K., & Mailewa, A. (n.d.). Neural network assisted IDS/IPS: An overview of implementations, benefits, and drawbacks. *International Journal of Computer Applications, 975*, 8887.

Sarker, I. H., Abushark, Y. B., Alsolami, F., & Khan, A. I. (2020). IntruDTree: A machine learning based cyber security intrusion detection model. *Symmetry, 12*, 754. https://doi.org/10.3390/sym12050754

Sarker, I. H., Furhad, M. H., & Nowrozy, R. (2021). AI-driven cybersecurity: An overview, security intelligence modeling and research directions. *SN Computer Science, 2*, 1–18.

Siirtola, P., & Röning, J. (2019). Incremental learning to personalize human activity recognition models: The importance of human AI collaboration. *Sensors, 19*, 5151. https://doi.org/10.3390/s19235151

Siriwardhana, Y., Porambage, P., Liyanage, M., & Ylianttila, M. (2021). AI and 6G security: Opportunities and challenges. In *2021 Joint European conference on networks and communications & 6G summit (EuCNC/6G summit), Porto, Portugal* (pp. 616–621). https://doi.org/10.1109/EuCNC/6GSummit51104.2021.9482503

Sommestad, T., Holm, H., & Steinvall, D. (2022). Variables influencing the effectiveness of signature-based network intrusion detection systems. *Information Security Journal: A Global Perspective, 31*(6), 711–728.

Veiga, A. P. (2018) Applications of artificial intelligence to network security. *arXiv preprint* arXiv:1803.09992.

Visner, S. S. (2016). The cybersecurity storm front—Forces shaping the cybersecurity landscape: A framework for analysis. *Georgetown Journal of International Affairs, 17*(3), 85–99. http://www.jstor.org/stable/26395978

Waseem, Q., Alshamrani, S. S., Nisar, K., Wan Din, W. I., & Alghamdi, A. S. (2021). Future technology: Software-defined network (SDN) forensic. *Symmetry, 13*(5), 767.

Zeadally, S., Adi, E., Baig, Z., & Khan, I. A. (2020). Harnessing artificial intelligence capabilities to improve cybersecurity. *IEEE Access, 8*, 23817–23837. https://doi.org/10.1109/ACCESS.2020.2968045

Zhang, Z., Ning, H., Shi, F., Farha, F., Yang, X., Jiabo, X., Zhang, F., & Choo, K.-K. R. (2022). Artificial intelligence in cyber security: Research advances, challenges, and opportunities. *Artificial Intelligence Review*, 1–25.

Chapter 5
AI for Software Security

5.1 Introduction

AI and ML Methods play a crucial role in enhancing the security of software applications. In this chapter, we first explore the various cybersecurity threats and vulnerabilities that pose risks to software applications across platforms, including mobile, web, and desktop applications. Following this, we delve into the application areas of AI and ML methods for enhancing security. A range of AI and ML methods (e.g., machine learning, deep learning, and other predictive modeling methods) can be used to analyze large amounts of data and identify patterns for potential cyber threats. Advanced AI and ML methods provide robust, adaptive, and intelligent solutions to enhance the security of smartphone, web, and desktop applications. User authentication, threat detection and prevention, and vulnerability and patch management are the common application areas of AI and ML methods for the security of the application. Integration of these advanced AI and ML methods to security and monitoring software such as antivirus software, IDS, IPS, and firewalls has significantly enhanced the accuracy and effectiveness in detecting and preventing malware infections and other cyberattacks.

Mobile devices and smartphones are an important part of our everyday lives since they enable us to access many ubiquitous services. However, Smartphone applications face numerous threats, including malware, phishing attacks, insecure data storage, and unauthorized access to sensitive information. AI-powered security solutions address these challenges by using machine learning algorithms to detect abnormal app behavior, identify malicious software, and analyze user patterns in real-time. AI-driven security tools can continuously monitor mobile app activities, block suspicious actions, and provide real-time alerts. In addition, smartphone app security is a shared responsibility mainly between two parties including developers and users. Developers should adhere to the best security practices, recent technology, and standards for smartphone app development. Users should be aware of the

D. P. Sharma et al., *Understanding AI in Cybersecurity and Secure AI*, Progress in IS, https://doi.org/10.1007/978-3-031-91524-6_5

cybersecurity risks of using the apps, and take precautions to protect their devices, data, and privacy.

Web applications pose significant risks to online platforms by exploiting vulnerabilities (e.g., SQL injections, cross-site scripting (XSS), DDoS attacks, etc.) in code and user inputs. Similarly, desktop applications also face numerous security threats including malware, ransomware, unauthorized access, and data exfiltration. These threats can exploit vulnerabilities in software, user credentials, and system configurations. AI-powered solutions enhance both web and desktop application security by providing real-time threat detection, behavior analysis, identifying patterns associated with attacks, and automated threat responses. Machine learning methods can identify abnormal patterns, flag suspicious activity, and block potential attacks like phishing or malware before they cause harm. Additionally, AI-driven application software continuously adapts to new threats, enabling proactive defense and minimizing the risk of security breaches on applications.

This chapter explores the security and privacy threats associated with smartphone, web, and desktop applications, highlighting key vulnerabilities that cybercriminals exploit to compromise user data and system integrity. It examines how malicious applications, improper OS configurations, insecure storage, and network threats make mobile applications susceptible to attacks. Similarly, it delves into web application security risks, focusing on the Open Web Application Security Project (OWASP) Top 10 vulnerabilities, including broken access control, cryptographic failures, injection attacks, security misconfigurations, and outdated components. The discussion extends to desktop application security, detailing injection flaws, authentication failures, data exposure, insecure communication, and poor code quality.

Furthermore, the chapter introduces AI and ML-driven security methods that enhance application security through user authentication, threat detection, malware analysis, and vulnerability assessment. AI-driven techniques such as biometric authentication, anomaly detection, deep learning-based malware classification, and automated vulnerability assessment are presented as proactive solutions for strengthening security measures. The chapter also highlights the role of AI-powered defensive mechanisms like intrusion prevention systems, anti-malware tools, deception techniques, and automated patch management. By addressing both threats and AI-based countermeasures, this chapter provides a comprehensive understanding of application security challenges and modern mitigation strategies to protect users, systems, and sensitive data from cyber threats.

5.2 Smartphone App Security Threats and Vulnerabilities

Smartphones are general-purpose handheld computing and communications devices that support multimedia communications and applications for entertainment and work. One of the distinct features of smartphones is that they allow users to install and run third-party Apps. These apps are officially distributed via online stores App markets such as Apple App Store for the iOS platform, and Google Play Store for the Android platform. Users may download an application while browsing or from the third-party application store, which may result in the download of malware. Once the malicious application enters your mobile device, it collects sensitive information about the users and transmits it to attackers. Malicious applications may cause financial loss to the users by stealing personal information (He et al., 2015). The following factors make smartphone applications more vulnerable to cybersecurity attacks:

- **Improper usage of mobile operating system (OS)**: Improper usage of smartphone OS may lead to misconfiguration of security features provided by the operating system, such as secure APIs, sandboxing, and permission management.
- **Insecure storage of personal sensitive data in smartphones**: Users carry out financial transactions such as online banking and shopping from their smartphones, and some data can be very sensitive. Sensitive data like passwords, personal information, or payment details stored in plain text can be easily accessed by attackers. Weak or improperly implemented encryption can be bypassed, exposing stored data. Attackers can have substantial financial gain from such sensitive data and thus find smartphones to be lucrative targets.
- **Insecure network traffic and API calls**: data transmitted without encryption or with a weak encryption algorithm can be intercepted and read by attackers.
- **App Store policy and jailbroken or rooted devices:** Many smartphones are based on the open-source platform (e.g., Android). With Android's policy of open-source kernel, malware writers can gain a deeper understanding of the mobile platform. According to Google's marketing strategy, the development of third-party apps is encouraged, and the publishing of apps makes it easy to gain market share. As a result, there are many opportunities for hackers to create and publish malware. At the same time, as users are in the habit of downloading and installing apps for their smartphones, the chances of installing malware increase as well. While major app stores (like Google Play and Apple App Store) have vetting processes, malicious apps can still occasionally bypass these checks. Jailbreaking (iOS) or rooting (Android) a device removes many of the built-in security controls and makes it easier for attackers to gain full control over the device. Jailbroken or rooted devices can run apps from untrusted sources which increases the risk of malware infections.

5.3 Web Application Security Threats and Vulnerabilities

A web application is a distributed application that executes over the Internet and Web platform. Web applications are platform-independent and run with a web browser on any device including desktops, laptops, tablets, and smartphones. These applications are now widely used in businesses, governments, and individuals;

however, the Internet & Web are vulnerable (Stallings, 2013). The common web security threats are as follows:

- **Integrity:** It includes the modification of user data, trojan horse browser, modification of memory, modification of message traffic in transit, etc.
- **Confidentiality:** It includes eavesdropping on the net, theft of information from web servers and clients, etc.
- **Denial of service:** It includes the killing of user threads, filling up disk or memory.
- **Authentication:** It includes the impersonation of legitimate users, data forgery, etc.

The OWASP is an open community that enables organizations to develop, purchase, and maintain applications and APIs secure and trustworthy. It provides cutting-edge research for application security tools and standards, standard security controls and libraries, secure code development, secure code review, etc. OWASP provides a well-known list of the top vulnerabilities for web applications that are known as the OWASP Top 10 vulnerabilities. The OWASP top 10 web application security risks list outlines the most common web application vulnerabilities that organizations need to be aware of, and it regularly updates this list to reflect the evolving threat landscape. Following are the OWASP top 10 vulnerabilities (OWASP, 2021a):

1. Broken access control
2. Cryptographic failures
3. Injection
4. Insecure design
5. Security misconfiguration
6. Vulnerable and outdated components
7. Identification and authentication failures
8. Software and data integrity failures
9. Security logging and monitoring failures
10. Server-side request forgery (SSRF)

Understanding these web application security vulnerabilities and implementing suitable security measures enable organizations to protect themselves from cyberattacks.

5.3.1 Broken Access Control

Access control mechanisms ensure the restriction of accessing web resources such as web pages, database tables, etc. and it is the security configuration for preventing unauthorized access from the attackers. It enforces an authentication and authorization policy such that users cannot act outside of their intended permissions. Failures typically lead to unauthorized information disclosure, modification, or destruction of all data or performing a business function outside the user's limits. A web application is vulnerable to access control (broken access control) attacks when (OWASP Top 10:2021, A01:2021—Broken Access Control, 2021):

- Violation of the principle of least privilege or denial by default.
- Bypassing access control checks by modifying the URL, internal application state, or the HTML page, or by using an attack tool to modify API requests.
- Permitting viewing or editing someone else's account by providing its unique identifier.
- Accessing API with missing access controls for POST, PUT, and DELETE.
- Elevation of privilege that includes acting as a user without being logged in or acting as an admin when logged in as a user.
- Replaying or tampering with a JSON Web Token (JWT) access control token.
- Cross-Origin Resource Sharing (CORS) misconfiguration allows API access from unauthorized/untrusted origins.
- Force browsing to authenticated pages as an unauthenticated user or to privileged pages as a standard user.

5.3.2 Cryptographic Failures

Cryptographic failures are the second most common vulnerability in web applications. It exposes sensitive data, including passwords, credit card numbers, health records, personal information, and business secrets. These data-sensitive data require extra protection. The cryptographic failures include broken or weak algorithms that can be easily or quickly hacked or broken; outdated or hardcoded passwords; or a lack of security around data assets in motion. A web application is vulnerable to cryptographic failure threats when (OWASP Top 10:2021, A02:2021—Cryptographic Failures, 2021):

- Transmission of plain or clear text
- Use of old or weak cryptographic algorithms
- Use of default cryptographic keys or use of weak crypto-generated keys
- Lack of validation of the server certificate and the trust chain
- Use of the deprecated hash functions such as MD5 or SHA1, or use of non-cryptographic hash functions

5.3.3 Injection

An injection attack is a common type of web attack that inserts malicious code into a program which can lead to unauthorized command execution or data access. A web application is vulnerable to injection attack when:

- User-supplied data is not validated, filtered, or sanitized by the application.

- Dynamic queries or non-parameterized calls without context-aware escaping are used directly in the interpreter.
- Hostile data is used within object-relational mapping (ORM) search parameters to extract additional, sensitive records.
- Hostile data is directly used or concatenated. The SQL or command contains the structure and malicious data in dynamic queries, commands, or stored procedures.

Injection attacks target various software-intensive systems including web applications, databases, operating systems, software applications, and web servers by exploiting vulnerabilities. Different forms of injection attacks include:

- **SQL injection**: SQL injection is a type of injection attack that targets SQL databases and allows a malicious user to either provide their parameters to an existing SQL query or to escape a SQL query and provide their query. It exploits database vulnerabilities through malicious SQL statements and affects data integrity and availability. Modern attackers might employ simple methods like exploiting unsensitized input fields for SQL injection to more robust advanced tools to automate vulnerability discovery and execute complex injection attacks. SQL injection can be classified in many ways based on several factors. A general classification of the SQL injection attacks is as follows (Tajpour et al., 2012).
- **In-band SQL injection:** This attack uses the same channel for launching and receiving the result of the attack. Error-based SQL and union-based SQL attacks are two sub-types of in-band SQL injection attacks.
- **Inferential SQL injection:** This attack does not transfer data via a web application or database. There is no output on the webpage in response to any request. This type of attack generally takes more time to exploit. Boolean-based blind SQL and time-based SQL are two common sub-types of inferential SQL injection attacks.
- **Code injection:** This attack tries to add additional SQL queries or commands at the end of SQL statements in any application. For example, using LIKE queries where the user input is incorporated into the LIKE query can sabotage the whole query and slow down the response time of the query. When these LIKE queries are used multiple times, it can work as a Denial of Service (DoS) attack by overloading the database.
- **Functional call injection:** It is the injection of database functions into an SQL statement which can be used to manipulate or access data in the database. Role foundation and System stored procedure are two sub-types of function call injection attacks.
- **Command injection:** It is an attack that executes unauthorized commands on the host operating system and takes control of the system (Rai et al., 2021). This attack is possible when an application passes unsafe user-supplied data via forms, cookies, and HTTP headers, to a system shell. Command injection attacks are possible largely due to insufficient input validation. In addition, it can potentially open an entire host of potential attacks that include:

  - Steal data from the server.

  - Rewrite log files to hide our tracks.
  - Add database user with write access for later use.
  - Delete important files on the server.
  - Wipe the server and kill it.
  - Make use of integrations with other servers or APIs.
  - Change a single login form in the web app to a phishing form that sends unencrypted passwords.
  - Lock the admins out and blackmail them.

- **XML injection:** XML Injection is a type of injection attack that targets web applications generating XML content. It aims at manipulating the logic of XML-based applications or services (Jan et al., 2019). It compromises XML applications by manipulating the processing of XML data or documents. Attackers can exploit XML documents if user-supplied input isn't properly sanitized before being added and inject the malicious code into it by manipulating its content. It can cause unauthorized access to sensitive data including user credentials, credit card data, DoS attacks by overwhelming the application, and data manipulation or corruption. Different search-based algorithms such as Standard Genetic Algorithm (SGA), Real-coded Genetic Algorithm (RGA), Hill Climbing (HC), and Random Search (RS) can be used for the automatic generation of tests to exploit XML injection vulnerabilities in web applications.
- To safeguard your systems against injection attacks, consider implementing robust prevention and mitigation strategies. These measures will protect system data and maintain system integrity, thereby ensuring business continuity and preserving customer trust. Key defensive strategies include:
- **Input validation and sanitization:** Implement strict validation rules for user inputs, processing only expected and safe inputs. Sanitize inputs by removing or neutralizing potentially malicious code before it can be executed.
- **Secure coding practices:** Adopt secure coding standards that expressly address injection vulnerabilities. Examples include the use of prepared statements and parameterized queries when working with database transactions.
- **Regular security audits and updates:** Conduct periodic security audits to identify and rectify vulnerabilities in your systems. Keep your systems and software up to date with the latest security patches.
- **Leverage AI-native security solutions:** Modern cybersecurity solutions leverage AI technologies to provide automated threat detection, behavioral analytics, and enhanced threat intelligence. With the ability to analyze vast amounts of data, AI can identify subtle signs of injection attacks or their attempts, enabling quicker and more effective responses.

5.3.4 *Insecure Design*

It is a vulnerability category based on risks to design and architectural flaws including threat modeling, secure design patterns, and reference architectures. Insecure design represents different weaknesses that can be expressed as missing or ineffective control design (OWASP, A04:2021—Insecure Design, 2021b). Secure design is a culture and methodology that constantly evaluates threats and ensures that code is robustly designed and tested to prevent known attack methods. However, a secure design can still have implementation defects leading to vulnerabilities that may be exploited. An insecure design cannot be fixed by a perfect implementation as by definition, needed security controls were never created to defend against specific attacks. Insecure design is a software design flaw that can make an application vulnerable to attack. This category encompasses a wide range of weaknesses, such as lack of input validation, improper session management, insecure data storage, and insecure communication.

5.3.5 *Security Misconfiguration*

Security misconfigurations expose an application to a cyberattack. Attackers gain access that leads to a major impact on the business causing loss of money, customers, and reputation. A web application is vulnerable to security misconfiguration when (OWASP Top 10:2021 A09:2021—Security Logging and Monitoring Failures, 2021):

- Missing appropriate security hardening across any part of the application stack or improper configuration of the permissions on web or cloud services.
- Unnecessary features are enabled or installed.
- Default accounts and their passwords are still enabled and unchanged.
- Error handling reveals stack traces or other overly informative error messages to users.

5.3.6 *Vulnerable and Outdated Components*

Vulnerable and outdated components can have security vulnerabilities because these components are no longer supported by their developers making them susceptible to new security threats. Outdated components are incompatible with newer systems, have compliance violations, and have known security flaws that can be exploited by attackers. A web application is likely vulnerable when (OWASP, OWASP Top 10:2021, A06:2021—Vulnerable and Outdated Components, 2021c):

- Unknown versions of components used in both client-side and server-side, and nested dependencies.
- Use of components that have no longer support or are out of date. This includes the OS, web/application server, database management system (DBMS), applications, APIs and all components, runtime environments, and libraries.
- No regular scanning of vulnerabilities and bugs.
- No proper test for the compatibility of updated, upgraded, or patched libraries.

5.3.7 Identification and Authentication Failures

Identification and authentication failures can significantly compromise the security of a web application leading to various vulnerability risks. These failures occur when a web application does not properly verify the identity of users or fails to protect the authentication mechanisms. The verification of the user's identity, authentication, and session management is crucial to protect against authentication-related web attacks. A web application is vulnerable to identification and authentication failures when (OWASP Top 10:2021, A07:2021—Identification and Authentication Failures, 2021):

- It permits automated attacks such as credential stuffing, where the attacker has a list of valid usernames and passwords.
- It allows brute force or other automated attacks.
- It permits default, weak, or well-known passwords, such as "Password1" or "admin/admin."
- It uses weak or ineffective credential recovery and forgotten-password processes, such as "knowledge-based answers," which cannot be made safe.
- It uses plain text, encrypted, or weakly hashed password data stores.
- It has missing or ineffective multi-factor authentication.
- It exposes the session identifier in the URL.
- It reuses the session identifier after a successful login.
- It does not correctly invalidate Session IDs.

5.3.8 Software and Data Integrity Failures

Software and data integrity failures occur when the integrity of software or data is not properly maintained. These failures can compromise the security and functionality of a web application which are related to code and infrastructure that do not protect against integrity violations (OWASP Top 10:2021, A08:2021—Software and Data Integrity Failures, 2021). For example, an application relies upon plugins, libraries, or modules from untrusted sources, repositories, and content delivery networks. An insecure continuous development and deployment pipeline can introduce the potential for unauthorized access, malicious code, or system compromise. Code injection, invalidated inputs, use of unpatched software, lack of integrity checks, use of weak cryptographic protocols, and many more are the vulnerabilities due to the software and data integrity failures. A web application is vulnerable to software and data integrity failures when:

- It allows attackers to inject malicious code into the application which can lead to compromising its functionality and data integrity.
- It accepts unvalidated input from users that can lead to data corruption and exploitation of the application.
- It has inadequate access controls that can allow unauthorized users to modify data or software components.
- It fails to implement integrity checks that can lead to undetected alterations in code or data.
- It has compromised third-party libraries or dependencies that can introduce malicious code into the application.
- It uses weak or improper cryptographic algorithms that can compromise the integrity of data.

5.3.9 Security Logging and Monitoring Failures

Security logging and monitoring failures is one of a common web application vulnerability that can significantly impact the ability of a web application to detect and respond to security incidents which leads to increased risk of cyberattacks and prolonged undetected breaches (OWASP Top 10:2021, A09:2021—Security Logging and Monitoring Failures, 2021). A web application is vulnerable to security logging and monitoring failure attacks if:

- It cannot keep the log records of auditable events such as logins, failed logins, and high-value transactions.
- It cannot monitor logs of applications and APIs for suspicious activity.
- It does not have any appropriate alerting threshold and response escalation processes in place.
- It does not have any penetration testing and scanning tools for dynamic application security testing.
- It cannot detect, escalate, or alert for active attacks in real-time or near real-time.

5.3.10 Server-Side Request Forgery (SSRF)

Server-side request forgery (SSRF) is a web application vulnerability that allows a cybercriminal to make requests from a vulnerable server to other internal or external resources. SSRF flaws occur whenever a web application is fetching a remote resource without validating the user-supplied URL. It allows an attacker to coerce the application to send a crafted request to an unexpected destination, even when protected by a firewall, VPN, or another type of network access control list (OWASP Top 10:2021, A10:2021—Server-Side Request Forgery [SSRF], 2021). Some of the common SSRF vulnerabilities in a web application are as follows:

- Attackers can perform internal network scans to identify services, open ports, and other vulnerabilities within the internal network.
- SSRF can be used to make requests to internal systems that are not exposed to the public internet and reveal sensitive information or compromise internal services.
- Attackers can leverage SSRF to bypass firewalls and access internal network resources including databases, application servers, and other infrastructure components.
- SSRF can be used to exfiltrate sensitive data from internal systems by making requests that return data to the attacker.

5.4 Desktop Application Security Threats and Vulnerabilities

Desktop applications are software application programs designed that run on desktop or laptop computers. These applications are typically installed on operating system platforms such as Windows, macOS, and Linux. Desktop application security refers to the security measures and practices that are used to protect these applications from unauthorized access, data breaches, malware, and other cybersecurity attacks. Security measures include secure coding practices, user authentication and authorization, data encryption, regular software updates, attack detection, and response mechanisms. Robust encryption methods ensure the protection of data at rest and in transit, strong authentication and authorization mechanisms such as multi-factor authentication and role-based access control mechanisms protect the applications from unauthorized access, and the secure coding practice implementation helps to prevent common vulnerabilities such as SQL injection and buffer overflows. Additionally, regular patch management and automated updates ensure that the software applications remain protected against emerging cyber threats. Like the Web's top 10 vulnerabilities, OWASP also provides a well-known list of the top 10 vulnerabilities for desktop applications (OWASP Top 10 Desktop Application Security Risks, 2021). The OWASP Top 10 vulnerabilities for desktop applications are as follows:

- **Injections**: Injections occur when untrusted input is passed to the interpreter as a part of a query/command. An attacker can trick interpreters to execute arbitrary commands to perform unwanted operations or gather unauthorized data. The common injection vulnerabilities include SQL, LDAP (Lightweight Directory Access Protocol), XML, OS command injection, etc.

- **Broken authentication and session management:** This is due to insecure authentication implementation, authentication bypass, improper session, etc. An attacker can exploit insecure implementations to compromise user sessions, passwords, and keys or to assume the identity of the user of the application.
- **Sensitive data exposure:** This is due to the unintentional exposure of sensitive information such as personal identity information, financial information, healthcare information, or application keys and secrets. For example, logs with sensitive info, and hardcoded secrets in files. An attacker can use this information to carry out identity fraud and future attacks.
- **Improper cryptography usage:** It includes the usage of weak cryptographic algorithms, weak keys or secrets, custom cryptographic functions, and insecure key management. An attacker can exploit these flaws to retrieve sensitive information or to attack the users of the different instances of the same application.
- **Improper authorization:** This risk is due to authorization flaws that include weak file permission per user role, missing principle of least privilege approach, improper user roles, unauthorized access to registry or environment variables, etc. An attacker can gain elevated privileges of the application or the target system.
- Security Misconfiguration: These flaws include misconfigured group policies, registry, firewall rules, etc. An attacker can gain system access by exploiting these flaws.
- **Insecure communication:** This vulnerability includes the usage of weak transport layer security (TL) or cipher-suites, protocols, plaintext database connections, usage of plaintext communication protocols, etc. These vulnerabilities allow an attacker to perform main in-the-middle attacks to sniff and manipulate the data of an active connection.
- **Poor code quality:** This vulnerability occurs due to the absence of secure coding practices such as missing code-signing and verification of file integrity, missing code obfuscation, lack of binary protection, memory leaks, buffer overflows, etc. An attacker can reverse engineer the application to obtain information about the application logic, and business-specific proprietary logic or can exploit the application.
- **Using components with known vulnerabilities:** It includes usage of outdated software and obsolete components/services of OS/Third-party vendors. An attacker can exploit the vulnerable components to retrieve information or to compromise the target system either locally or remotely depending upon the exploit.
- **Insufficient logging and monitoring:** This vulnerability Includes the missing or insecure implementation of logs, improper parameters within audit logs, missing regular monitoring to detect abuse, etc.

5.5 AI and ML Methods for Application Security

AI and ML technology provide advanced methods for detecting, preventing, and responding to security threats. A range of AI and ML techniques such as machine learning, deep learning, and other predictive modeling methods can be used to analyze large amounts of data and identify patterns for potential cyber threats. Integration of AI and ML methods to security and monitoring software (e.g. antivirus software, IDS, IPS, firewall, etc.) has significantly enhanced the accuracy and effectiveness in detecting and preventing malware infections and other cyberattacks. Advanced AI and ML techniques provide robust, adaptive, and intelligent solutions to enhance the security of smartphone, web, and desktop applications. User authentication, threat detection and prevention, and vulnerability and patch management are the common application areas of AI and ML methods for the security of the application. Figure 5.1 shows three common application areas of AI and ML methods for software application security:

1. User authentication and authorization.
2. Threat detection and prevention.
3. Vulnerability assessment and patch management.

5.5.1 User Authentication and Authorization

User authentication and authorization play a vital role in protecting from unauthorized access. It is one of the top 10 application vulnerabilities. Implementing strong passwords, biometrics, and multi-factor authentication are the common methods used in user authentication and authorization. Machine Learning (ML) and Deep Learning (DL)-based user authentication and authorization methods offer several benefits including improved security through robust identification methods, adaptive access control based on user behavior, and faster detection of suspicious activity (Pritee et al., 2024). The advanced ML and DL-based methods help to identify and prevent cyber threats by processing extensive data, discovering patterns, and

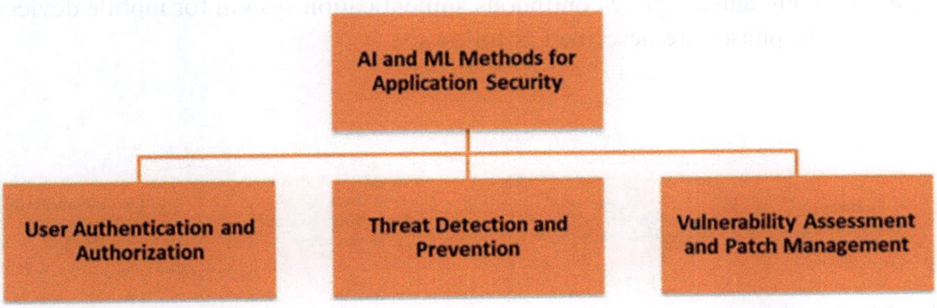

Fig. 5.1 Three common application areas of AI and ML methods for software application security

learning from past incidents to improve threat detection and response. K-Nearest Neighbors, Logistic Regression, Support Vector Machines, Convolutional Neural Networks, Recurrent Neural Networks, Long Short-Term Memory, etc. are some popular ML and DL algorithms used in cybersecurity.

AI and ML improve user authentication with physical biometrics, behavioral biometrics, or multi-factor authentication instead of easily compressible usernames, passwords, and even one-time text tokens (Kaur et al., 2023).

5.5.1.1 Biometric Methods for User Authentication

- **Physical biometric**: Biometrics is a set of advanced technologies that use the physical or behavioral characteristics of individuals to provide reliable access control (Awad et al., 2024). Physical biometrics typically refers to the innate physical characteristics of users that can be used for identification such as fingerprints, iris, and bio-signals (Siam et al., 2021).
- **Gait-based human identification:** Gait is defined as the walking pattern in humans such as walking, jogging, or running. Gait-based human identification (GHID) is a promising biometric technology that recognizes individuals based on their unique walking patterns. Temporal and spatial network neural networks can be used for capturing temporal and spatial features in the GHID task (Geng et al., 2023).
- **Behavioral biometrics for continuous authentication:** Behavioral biometrics are related to the uniquely identifiable and measurable patterns in human activities such as usage behavior that can provide continuous and user-friendly security. ML methods can analyze user behavior, such as typing patterns, mouse movements, and touch interactions, to create unique biometric profiles. A continuous authentication method ensures that the person interacting with the application is a legitimate user (Jorquera Valero et al., 2018). The use of behavior patterns related to a user's interaction with their device is the main basis of continuous authentication systems. It monitors users' behaviors by considering data coming from applications' usage statistics and sensors from interactions with different applications and determines whether the current user is the same as the one previously authenticated. Figure 5.2 shows four phases of a typical design of an intelligent and adaptive continuous authentication system for mobile devices. These four phases are described as follows:

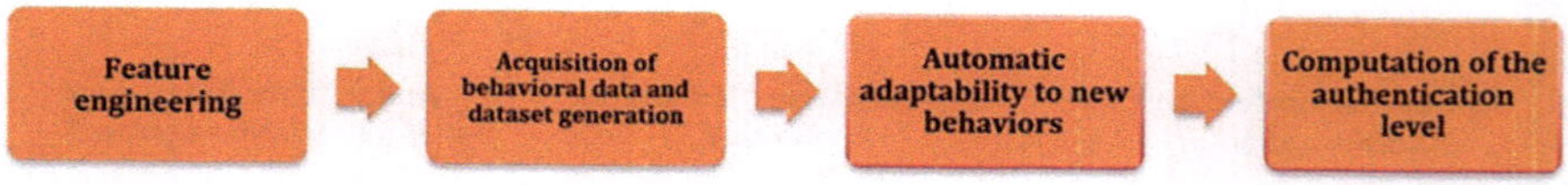

Fig. 5.2 Four Phases adaptive and continuous authentication system in (Jorquera Valero et al., 2018)

- **Feature engineering:** This is an initial noninteractive stage where that makes the selection of dimensions and features. This initial feature set is subsequently refined by using feature selection techniques.
- **Acquisition of behavioral data and dataset generation:** This phase acquires data from the mobile device and extracts the relevant features selected in the feature selection.
- **Computation of the authentication level**: In this phase, the ML algorithm is trained to fit a model from the user's behavior. Repeatedly, the new user's behavior is sampled and then evaluated by the fitted model which returns an authentication level score.
- **Automatic adaptability to new behaviors.** This is the last phase that focuses on enabling system adaptability through the elimination/inclusion of old/new behaviors in the dataset.

5.5.1.2 AI-Based Device Authentication

AI and ML models can be used for device authentication. AI-supported device authentication is the process of authenticating devices based on their credentials or behavior in the network to ensure the security of machine-to-machine communication. AI-based sensor identification and authentication methods to ensure the security of cyber-physical systems or the automotive sector (Kaur et al., 2023).

5.5.1.3 Automated Access Control

Automated access control restricts system access to authorized users based on situations or their roles and regulations within an organization. AI techniques can be used for maintenance of the access control state, role mining, policy mining, and situation-aware decision-making to prevent unauthorized access and its consequences.

Attribute-Based Access Control (ABAC) An attribute-based access control (ABAC) model leverages the machine-learning approach for automatic policy mining. An ABAC approach grants access rights to users based on attributes of entities in the system (i.e., user attributes, object attributes, and environmental conditions) and a set of authorization rules. Unsupervised learning-based algorithms detect the patterns in access logs and extract ABAC authorization rules from these patterns (Karimi et al., 2022).

5.5.1.4 Deep Learning in Biometrics

Biometrics involves identifying or verifying individuals based on their physical or behavioral characteristics such as facial features, fingerprint, voice, iris, palmprint, ear, signature, gait, etc. Deep learning-based models have increasingly been leveraged to improve the accuracy of different biometric recognition systems in recent years. These models outperformed previous state-of-the-art methods in various domains including biometric applications. The following driving factors are behind the success of deep learning models (Sundararajan & Woodard, 2018):

- **Feature learning:** Deep learning methods learn features from data which help to generalize for other related tasks.
- **Hierarchical representations:** Deep learning models learn hierarchical representations where lower-level layers learn simple features, and higher-level layers learn increasingly complex features composed of lower-level features. This helps encode both local and global properties in the final feature representation.
- **Distributed representations:** The learned representations are distributed because a single factor can explain many factors.
- **Computational resources**: GPUs and other parallel computing resources have made possible the training of large, deep neural networks with millions of training examples.
- **Large-scale datasets:** Large-scale datasets with huge amounts of training samples have helped deep learning create a significant impact in computer vision and natural language processing.

Deep learning-based models have increasingly been leveraged to improve the accuracy of different biometric recognition systems in recent years (Minaee et al., 2023). Figure 5.3 shows the common biometrics used for user or device

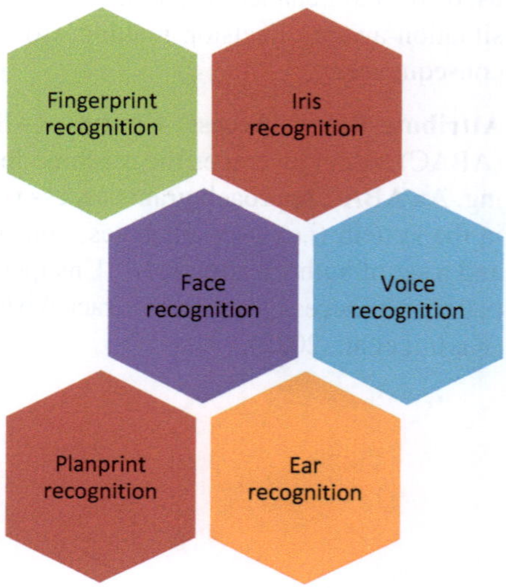

Fig. 5.3 Common biometric used for user or device authentication with deep learning

authentication with deep learning. The deep learning-based method uses neural networks with multiple layers to automatically learn and extract features from the biometric datasets. Figure 5.4 shows the sample biometric datasets for six different biometrics face, fingerprint, iris, palmprint, ear, and gait, respectively (Minaee et al., 2023).

- **Face recognition:** Face is one of the most popular biometrics with a wide range of applications including security cameras in airports, government offices, and smartphone authentication. Face recognition systems often use face detection, facial landmark detection for alignment, and face normalization as pre-processing, and then perform face recognition. Countless works are using deep learning for face recognition. DeepFace (Taigman et al., 2014) and DeepID (Sun et al., 2014) mark the beginning of deep-learning-based face recognition. Many of the models after 2017 have focused on developing new loss functions for more discriminative feature learning (Minaee et al., 2023).
- **Fingerprint recognition:** Fingerprints are perhaps the most widely used physical/physiological biometric as they consist of ridges and valleys, which form unique patterns. Minutiae are major local portions of the fingerprint that can be used to determine people's identity based on their fingerprint. Its extraction plays a major role in fingerprint identification. Important features in a fingerprint include ridge endings, bifurcations, islands, bridges, crossovers, and dots. There have been numerous research works on using deep learning for fingerprint recognition. Minutiae Extraction Network-MENet (Darlow & Rosman, 2017) is a deep learning model that proposed to extract fingerprint minutiae. Similarly, FingerNet (Tang et al., 2017) is another deep learning-based model for fingerprint minutiae extraction that jointly performs feature extraction, orientation estimation, and segmentation and uses them to estimate the minutiae maps.
- **Iris recognition:** The color, texture, and pattern of each person's iris are as unique as a fingerprint. Iris images contain a rich set of features embedded in their texture and patterns which do not change over time, such as rings, corona, ciliary processes, freckles, etc. Iris detection using deep learning has become a popular area of research in biometric identification systems. Deep learning-based models including CNN, RNN, and LSTM can achieve high accuracy in detecting and recognizing iris patterns that are unique to individuals. UniNet (Zhao & Kumar, 2017) is a deep learning framework for iris recognition that deeply learned spatially corresponding features with extended triplet loss (ETL) function to include bit shifting and non-iris masking. A conditional generative adversarial network (cGAN) based data augmentation method was proposed for improving the Iris recognition accuracy (Lee et al., 2019). In this iris recognition method, CNN networks are trained with training data generated by the pix2pix GAN model, and recognition is performed.
- **Voice recognition:** Voice Recognition is the task of determining a person's ID using the attributes of one's voice. It is also known as speaker recognition where it includes both behavioral and physical/physiological features, such as accent and pitch respectively. In recent years, it has become more and more popular to

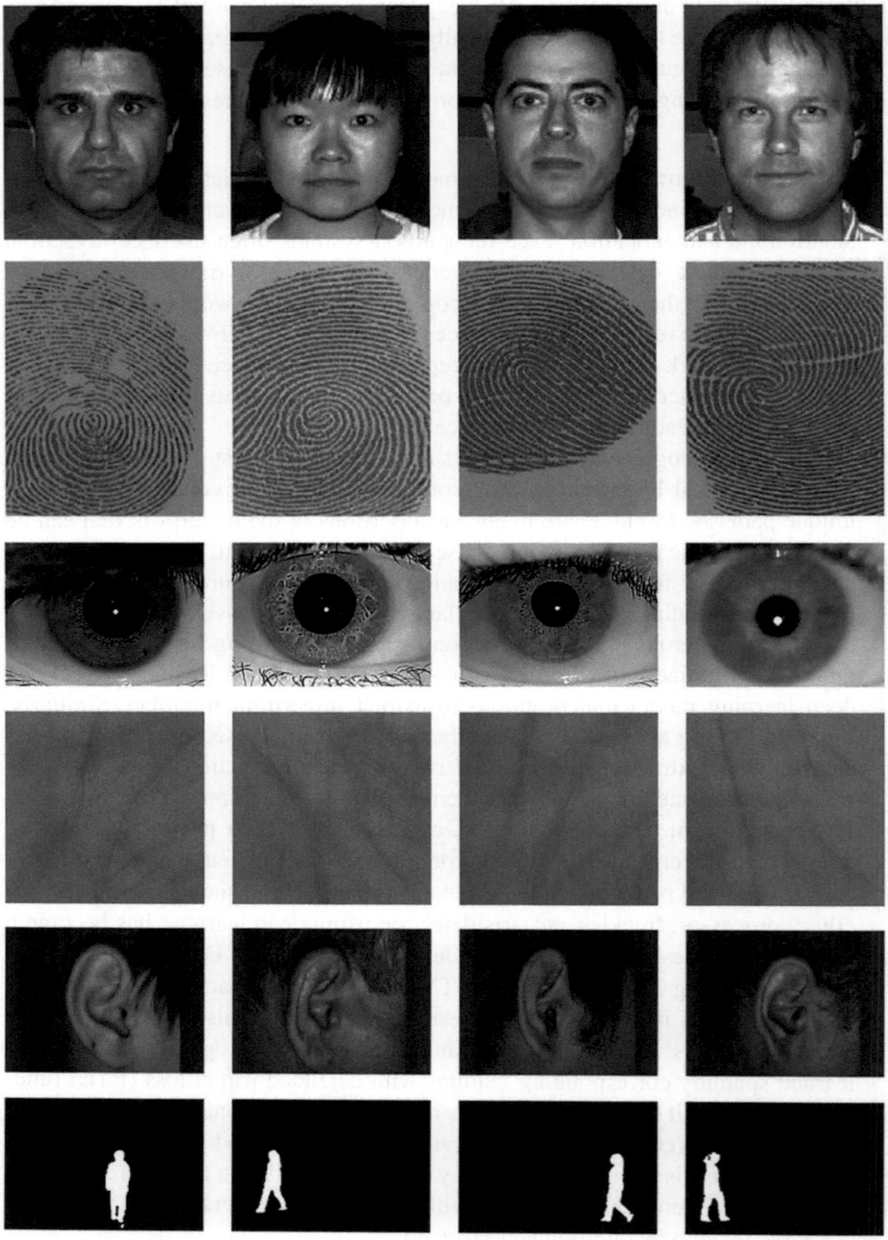

Fig. 5.4 Sample images of various biometrics including face, fingerprint, iris, palmprint, ear, and gait, respectively (Minaee et al., 2023)

explore deep learning approaches to identify or verify a person's identity based on their voice characteristics. These methods are widely used in security systems, authentication, and fraud prevention. Below are some key methods and approaches to voice recognition for biometrics using AI and ML including deep learning. ASR-DNN (Lei et al., 2014) is one of the first approaches that incorporate deep neural network-based acoustic models into the i-vector framework. This method uses a DNN acoustic model trained for Automatic Speech Recognition (ASR) to gather speaker statistics for i-vector model training.

- **Palmprint recognition** and **ear recognition** are two important biometric identification techniques that leverage the unique physical features of an individual for identity verification and have been gaining more attention recently (Minaee et al., 2023). The use of deep learning models can help to improve the accuracy of these methods.

5.5.2 Threat Detection and Prevention

Machine learning (ML) algorithms can help detect and prevent threats by analyzing data from past incidents and learning patterns. These algorithms identify unusual behavior and forecast potential threats.

5.5.2.1 Anomaly Detection

Anomaly detection is one of the common methods used for threat detection and prevention. Anomalies are patterns in data that do not conform to a well-defined notion of normal behavior (Chandola et al., 2009). Anomaly detection methods find patterns in data that do not conform to expected behavior. These nonconforming patterns are often referred to as anomalies or outliers. These methods are used in a wide variety of applications such as intrusion detection, user behaviors analysis, fraud detection for credit cards, fault detection in safety-critical systems, etc. Anomalies can be classified into the following three categories:

- **Point anomalies:** A point anomaly refers to an individual data instance that can be considered anomalous to the rest of the other data. It is the simplest type of anomaly and is the focus of most of the research on anomaly detection.
- **Contextual anomalies:** A contextual anomaly is an instance that is anomalous in a specific context. The context is induced by the structure of the data set and must be specified as a part of the problem formulation. Contextual attributes are used to determine the context for that instance and behavioral attributes define the non-contextual characteristics of an instance.
- **Collective anomalies:** A collective anomaly is a collection of related data instances that are anomalous to the entire data set. The individual data instances in a collective anomaly may not be anomalies by themselves, but their occur-

rence together as a collection is anomalous. Collective anomalies have been explored for sequence data, graph data, and spatial data. It should be noted that while point anomalies can occur in any data set, collective anomalies can occur only in data sets in which data instances are related. In contrast, the occurrence of contextual anomalies depends on the availability of context attributes in the data. A point anomaly or a collective anomaly can also be a contextual anomaly if analyzed in a context.

Supervised, semi-supervised, or unsupervised methods can be used for anomaly detection. Supervised anomaly detection models trained in supervised mode assume the availability of a training data set that has labeled instances for normal as well as anomaly classes. A typical approach in such cases is to build a predictive model for normal vs. anomaly classes. Semi-supervised anomaly detection methods operate in a semi-supervised mode and assume that the training data has labeled instances only for the normal class. Since they do not require labels for the anomaly class, they are more widely applicable than supervised techniques. Unsupervised anomaly detection methods that operate in unsupervised mode do not require training data and thus are most widely applicable.

5.5.2.2 Malware Analysis

Malware is one of the main attack vectors in smartphones and its detection is a key to smartphone application security. Malware analysis is the process of examining malicious software by understanding its behavior, origin, functionality, and potential impact on systems. ML learning-based methods have been increasingly used in malware detection (Muzaffar et al., 2022). The common approaches for malware analysis are:

- **Static analysis:** Static analysis involves examining the code, binaries, or other app artifacts without executing or running it. This can be achieved by techniques ranging from simply opening an APK header as a text file and reading printable strings in it, to unpacking and reverse engineering an APK file and then scanning the processed code file(s) for key information. In most cases, static analysis is generally quicker and easier to perform. This method includes techniques like reverse engineering, control flow analysis, data flow analysis, and pattern matching. ML techniques are applied to features extracted by static analysis.
- **Dynamic analysis:** Dynamic analysis involves executing the app in a controlled environment. Monitoring the application behavior in runtime is called a dynamic analysis where features are extracted while the application is executed and can then be used to train ML models. The application is run on an emulator/virtual device or a real mobile device. This can result in a greater use of resources and time for analysis compared to static analysis but is likely to result in more information. Dynamic analysis techniques can detect runtime behaviors like network communication, API calls, and interactions with the system that are not visible in static analysis.

- **Hybrid analysis:** This method combines both static and dynamic analysis methods. This approach can provide a more comprehensive understanding of an app's behavior by correlating the results of static code analysis with dynamic runtime behavior observations. MARVIN (Lindorfer et al., 2015) is a malware analysis tool that classifies mobile apps by using a hybrid analysis approach. It combines static with dynamic analysis and leverages machine learning techniques to assess the risk associated with unknown Android apps in the form of a malicious score.

Malware analysis methods using AI and machine learning (ML) have become crucial in enhancing app security, particularly as threats grow more sophisticated. These techniques leverage large datasets of known malware and benign software to train models that can identify patterns, behaviors, and characteristics indicative of malicious code. AI and ML algorithms can dynamically analyze applications in real-time, detecting anomalies and previously unseen threats through predictive modeling. With continuous learning from new data, AI and ML-based malware analysis tools can adapt to emerging threats and provide a more robust and proactive defense for application security. DroidDetector (Yuan et al., 2016) is a deep learning-based Android malware analysis tool that can automatically detect whether an app is malware or not. Web Application Security Threats and Vulnerabilities.

5.5.2.3 Protective Security Solutions

Various AI and ML-based methods provide protective security solutions to the application software in the form of log analysis tools, intrusion prevention systems, anti-virus/anti-malware software, and deception protection (Kaur et al., 2023).

- **Log analysis**: Log analysis is the process of reviewing computer-generated event logs to proactively identify bugs, security concerns, or other risks. AI-based log analysis tools can automate routine and repeated tasks to handle large amounts of distributed log data efficiently. Big data technology with AI methods helps to collect and process the different data formats collected from heterogeneous sources for automated feature extraction and feature selection techniques (Sisiaridis & Markowitch, 2018).
- **Intrusion Prevention System (IPS):** IPS systems monitor the network traffic and then take appropriate action to thwart the attack by reporting, blocking, dropping, or resetting the connection. Isolation forest and other unsupervised learning methods can be used with the intrusion prevention system.
- **Anti-virus or anti-malware software:** Anti-virus or anti-malware software analyzes thousands of files and extracts useful features to classify them as benign or malware using machine learning methods. Anti-virus programs integrate AI/ML models for detecting malware using the features retrieved from the executables or dynamic data analysis and used then with the artificial neural networks (ANNs) or recurrent neural network (RNN) models (Pedro et al., 2021).

- **Deception:** It is an advanced technique to protect critical documents after an attacker. AI-based deception methods have been used to generate credible fake text documents to mislead cyberattacks.

5.5.3 Vulnerability Assessment and Patch Management

An automated vulnerability assessment is the process of systematically reviewing security weaknesses in a system using automated tools for vulnerability identification, classification, exploration, and prioritization (Kaur et al., 2023). The AI and ML-based risk assessment process supports the risk management team.

- Deep learning and transfer learning methods can be used to detect software vulnerabilities by checking the source code.
- AI methods discover vulnerabilities in software and hardware interfaces and software applications by injecting erroneous, unexpected, or randomly generated data into a program or interface and then monitoring for events like crashes, failed code assertions, undocumented jumps or debug routines, and possible memory leaks.
- AI techniques are leveraged to develop an automated system for identifying potential attack options, input generation, the generation of probable test cases, and analyzing crashes.
- AI and ML methods can be used for automated penetration testing to penetrate an attack surface by exploiting known or zero-day vulnerabilities to identify what the attacker can gain from current environments.

5.6 Summary

In this chapter, we explore the application of AI and ML methods techniques in enhancing software application security across various platforms including smartphone apps, web applications, and desktop applications. The chapter begins by addressing common security vulnerabilities highlighted by the OWASP Top 10, such as injection attacks, cross-site scripting (XSS), and insecure authentication, etc. It then delves into how AI-powered security solutions can be used to detect and mitigate these vulnerabilities. We discussed AI and ML methods for user authentication, threat detection, and prevention methods, vulnerability assessment, and patch management. After understanding the various security threats and vulnerabilities of software applications across the platform (mobile, web, and desktop apps) and AI and ML methods for enhancing their security, the following questions are addressed in this chapter:

1. What are the common security threats and vulnerabilities in smartphone, web, and desktop applications?

2. What are the OWASP Top 10 security threats and vulnerabilities for web and desktop applications?
3. What are the common application areas of AI and ML in application security?
4. What are the AI and ML approaches for software application security?
5. What are the biometric methods for user authentication and authorization?
6. How are AI and ML models used for behavioral biometrics for continuous authentication?
7. What is automatic access control?
8. How are deep learning-based methods used in biometrics for user and device authentication?
9. What are the common biometric methods used with deep learning?
10. What are the threat detection and prevention methods?
11. How does the anomaly detection method monitor and detect security threats?
12. What is malware analysis? What are the types of malware analysis?
13. How does the malware analysis method monitor and detect security threats in smartphone applications?
14. How do AI and ML methods provide protective security solutions to the application software?
15. What are the AI and ML methods for vulnerability assessment and patch management?

References

Awad, A. I., Babu, A., Barka, E., & Shuaib, K. (2024). AI-powered biometrics for Internet of Things security: A review and future vision. *Journal of Information Security and Applications, 82*, 103748. https://doi.org/10.1016/j.jisa.2024.103748

Chandola, V., Banerjee, A. A., & Kumar, A. V. (2009). Anomaly detection: A survey. *ACM Computing Surveys, 41*, 1–58. https://doi.org/10.1145/1541880.1541882

Darlow, L. N., & Rosman, B. (2017). Fingerprint minutiae extraction using deep learning. In *2017 IEEE International Joint Conference on Biometrics (IJCB)* (pp. 22–30). IEEE.

Geng, Y., Wang, Y., Wang, X., Lu, C., Yu, H., & Yuan, M. (2023). Gait-based human identification using deep learning and multiple-position wearable data. In *2023 international conference on advanced mechatronic systems (ICAMechS)* (pp. 1–6). IEEE.

He, D., Chan, A. S., & Guizani, A. M. (2015). Mobile application security: Malware threats and defenses. *IEEE Wireless Communications, 22*, 138–144.

Jan, S., Panichella, A., Arcuri, A., & Briand, L. (2019). Automatic generation of tests to exploit XML injection vulnerabilities in web applications. *IEEE Transactions on Software Engineering*, 335–362. https://doi.org/10.1109/TSE.2017.2778711

Jorquera Valero, J. M., Sanchez Sanchez, P. M., Fernandez Maimo, L., Huertas Celdran, A., Arjona Fernandez, M., De Los Santos Vilchez, S., & Martinez Perez, G. (2018). Improving the security and QoE in mobile devices through an intelligent and adaptive continuous authentication system. *Sensors, 18*, 3769.

Karimi, L., Aldairi, A. M., Joshi, A. J., & Abdelhakim, A. M. (2022). An automatic attribute-based access control policy extraction from access logs. *IEEE Transactions on Dependable and Secure Computing*, 2304–2317.

Kaur, R., Gabrijelčič, A. D., & Klobučar, A. T. (2023). Artificial intelligence for cybersecurity: Literature review and future research directions. *Information Fusion, 101804*. https://doi.org/10.1016/j.inffus.2023.101804
Lee, M. B., Kim, Y. H., & Park, K. R. (2019). Conditional generative adversarial network- Based data augmentation for enhancement of iris recognition accuracy. *IEEE Access*, 122134–122152.
Lei, Y., Scheffer, N., Ferrer, L., & McLaren, M. (2014). A novel scheme for speaker recognition using a phonetically-aware deep neural network. In *2014 IEEE international conference on acoustics, speech and signal processing (ICASSP)* (pp. 1695–1699). IEEE.
Lindorfer, M., Neugschwandtner, M., & Platzer, C. (2015). MARVIN: Efficient and comprehensive mobile app classification through static and dynamic analysis. In *2015 IEEE 39th annual computer software and applications conference* (pp. 422–433). IEEE.
Minaee, S., Abdolrashidi, A., Su, H., Bennamoun, M., & Zhang, A. D. (2023). Biometrics recognition using deep learning: A survey. *Artificial Intelligence Review, 56*, 8647–8695. https://doi.org/10.1007/s10462-022-10237-x
Muzaffar, A., Hassen, A. H., Lones, A. M., & Zantout, A. H. (2022). An in-depth review of machine learning based Android malware detection. *Computers & Security, 121*, 102833.
OWASP. (2021a). Retrieved from OWASP Top 10–2021: https://owasp.org/Top10/ Accessed on July 15, 2024.
OWASP. (2021b). *OWASP Top 10:2021, A04:2021—Insecure Design*. Retrieved from: https://owasp.org/Top10/A04_2021-Insecure_Design/
OWASP. (2021c). *OWASP Top 10:2021, A06:2021—Vulnerable and Outdated Components*. Retrieved from: https://owasp.org/Top10/A06_2021-Vulnerable_and_Outdated_Components/
OWASP Top 10 Desktop Application Security Risks. (2021). Retrieved from https://owasp.org/www-project-desktop-app-security-top-10/
OWASP Top 10:2021, A01:2021—Broken Access Control. (2021). Retrieved from https://owasp.org/Top10/A01_2021-Broken_Access_Control/
OWASP Top 10:2021, A02:2021—Cryptographic Failures. (2021). Retrieved from https://owasp.org/Top10/A02_2021-Cryptographic_Failures/
OWASP Top 10:2021, A07:2021—Identification and Authentication Failures. (2021). Retrieved from https://owasp.org/Top10/A07_2021-Identification_and_Authentication_Failures/
OWASP Top 10:2021, A08:2021—Software and Data Integrity Failures. (2021). Retrieved from https://owasp.org/Top10/A08_2021-Software_and_Data_Integrity_Failures/
OWASP Top 10:2021 A09:2021—Security Logging and Monitoring Failures. (2021). Retrieved from OWASP Top 10:2021: https://owasp.org/Top10/A09_2021-Security_Logging_and_Monitoring_Failures/
OWASP Top 10:2021, A09:2021—Security Logging and Monitoring Failures. (2021). Retrieved from https://owasp.org/Top10/A09_2021-Security_Logging_and_Monitoring_Failures/
OWASP Top 10:2021, A10:2021—Server-Side Request Forgery (SSRF). (2021). Retrieved from https://owasp.org/Top10/A10_2021-Server-Side_Request_Forgery_%28SSRF%29/
Pedro, M., Matilda, A. R., & Ilir, A. G. (2021). Waste not: Using diverse neural networks from hyperparameter search for improved malware detection. *Computers & Security, 102339*.
Pritee, Z. T., Anik, A. M., Alam, A. S., Jim, A. J., Kabir, A. M., & Mridha, M. (2024). Machine learning and deep learning for user authentication and authorization in cybersecurity: A state-of-the-art review. *Computers & Security, 140*, 103747. https://doi.org/10.1016/j.cose.2024.103747
Rai, A., Miraz, M. M., Das, D., Kaur, H., & Swati. (2021). SQL injection: Classification and prevention. In *2021 2nd international conference on intelligent engineering and management (ICIEM)* (pp. 367–372). IEEE.
Siam, A. I., Sedik, A., El-Shafai, W., Elazm, A. A., El-Bahnasawy, N. A., El Banby, G. M., et al. (2021). Biosignal classification for human identification based on convolutional neural networks. *International Journal of Communication Systems, 34*.
Sisiaridis, D., & Markowitch, O. (2018). Reducing data complexity in feature extraction and feature selection for big data security analytics. In *2018 1st international conference on data intelligence and security (ICDIS)* (pp. 43–48). IEEE.

Stallings, W. (2013). *Network security essentials: Applications and standards, international edition: Applications and standards*. Pearson Education, Limited.

Sun, Y., Wang, X., & Tang, X. (2014). Deep learning face representation from predicting 10,000 classes. In *2014 IEEE conference on computer vision and pattern recognition* (pp. 1891–1898). https://doi.org/10.1109/CVPR.2014.244

Sundararajan, K., & Woodard, A. D. (2018). Deep learning for biometrics: A survey. *ACM Computing Surveys (CSUR), 51*, 1–34. https://doi.org/10.1145/3190618

Taigman, Y., Yang, M., Ranzato, M., & Wolf, A. L. (2014). DeepFace: Closing the gap to human-level performance in face verification. In *2014 IEEE conference on computer vision and pattern recognition* (pp. 1701–1708). IEEE. https://doi.org/10.1109/CVPR.2014.220

Tajpour, A., Ibrahim, S., & Sharifi, M. (2012). Web application security by SQL injection detection tools. *International Journal of Computer Science Issues*, 332–339.

Tang, Y., Gao, A. F., Feng, A. J., & Liu, A. Y. (2017). FingerNet: An unified deep network for fingerprint minutiae extraction. In *2017 IEEE International Joint Conference on Biometrics (IJCB)* (pp. 108–116). IEEE. https://doi.org/10.1109/BTAS.2017.8272688

Yuan, Z., Lu, Y., & Xue, Y. (2016). Droiddetector: Android malware characterization and detection using deep learning. *Tsinghua Science and Technology, 21*, 114–123. https://doi.org/10.1109/TST.2016.7399288

Zhao, Z., & Kumar, A. (2017). Towards more accurate iris recognition using deeply learned spatially corresponding features. In *2017 IEEE international conference on computer vision (ICCV)* (pp. 3829–3838). IEEE. https://doi.org/10.1109/ICCV.2017.411

Chapter 6
AI for Cloud Security

6.1 Introduction

Over the years, cloud computing has grown and made a substantial contribution to numerous businesses and academic disciplines. Parallel computing was the first step in the evolution process, followed by distributed, utility, cluster, grid, and finally, cloud computing (Bhardwaj & Rama Krishna, 2021). Instead of locally deploying the application and resources, hardware, and software on the user side, cloud computing facilitates sharing a broad range of computing resources, storage, and services over the internet. Different users utilize the same computing infrastructure and can easily access services and applications hosted on the cloud by public providers from any location known as the multi-tenancy feature (Kaaniche & Laurent, 2017). It increases the system resource utilization with cost-effective services among different cloud providers (Sabireen & Neelanarayanan, 2021; Kumar et al., 2021).

Depending on the services needed by organizations and individuals and the required services, cloud computing can be characterized by three existing models: software as a service (SaaS), platform as a service (PaaS), and infrastructure as a service (IaaS) (Opara-Martins et al., 2016; Ardagna et al., 2015; Allakonda & Sagar, 2021). SaaS includes software applications that are provided to customers for use in the cloud without any installation on their desktops, laptops, and so on. Today, various SaaS platforms around the world can be used (AlZain et al., 2012). The well-known examples of SaaS platforms are Amazon's EC2 (Thillaiarasu & ChenthurPandian, 2016), Amazon's S3 (Imran et al., 2020), IBM's Blue Cloud (Tomarchio et al., 2020), Google App Engine (Viswanath & Krishna, 2021), Yahoo Pig, Google Apps (Pachala et al., 2021), Dropbox (Subashini & Kavitha, 2011), and Salesforce's Customer Relation Management (CRM) system (Torkura et al., 2020). PaaS provides a platform for developing software applications provided by cloud computing, e.g., Amazon Web Services (Thillaiarasu & ChenthurPandian, 2016) and Window Azure (Wueest et al., 2015). IaaS comprises infrastructure, such as

D. P. Sharma et al., *Understanding AI in Cybersecurity and Secure AI*, Progress in IS, https://doi.org/10.1007/978-3-031-91524-6_6

servers, operating systems, networks, and so on, that is provided to users through virtualization. Virtualization is the principal enabling core of cloud computing; it uses software to split one computer device into multiple independent computing devices, where each can be used to perform computing tasks. This helps to efficiently allocate and use the usually idle computing resources, reduces cost, and reliably increases infrastructure use. Among IaaS systems are DigitalOcean, Linode, Rackspace, Microsoft Azure, GCE, and so forth (Bhonde & Devane, 2021; Masud et al., 2021; Chinnasamy & Deepalakshmi, 2021). These systems significantly increase work efficiency in organizations at a relatively low price.

Despite the global trend toward cloud computing and its benefits, some operational issues make it challenging to move towards the ubiquitous computing environment. Several challenges constrain its deployment, including security concerns, lack of interoperability and portability as a utility, high latency, flexibility and timely responsiveness to cloud users, data storage and access regulation, vendor lock-in problems, unavailability of resource and services provisioning leaving cloud users with no access to their paid cloud resources, interruption of services, the obligation of trust, quality of service degradation due to the distance between cloud and customer, and heterogeneity (Dewangan et al., 2016; Opara-Martins et al., 2016).

Muti cloud shows a predominant area over cloud computing architecture. It relies on using more than one cloud service provider (CSP). In fact, several cloud networks are combined together for different roles, intending to reduce the necessary trust requirements among the CSPs (Ardagna et al., 2015). It overcomes the limitations of cloud computing and brings a wide range of benefits. For example, it avoids vendor lock-in problems by providing more than one distributed cloud and thus limiting the dependence on only one external provider. Moreover, combining various clouds eliminates the risk of manipulating cloud user data; it is far more challenging for a malicious outsider to hack the system and access the user's data distributed across different clouds. The user's data stored in the cloud are divided according to the cloud's reliability and the data's degree of sensitivity (Allakonda & Sagar, 2021; AlZain et al., 2012; Thillaiarasu & ChenthurPandian, 2016).

A multiple-clouds structure can deal with the peaks in service and resource requests from various clients. It responds to changes in service providers' offers by abiding by constraints like new locations or laws. It provides a flexible and transparent service delivery under varying workloads and network constraints while maintaining interoperability characteristics. Moreover, users do not need to be concerned about the complexity of the underlying infrastructure while using multiple clouds from various providers (Imran et al., 2020; Tomarchio et al., 2020).

The benefits of multiple-cloud are varied and can be briefly stated; supporting the single web interface to access the resources from heterogeneous cloud platforms, improving data sharing, preventing information corruption and unethical issues from the vendors, assurance of data protection, and providing flexibility of sharing the data by the data owners in the cloud, react to changes of the offers by the providers, ensuring backup-ups to deal with disasters or scheduled activity, acting as an intermediary, enhancing the cloud resource and service offers based on agreements with other providers—the significant advantage of using the multiple-cloud for big data storage (Ardagna et al., 2015; Viswanath & Krishna, 2021; Pachala et al., 2021).

Security and privacy are vital with adopting cloud and multiple-cloud computing. The success of cloud computing and a trustworthy environment is primarily driven by cloud security and data privacy (AlZain et al., 2012; Thillaiarasu & ChenthurPandian, 2016). Building a trustworthy cloud environment mainly depends on a secure underlying architecture and maintaining the security and privacy of users' data and sensitive attributes. Cloud collaboration and communication impact the security and privacy of users' data in an open, unreliable environment. It raises the possibility that outsourcing, transmitting, and accessing data from one cloud to another could compromise users' data security and privacy.

Different security and privacy-preserving techniques were put into practice in the context of the cloud. It ranges from applying cryptographic and non-cryptographic techniques to setting security and privacy policies and service level agreements. It extends to relying on externally trusted parties like brokers or middleware to facilitate reliable and trustworthy communication at the infrastructure and platform levels.

This chapter explores the critical security and privacy challenges associated with cloud computing, particularly as organizations increasingly migrate IT operations to cloud infrastructure. It will address key security vulnerabilities such as misconfiguration, unauthorized access, data breaches, malware injections, insecure APIs, abuse of cloud services, account hijacking, and insider threats. Each of these threats poses significant risks to data confidentiality, integrity, and availability, impacting businesses and cloud users. The chapter also discusses AI-based security protection in cloud computing, highlighting how AI-driven solutions can enhance threat detection, predictive analytics, proactive defense mechanisms, behavioral analysis, and automated security responses. Additionally, AI-powered compliance monitoring, security automation, and threat intelligence sharing will be explored as critical measures to strengthen cloud security. The discussion also highlights the challenges of AI-based cloud security, including adversarial AI threats, evolving attack strategies, and regulatory compliance issues. By analyzing current and emerging threats, along with AI-enhanced defense mechanisms, this chapter aims to provide a comprehensive understanding of cloud security risks and mitigation strategies, ensuring more resilient and secure cloud environments.

6.2 Security and Privacy Issues with the Cloud Computing

Companies are increasingly moving their IT operations to infrastructure-as-a-service (IaaS) solutions. In an IaaS environment, the cloud provider allows the customer to virtually access underlying IT infrastructure. This gives the customer the ability to provision these resources on demand (Wueest et al., 2015). The main elements that determine the success and reliability functions of cloud computing are creating a secure cloud infrastructure while protecting the privacy of cloud users' data and sensitive attributes. The main security threats in the cloud environment are information disclosure/leakage and data unavailability, a.k.a., data loss. The security threats occur due to several breaches or account hijacking from malicious insiders that don't behave legally to their access rights or untrusted cloud providers. Basically, security issues in cloud computing can be classified into following issues.

6.2.1 Misconfiguration

Most cyber-attacks and data breaches in cloud infrastructure are due to human errors and misconfiguration vulnerabilities (Subashini & Kavitha, 2011). Misconfiguration generally occurs due to incorrect set up of computing assets which lead to exploitation of the vulnerability in the future. Some of the common examples are unsecured data storage elements or containers, excessive permissions, forgetting to change the default credentials, disabled standard security controls. Misconfiguration of cloud resources due to lack of knowledge causes data breaches and has the potential to modify or even deletion of resources resulting in data tampering, repudiation, information disclosure or even denial of services (Bhonde & Devane, 2021).

Cloud misconfiguration refers to any glitches, gaps, or errors that could expose the cloud environment to risk during adoption. Misconfiguration vulnerabilities e.g., excessive permissions, disabled logging features and publicly accessible cloud storage buckets, may lead to the form of security breaches, such as external hackers, ransomware, malware, or insider threats that use vulnerabilities to access the network (Torkura et al., 2020). For instance, misconfiguration in AWS Simple Storage Service (S3) cloud storage bucket in 2017, exposed private data of 123 million American households which belonged to Experian, a credit bureau, which sold the data to an online marketing and data analytics company named Alteryx. It affects the software, platform as well as infrastructure layer of service Models (Bhonde & Devane, 2021). In 2019, a telecom company named Voipo, that provides voice over internet services, exposed around 7 million of customer call logs, short message service logs, call records and credentials. The reason was due to misconfigured security control as one of their backend Elasticsearch databases.

6.2.2 Unauthorized Access

Data access is a significant aspect of the service of the cloud, without which the platform would not be able to operate or be so popular among users. Therefore, unauthorized access in a cloud system is one of the important problems that must be solved or prevented so that every user is able to trust the provider with their sensitive data (Masud et al., 2021). Figure 6.1 shows general security issues which lead to unauthorized access in cloud computing.

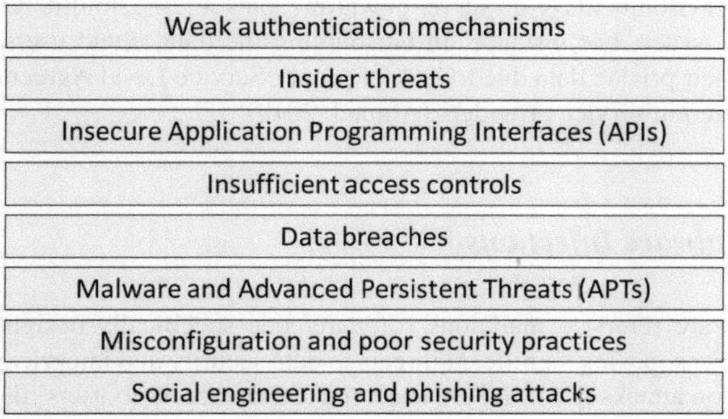

Fig. 6.1 Security issues lead to unauthorized access in cloud computing

In the cloud, the hardware and software should be protected from unauthorized access. A cloud service provider in cloud computing offers computational services and virtualization over the Internet. It provides critical services such as restricting unauthorized access, maintaining data integrity, and ensuring data availability. To ensure cloud security, security challenges must be addressed to take full advantage of this computing paradigm (Chinnasamy & Deepalakshmi, 2021). For instance, Zero Trust frameworks can exclusively provide cloud users with access to the cloud-based applications and resources. The Zero Trust approach utilizes micro-segmentation and rigorous policies to enhance the security of workloads and other critical traffic in the cloud (Mallikarjunaradhya et al., 2023).

6.2.3 *Data Breach (Loss/Leakage)*

Data breach is a major users' data related issues which have been one of the biggest fears that users face in cloud computing services. Based on the 2023 Thales Global Cloud Security Study,[1] 39% of businesses experienced a data breach in their cloud environment in 2022, an increase of 4 points from the previous year (35%). It can be considered as the data loss or leakage. Data loss happens when data may be physically or logically removed from the cloud servers either intentionally (e.g., malicious actions) or unintentionally (e.g., misconfiguration). Data Leakage is an incident when the confidentiality of information has been compromised. It may be caused by an unauthorized transmission of data from within a cloud resource to an external or third-party server. The data that is leaked out can either be private in nature or are deemed confidential whereas the data loss is loss of data due to deletion, system crash etc. (Purohit & Singh, 2013). Some conditions in cloud

[1] 2023 Thales Cloud Security Study https://cpl.thalesgroup.com/about-us/newsroom/2023-cloud-security-cyberattacks-data-breaches-press-release

computing environments (e.g., server downtime, outsourcing, multitenancy) lead to data breach issues. For instance, in outsourcing the data, cloud users might lose control of their private data due to lack of proper Service Level Agreements (SLA) between different service providers (Ahmed, 2019).

6.2.4 Malware Injections

Cloud malware refers to malicious software/code specifically designed to target cloud platforms, posing significant threats to data security and integrity. Cloud malware injection attacks (CMIAs) are executed to gain access to users' data, which is stored and processed in the cloud (Aljumah & Ahanger, 2020). In this environment, a hacker (e.g., a malicious user or third party) inserts malicious code into applications to run arbitrary code with the privileges of a vulnerable process and so gain access to other users' computing resources, applications (i.e., Cross-Site scripting/HTML injection), or cloud databases (i.e., SQL injection). Malware injection can be network-based, or injections can be done via the hypervisor (Coppolino et al., 2017). Some of the most widely practiced CMIA threats are cross-site scripting attacks and structured query language (SQL) injection attacks. Such attacks are possible due to vulnerable cloud service providers such as the OpenStack cloud platform.[2] With the assistance of a malevolent cypher, adversaries can easily deliver scrambled information from a buffer by misusing a design flaw in present day mainframes (Aljumah & Ahanger, 2020). In this case, cloud providers must protect traffic inside the infrastructure to securely connect a user/resource to the other and the traffic coming from outside trying to leave the smallest number of access points. Many cloud providers implement al- most the same solutions in the field of network. They use common techniques such as Firewalls, IDSs, and Anti-Virus Gateway that are now widely deployed in edge networks to protect end-systems from attacks and to monitor the incoming and outgoing traffic (Coppolino et al., 2017).

6.2.5 Insecure APIs

In an ideal cloud environment, APIs streamline cloud computing processes and services. At all cloud infrastructure, platform and software service levels, APIs are used to provide effective communication with other services/resources. For instance, IaaS APIs are used to access and manage infrastructure resources, e.g., virtual machine and network, PaaS APIs give access to the cloud services such as storage, and SaaS APIs connect infrastructure with software applications (Sujatha &

[2] https://www.openstack.org/

Balachandran, 2016). Cloud services security depends on the APIs security. The challenge with the APIs is that they are specifically designed to share data (Macy, 2018). Public cloud APIs unlock numerous, productive possibilities for developers. These interfaces bring core features to applications and connect apps and programs to external services. Properly integrated APIs benefit all cloud users and bolster a service's value proposition on the software market. Security of the cloud APIs directly affects the security and availability of general cloud services. Third parties or cloud service providers in a multi-cloud environment often build upon APIs to offer their own value-added services to their customers. This leads to the complexity of the new layered API and increases risk, as organizations may be required to relinquish their credentials to third parties in order to enable their agency. Anonymous access and/or reusable tokens or passwords, clear-text authentication or transmission of content, inflexible access controls or improper authorizations, limited monitoring and logging capabilities, unknown service or API dependencies are some possible API related issues. From authentication and access control to encryption and activity monitoring, these interfaces must be designed to protect against both accidental and malicious attempts to circumvent policy (Cloud Security, n.d.; Mallikarjunaradhya et al., 2023).

6.2.6 Abuse of Cloud Services

Cloud users may abuse cloud services and exploit the cloud services to perform unethical or malicious activities to acquire benefits or financial gain. Due to shared technology vulnerabilities, threats are hard to control for massive parallelism infrastructure. Virtualization hypervisors are not enough to address the gap for strong compartmentalization multitenant architecture in cloud computing. Therefore, it exhibits flaws and risks of accessing compromising customers' sensitive data. Attackers can abuse this feature by renting VM to hack service engines through other customers' VMs to breach and compromise confidential data by breaking the isolation feature that separates customers' data (Ahmad & Bakht, 2019).

Depending on the services provided at different models, IaaS, SaaS, or PaaS, services may be abused differently. IaaS providers offer their customers the illusion of unlimited compute, network, and storage capacity often coupled with a 'frictionless' registration process where anyone with a valid credit card can register and immediately begin using cloud services. Some providers even offer free limited trial periods. By abusing the relative anonymity behind these registration and usage models, spammers, malicious code authors, and other criminals have been able to conduct their activities with relative impunity. PaaS providers have traditionally suffered most from this kind of attacks; however, recent evidence shows that hackers have begun to target IaaS vendors as well. Future areas of concern include password and key cracking, DDOS, launching dynamic attack points, hosting malicious data, botnet command and control, building rainbow tables, and CAPTCHA solving farms. IaaS offerings have hosted the Zeus botnet, InfoStealer trojan horses, and downloads for Microsoft Office and Adobe PDF exploits. Additionally, botnets have used IaaS servers for command-and-control functions. Spam continues to be a problem—as a defensive measure, entire blocks of IaaS network addresses have been publicly blacklisted (Cloud Security, n.d.).

6.2.7 Account Hijacking

Account or service hijacking is a kind of identity theft and has evolved to be one of the most rapidly increasing types of cyberattack in cloud computing aimed at deceiving end users. It is a process in which the attackers dishonestly gain access to an individual's uniquely identifiable information associated with an IT device or service (email account, bank account, computer account, etc.) and the information stolen is thus used for unlawful purposes. Typically, the compromised account information is used to impersonate the original account owner. Account hijacking is usually accomplished through tactics like phishing emails, spoofed emails, and faux pop-up windows. Users unaware of the actual motive unknowingly respond to these emails providing the attackers with credential information, which the attackers use to modify user accounts, create new accounts and leave little or no trace by deleting transaction history (Ahmad & Arce, 2008). For instance, The New York Times (NYT) website was attacked using cloud account hijacking which is considered as one of the most famous security breaches, where the site was down for almost 6 h (Tirumala et al., 2015).

6.2.8 Insider Threat

Insider threat means threat occurring from the employees of the cloud service providers (Deep et al., 2022). A malicious insider is an individual, such as current or ex-employee, supplier, vendor, client, contractor or other business partner, who has or had authorized access to organizational information processing facilities, like system, network or data and attempt to abuse the privileges by damaging employer's assets, reputation or by leaking sensitive information for financial gain or revenge (Ahmad & Bakht, 2019). Insider threat is well-known and is amplified for consumers of cloud services by the convergence of IT services and customers under a single management domain, combined with a general lack of transparency into provider process and procedure. For example, a provider may not reveal how it grants employees access to physical and virtual assets, how it monitors these employees, or how it analyzes and reports on policy compliance (Cloud Security, n.d.).

6.2.9 Security Protection Solutions in Cloud Computing

Cloud storage not only stores vast amounts of data but also supports the process of this data in query, sharing, and computations. However, the data outsourced to the cloud should be kept secure and private through different phases, starting from the transfer, access, sharing, analysis, archival, and destruction. Not only should the data be kept secure but also privacy concepts, like user identities, sensitive attributes, location, and user access patterns should be considered. The leakage of users' sensitive information can lead to critical and undesirable circumstances.

Achieving data security at the software level (SaaS) is the most important concern in a cloud environment. Cloud users face different challenges during cloud deployment. First, they lose control over their outsource data in different heterogeneous clouds; they need to trust the cloud service provider as they are not entirely sure that their data is not being used for other purposes other than that for which it is intended to be, and it is adequately destroyed in the end (Subashini & Kavitha, 2011). They are also unsure about the occurrence of any privacy breaches which may have exposed their information. They are also uncertain if their information is retained after they have stopped using a particular service. These uncertainties decrease the trust in a specific service provider and raise a risk to users' privacy and data security during its transmission, outsourcing, and access from one cloud to another. The situation will become more difficult in the multiple clouds context due to increased system complexity between different clouds as the data can be dynamically collected and fragmented across distributed clouds.

Traditionally, encryption techniques are used for confidentiality and to preserve cloud users' outsourced data, which prohibits the disclosure of sensitive information. Different encryption techniques are used to protect user data and sensitive attributes in the cloud and multi-cloud computing. The cryptographic techniques lead to a trade-off between security and efficiency, e.g., data encryption offers robust security but at the cost of reducing the efficiency and limiting the functions performed over the encrypted data (Sánchez & Batet, 2017).

Secure Multi-Party Computation (MPC) is used in the context of cloud computing to support different cloud interactions in the cloud dynamic environments. It enables two or more cloud enterprises, each with private input data, and they wish to jointly evaluate a function on their inputs without revealing them to other parties (e.g., health applications). It was first introduced by Yao, in 1986, to enable two parties to perform some computation over their encrypted data. Then (General MPC, n.d.) generalized the ideas to support a different number of parties which requires many rounds among different parties to get the results. The main drawback is the difficulty in controlling the interaction within an arbitrary number of parties (Patel & Alabisi, 2019).

Access control is context aware specifically in federated and cross-federated clouds in which different administrative domains can communicate and dynamically access and provision resources during the application life cycle (Taherkordi et al., 2018).

6.2.9.1 AI-Based Security Protection in Cloud Computing

In comparison to the conventional systems that depend on predetermined rules, AI-driven systems possess the capability to acquire knowledge from data, hence enabling them to adjust and develop their abilities to identify emerging risks. Predictive analytics extends the capabilities of enterprises by enabling them to proactively anticipate and mitigate potential threats before they occur. Automation, which is another characteristic of AI, holds the potential to deliver improvements in efficiency. Automating regular danger responses enables businesses to allocate their human resources more strategically, thereby enhancing their efficiency and effectiveness. Lastly, the ability of AI to tailor security solutions based on user behavior offers an opportunity to create user-centric solutions, enhancing both security and user experience (Mallikarjunaradhya et al., 2023).

AI-driven strategies leverage machine-gaining knowledge of algorithms, anomaly detection, and predictive analytics to identify patterns, come across anomalies, and automate reaction mechanisms in real time. These strategies can enhance the visibility and situational attention of security operations, enabling proactive threat detection, incident response, and vulnerability management. Furthermore, AI can facilitate the automation of routine security responsibilities, releasing up security resources to focus on strategic security tasks and reaction to complicated security incidents. AI-driven techniques also play a vital role in enhancing the resilience and scalability of security features in the cloud security framework. Through leveraging AI for dynamic access controls, context-based anomaly detection, and dynamic risk modeling, companies can enhance their cloud security posture and mitigate the effect of increasing threats. Moreover, AI-powered security solutions can continuously analyze security activities and adapt their defenses, thereby evolving along the dynamic nature of cloud-native environments (Rangaraju et al., 2023).

As shown in Fig. 6.2, AI-driven techniques in cloud security can be classified into the following categories.

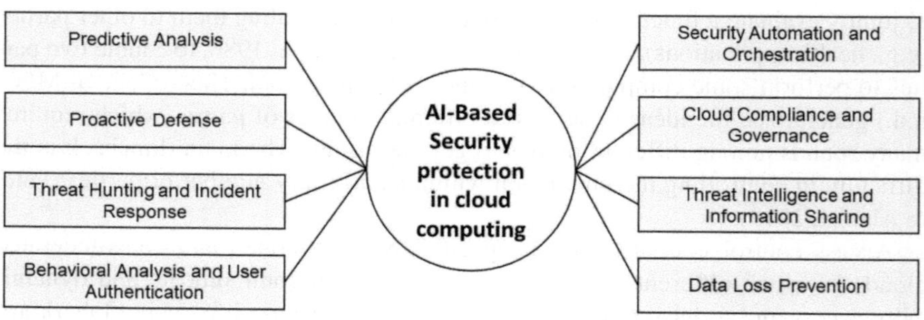

Fig. 6.2 AI-Based security protections in cloud computing

6.2.9.2 Predictive Analysis

Capability to predict potential threats in cloud environments is one of the main features of AI. AI-based predictive analysis in cloud computing leverages ML and advanced analytics to forecast future events, trends, and behaviors based on historical and real-time data. Analyzing historical attack data and classifying their patterns enhances decision-making, resource optimization, and security by providing insights that allow security engineers to predict emerging threats and vulnerabilities and anticipate/mitigate potential issues before they arise. This capability allows cloud service providers to take preventive measures, such as patching vulnerabilities or adjusting security policies, before an attack occurs (Tahir & Lulwani, 2023).

6.2.9.3 Proactive Defense

AI-based proactive defense in cloud computing refers to the use of AI-powered techniques to anticipate, identify, and mitigate security threats before they can cause significant harm. These approaches leverage AI's capabilities to analyze large volumes of data, detect anomalies, and automate responses, enhancing the overall security posture of cloud environments. Based on AI's automated incident response capability, AI-driven systems can initiate predefined actions to contain or mitigate the threat. When a potential threat is detected, they isolate compromised systems, block malicious IP addresses, or adjust access controls in real-time. This automation accelerates the incident response process, reducing the time and resources required to mitigate security breaches (Pothukuchi et al., 2023). For instance, AI-based security information and event management (SIEM) (e.g., IBM Security QRadar SIEM (IBM, n.d.)) technology not only automates the complex processes of data aggregation and normalization but also enables proactive threat detection and response through machine learning and predictive analytics.

6.2.9.4 Behavioral Analysis and User Authentication

By analyzing users' behavior and biometric information, AI introduces advanced authentication mechanisms. Behavioral analysis involves monitoring the way users interact with cloud systems. AI algorithms build profiles of typical user behavior, considering factors such as login times, locations, devices, and usage patterns. If a user's behavior deviates significantly from their established profile, the AI system may request additional authentication steps, such as multi-factor authentication (MFA) or revalidation (Singh, 2012). Additionally, AI can incorporate biometric authentication, such as fingerprint recognition or facial recognition, for secure access to cloud resources. These methods provide a higher level of security, as they are difficult to forge or replicate (Tahir & Lulwani, 2023).

6.2.9.5 Threat Hunting and Incident Response

Threat hunting involves proactively searching for signs of compromise within a cloud environment, even before automated security systems raise alarms. AI-driven threat hunting platforms use advanced analytics to identify subtle indicators of compromise, helping security teams uncover hidden threats. Once a security incident is confirmed, AI aids in incident response. It can quickly assess the scope of the breach, determine affected systems, and classify the severity of the incident. This information enables security teams to prioritize their response efforts and allocate resources efficiently. In digital forensics applications, AI can assist by collecting and analyzing evidence related to the incident. It can identify the attack vector, the techniques used by the threat actor, and potential data exfiltration. This information is invaluable for post-incident analysis and can inform future security enhancements (Dittakavi, 2023).

6.2.9.6 Data Loss Prevention

AI-driven data loss prevention (DLP) systems monitor and control data movement within cloud environments. These systems can classify data based on its sensitivity and apply policies to prevent unauthorized access or sharing. For instance, AI can detect when a user attempts to upload sensitive financial data to a public cloud storage service and trigger alerts or block the action if it violates organizational policies. Similarly, AI can recognize patterns indicative of data exfiltration attempts and take preventive actions in real-time. AI also assists in encryption key management, ensuring that data remains encrypted at rest and in transit. It can automatically generate, rotate, and protect encryption keys, reducing the risk of data exposure due to compromised keys (Tahir & Lulwani, 2023).

6.2.9.7 Security Automation and Orchestration

Without human intervention, AI can automate routine security operations, e.g., system patching, vulnerability scanning, and access control management (Allakonda & Sagar, 2021). Orchestration, on the other hand, involves coordinating multiple security processes to respond to complex security incidents. AI-driven orchestration platforms can integrate various security tools and systems, allowing them to work together seamlessly during incident response. For example, when a security incident is detected, an orchestration platform can automatically isolate compromised systems, notify relevant teams, initiate forensic analysis, and update security policies. This automation and orchestration not only accelerate incident response but also reduce the risk of human errors, which can be costly in terms of both security and operational impact.

6.2.9.8 Cloud Compliance and Governance

Due to cloud's distributed nature, regulations and laws may differ and customers and cloud providers must find a way to balance increasing compliance pressures with cloud computing benefits. Cloud organizations and users need to cope with compliance aspects in their cloud-oriented environments, which can be rooted in internal and external regulations (Brandis et al., 2019). AI-based systems can assist cloud users/providers in achieving and maintaining compliance by continuously monitoring cloud environments and ensuring adherence to security and privacy standards. AI-driven compliance tools can automatically scan cloud configurations to identify non-compliance issues. For instance, they can detect misconfigured access controls, insecure storage settings, or improper encryption settings. Upon detection, AI can generate compliance reports, suggest remediation steps, and, in some cases, automate the correction of non-compliant configurations (Mallikarjunaradhya et al., 2023).

6.2.9.9 Threat Intelligence and Information Sharing

Generally, the cloud providers provision the shared information in enormous server farms outside the faith space by information proprietors, which may activate the issue of information congeniality. It is needed to protect the communication measure and collective information from unapproved admission (Sharma et al., 2023). In this view, AI-enhanced cloud security benefits from global threat intelligence networks to collect and analyze data on emerging threats and vulnerabilities worldwide. AI algorithms can process this threat intelligence data and identify potential risks specific to an organization's cloud environment. AI facilitates information sharing and collaboration among organizations. When a new threat is detected by one organization, AI-driven systems can automatically share threat indicators, attack patterns, and mitigation strategies with other organizations in real-time. This collective defense approach helps organizations stay ahead of evolving threats and strengthens overall cloud security (Tahir & Lulwani, 2023).

6.3 Future of AI-Based Security Protection Solutions in Cloud Computing

The integration of AI with cloud security has introduced a novel range of prospects that may be leveraged from a business standpoint. The significance of AI in the proactive identification, mitigation, and prevention of cyber risks increases in importance as these threats get more complex (Mallikarjunaradhya et al., 2023).

6.4 Challenges and Issues

The advent of AI has transformed various sectors of the economy, including cloud computing. While AI's democratization has provided immense benefits, it still poses significant security challenges as it expands the threat landscape. More AI tools become available, more malicious purposes arise. This fact expands the possible attack vectors and security issues. However, one of the most alarming developments is adversaries using AI to identify cloud vulnerabilities and create malware. AI can automate and accelerate finding vulnerabilities, making it a potent tool for cyber criminals. They can use AI to analyze patterns, detect weaknesses and exploit them faster than security teams can respond. Additionally, AI can generate sophisticated malware that adapts and learns to evade detection, making it more difficult to combat (Sowinski, 2023).

Cybercriminals are progressively proficient in designing new devices that use AI to abuse vulnerabilities. This permits cybercriminals to hide their expectations when testing systems and sending malware (Butt et al., 2020). Highly targeted and evasive attacks in benign carrier applications, such as DeepLocker, have demonstrated the intentional use of AI for harmful purposes. Threat actors are constantly changing and improving their attack strategy with particular emphasis on the application of AI-driven techniques in the attack process, called AI-based cyberattack, which can be used in conjunction with conventional attack techniques to cause greater damage (Kaloudi & Li, 2020).

AI's lack of transparency complicates these security challenges. As AI systems, especially deep learning models, are complex to interpret, diagnosing and rectifying security incidents become arduous tasks. With AI now in the hands of a broader user base, the likelihood of such incidents increases. The automation advantage of AI also engenders a significant security risk: dependency. As more services become reliant on AI, the impact of an AI system failure or security breach grows. In the distributed environment of the cloud, this issue becomes harder to isolate and address without causing service disruption. AI's broader reach also adds complexity to regulatory compliance. As AI systems process vast amounts of data, including sensitive and personally identifiable information, adhering to regulations like the General Data Protection Regulation (GDPR) or the California Consumer Privacy Act (CCPA) becomes trickier. The wider range of AI users amplifies non-compliance risk, potentially resulting in substantial penalties and reputational damage (Sowinski, 2023).

6.5 Summary

In this chapter, we discussed AI-based security solutions used to address security issues with cloud computing. We reviewed general security issues with cloud computing and traditional security protections. Potential and practical features of

AI-driven solutions which are used in cloud computing were discussed. AI-driven solutions in cloud computing offer a wide range of potential and practical features that enhance efficiency, security, cost-effectiveness, and overall user experience. Generally, the security features can be categorized into threat detection, response, prevention, compliance, and operational efficiency. AI-driven security solutions in cloud computing offer significant advantages in terms of enhanced threat detection, improved efficiency, cost savings, and advanced data protection. However, they also present challenges related to complexity, costs, ethical concerns, and the inherent security risks of the AI systems themselves. Balancing these pros and cons requires careful planning, skilled personnel, and ongoing management to ensure that the benefits outweigh the potential drawbacks.

References

Ahmad, D., & Arce, I. (2008). The confused deputy and the domain hijacker. *IEEE Security & Privacy, 6*(1), 74–77. https://doi.org/10.1109/MSP.2008.25

Ahmad, I., & Bakht, H. (2019). Security challenges from abuse of cloud service threat. *International Journal of Computing and Digital Systems, 8*(01), 19–31.

Ahmed, I. (2019). A brief review: Security issues in cloud computing and their solutions. *Telkomnika (Telecommunication Computing Electronics and Control), 17*(6), 2812–2817.

Aljumah, A., & Ahanger, T. A. (2020). Cyber security threats, challenges and defence mechanisms in cloud computing. *IET Communications, 14*(7), 1185–1191.

Allakonda, M., & Sagar, K. (2021). A survey on data security challenges in multi cloud environment. In *2021 IEEE international conference on electronics, computing and communication technologies (CONECCT), Bangalore, India* (pp. 1–5). https://doi.org/10.1109/CONECCT52877.2021.9622722

AlZain, M. A., Soh, B., & Pardede, E. (2012). A new model to ensure security in cloud computing services. *Journal of Service Science Research, 4*, 49–70.

Ardagna, C. A., Asal, R., Damiani, E., & Vu, Q. H. (2015). From security to assurance in the cloud: A survey. *ACM Computing Surveys (CSUR), 48*(1), 1–50.

Bhardwaj, A., & Rama Krishna, C. (2021). Virtualization in cloud computing: Moving from hypervisor to containerization—A survey. *Arabian Journal for Science and Engineering, 46*(9), 8585–8601.

Bhonde, A., & Devane, S. (2021). Impact of cloud attacks on service level agreement. In *2021 International conference on communication information and computing technology (ICCICT), Mumbai, India* (pp. 1–6). https://doi.org/10.1109/ICCICT50803.2021.9510130

Brandis, K., Dzombeta, S., Colomo-Palacios, R., & Stantchev, V. (2019). Governance, risk, and compliance in cloud scenarios. *Applied Sciences, 9*(2), 320.

Butt, U. A., Mehmood, M., Shah, S. B., Amin, R., Shaukat, M. W., Raza, S. M., Suh, D. Y., & Piran, M. J. (2020). A review of machine learning algorithms for cloud computing security. *Electronics, 9*(9), 1379.

Chinnasamy, P., & Deepalakshmi, P. (2021). HCAC-EHR: Hybrid cryptographic access control for secure EHR retrieval in healthcare cloud. *Journal of Ambient Intelligence and Humanized Computing*, 1–19. https://doi.org/10.1007/s12652-021-02942-2

Cloud Security. (n.d.). *Insecure interfaces and APIs*. www.cloud-security.us

Coppolino, L., D'Antonio, S., Mazzeo, G., & Romano, L. (2017). Cloud security: Emerging threats and current solutions. *Computers & Electrical Engineering, 59*, 126–140.

Deep, G., Sidhu, J., & Mohana, R. (2022). Insider threat prevention in distributed database as a service cloud environment. *Computers & Industrial Engineering, 169*, 108278.

Dewangan, B. K., Agarwal, A., Venkatadri, & Pasricha, A. (2016). Credential and security issues of cloud service models. In *2016 2nd international conference on next generation computing technologies (NGCT), Dehradun, India* (pp. 888–892). https://doi.org/10.1109/NGCT.2016.7877536

Dittakavi, R. S. S. K. (2023). AI-optimized cost-aware design strategies for resource-efficient applications. *Journal of Science & Technology, 4*(1), 1–10.

IBM. (n.d.). IBM security QRadar SIEM, https://www.ibm.com/products/qradar-siem#experience

Imran, H. A., et al. (2020). Multi-Cloud: A comprehensive review. In *2020 IEEE 23rd international multitopic conference (INMIC), Bahawalpur, Pakistan* (pp. 1–5). https://doi.org/10.1109/INMIC50486.2020.9318176

Kaaniche, N., & Laurent, M. (2017). Data security and privacy preservation in cloud storage environments based on cryptographic mechanisms. *Computer Communications, 111*, 120–141.

Kaloudi, N., & Li, J. (2020). The ai-based cyber threat landscape: A survey. *ACM Computing Surveys (CSUR), 53*(1), 1–34.

Kumar, M., Kishor, A., Abawajy, J., Agarwal, P., Singh, A., & Zomaya, A. Y. (2021). ARPS: An autonomic resource provisioning and scheduling framework for cloud platforms. *IEEE Transactions on Sustainable Computing, 7*(2), 386–399.

Macy, J. (2018). API security: Whose job is it anyway? *Network Security, 2018*(9), 6–9.

Mallikarjunaradhya, V., Pothukuchi, A. S., & Kota, L. V. (2023). An overview of the strategic advantages of AI-powered threat intelligence in the cloud. *Journal of Science & Technology, 4*(4), 1–12.

Masud, M., Gaba, G. S., Choudhary, K., Alroobaea, R., & Hossain, M. S. (2021). A robust and lightweight secure access scheme for cloud based E-healthcare services. *Peer-to-Peer Networking and Applications, 14*, 3043–3057.

Opara-Martins, J., Sahandi, R., & Tian, F. (2016). Critical analysis of vendor lock-in and its impact on cloud computing migration: A business perspective. *Journal of Cloud Computing, 5*, 4. https://doi.org/10.1186/s13677-016-0054-z

Pachala, S., Rupa, C., & Sumalatha, L. (2021). An improved security and privacy management system for data in multi-cloud environments using a hybrid approach. *Evolutionary Intelligence, 14*, 1117–1133. https://doi.org/10.1007/s12065-020-00555-w

Patel, K., & Alabisi, A. (2019). Cloud computing security risks: Identification and assessment. *The Journal of New Business Ideas & Trends, 17*(2), 11–19.

Pothukuchi, A. S., Kota, L. V., & Mallikarjunaradhya, V. (2023). Impact of generative AI on the software development lifecycle (SDLC). *International Journal of Creative Research Thoughts, 11*(8).

Purohit, B., & Singh, P. P. (2013). Data leakage analysis on cloud computing. *International Journal of Engineering Research and Applications, 3*(3), 1311–1316.

Rangaraju, S., Ness, S., & Dharmalingam, R. (2023). Incorporating AI-driven strategies in DevSecOps for robust cloud security. *International Journal of Innovative Science and Research Technology, 8*(23592365), 10–5281.

Sabireen, H., & Neelanarayanan, V. J. I. E. (2021). A review on fog computing: Architecture, fog with IoT, algorithms and research challenges. *ICT Express, 7*(2), 162–176.

Sánchez, D., & Batet, M. (2017). Privacy-preserving data outsourcing in the cloud via semantic data splitting. *Computer Communications, 110*(2017), 187–201.

Sharma, V. P., Patil, K. S., Pavithra, G., Krishnan, S., & Asokan, A. (2023). A secured data sharing protocol for minimisation of risk in cloud computing and big data in AI application. In *Artificial intelligence for smart healthcare* (pp. 3–16). Springer.

Singh, G. (2012). *Analysis of shoe-floor slipperiness through computational modeling and measurements of hydrodynamic pressures with robotic slip simulator*. PhD diss., University of Wisconsin--Milwaukee.

Sowinski, D. (2023). Cloud security in the era of artificial intelligence, *SecurityIntelligence*. https://securityintelligence.com/posts/cloud-security-in-the-era-of-artificial-intelligence/

Subashini, S., & Kavitha, V. (2011). A survey on security issues in service delivery models of cloud computing. *Journal of Network and Computer Applications, 34*(1), 1–11.

Sujatha, P., & Balachandran, M. J. (2016). A survey on insecure API challenges and resolution mechanisms on cloud computing. *International Journal of Web Technology, 05*(01), 17–21.

Taherkordi, A., Zahid, F., Verginadis, Y., & Horn, G. (2018). Future cloud systems design: Challenges and research directions. *IEEE Access, 6*(2018), 74120–74150.

Tahir, F., & Lulwani, M.. (2023). *A narrative overview of latest trends of artificial intelligence in cloud computing security*.

Thillaiarasu, N., & ChenthurPandian, S. (2016). Enforcing security and privacy over multi-cloud framework using assessment techniques. In *2016 10th international conference on intelligent systems and control (ISCO), Coimbatore, India* (pp. 1–5). https://doi.org/10.1109/ISCO.2016.7727001

Tirumala, S. S., Sathu, H., & Naidu, V. (2015). Analysis and prevention of account hijacking based INCIDENTS in cloud environment. In *2015 International conference on information technology (ICIT), Bhubaneswar, India* (pp. 124–129). https://doi.org/10.1109/ICIT.2015.29

Tomarchio, O., Calcaterra, D., & Modica, G. D. (2020). Cloud resource orchestration in the multi-cloud landscape: A systematic review of existing frameworks. *Journal of Cloud Computing, 9*, 49. https://doi.org/10.1186/s13677-020-00194-7

Torkura, K. A., Sukmana, M. I. H., Cheng, F., & Meinel, C. (2020). CloudStrike: Chaos engineering for security and resiliency in cloud infrastructure. *IEEE Access, 8*, 123044–123060. https://doi.org/10.1109/ACCESS.2020.3007338

Viswanath, G., & Krishna, P. V. (2021). Hybrid encryption framework for securing big data storage in multi-cloud environment. *Evolutionary Intelligence, 14*, 691–698. https://doi.org/10.1007/s12065-020-00404-w

Wueest, C., Barcena, M. B., & O'Brien, L. (2015). Mistakes in the IaaS cloud could put your data at risk. *Symantec*.

Chapter 7
AI for IoT and OT Security

7.1 Introduction

Basically, Internet of Things (IoT) environments comprise many intelligent devices, like sensors, network communicating devices, cloud storage, and data processing, that can collect, process, transmitting, and receiving data from each other. Real-time data generated or collected by billions of connected devices, sensors, and other things leads to big data analysis. This ubiquitous level of connectivity, powered in different technologies, e.g., Cloud computing, results in enormous data sets. IoT big data processing comprises different steps, including data collecting, data storage, and data analysis through untrusted network players. Figure 7.1 shows a four-layer high-level architecture for IoT (Raj et al., 2022).

- **IoT device layer:** In this layer, there are IoT devices and sensors in plenty for collecting environmental and device data. Due to the unprecedented adoption of miniaturization technologies, Miniscule, disappearing yet indispensable IoT elements are getting produced and deployed across. Sensors have the inherent capability to form ad hoc networks dynamically to share their distinct capabilities and data. The prime idea behind the grand success of the IoT paradigm is that the IoT phenomenon could convert commonly found and cheap articles in our daily locations into digitized artifacts systematically. That is, all kinds of electrical, mechanical and physical systems in our hotels, homes, hospitals, etc., are digitized through the smart application of digitization and edge technologies. In short, the IoT paradigm represents scores of pioneering and path breaking technologies and tools to transition ordinary things into digital objects, which generate a lot of digital data. Now, with the faster stability of data transmission protocols, IoT sensor and device data gets transmitted to nearby IoT gateways/buses/brokers and any other middleware.
- **Network layer:** The bridge between IoT device layer and the cloud layer is this network or gateway layer. This layer acts as the middleware and performs

D. P. Sharma et al., *Understanding AI in Cybersecurity and Secure AI*, Progress in IS, https://doi.org/10.1007/978-3-031-91524-6_7

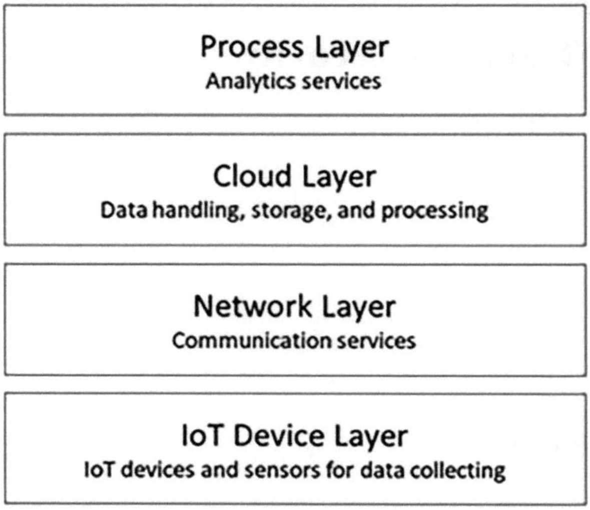

Fig. 7.1 IoT four-layer architecture

different communication services, namely data aggregation, intermediation, enrichment, and transformation. There are networking facilities such as LAN, WAN, and the Internet to take IoT data from the IoT gateway to cloud-based data analytics platforms. Further on, there are lightweight protocols (MQTT, AMQP, COAP, and HTTP) to establish the much-needed communication between IoT gateway and cloud-based servers.

- **Cloud layer:** This represents software-defined cloud environments. There are integrated analytics platforms (big, fast, and streaming data) and AI libraries for knowledge discovery in time. Further on, there are data lakes, and other data stores (SQL, NoSQL, and distributed SQL). Data handling, storage, processing, and analytics are fully accomplished in this layer.
- **Process layer:** The final layer of the IoT analytics architecture is the process layer. This layer is for hosting of different processes, which use the knowledge discovered in the previous layer.

AI-based algorithms have the potential of maximizing the benefits from deploying IoT systems, including Industrial IoT (IIoT), to improve their flexibility, productivity, and performance. Since IoT systems consist of a wide range of physical and communication devices and services involving electronics, sensors, actuators and software, they are remotely controlled and managed via connection to the Internet (Alcácer & Cruz-Machado, 2019). The significance of IoT is the use of heterogeneous sensors and actuators, computing appliances, network elements and internet connectivity and their smart machines, to offer increased manufacturing speed, faster recalibration and greater configuration. This, in turn, enables the flexible designs of new business models that meet user requirements (Moustafa, 2021a).

This chapter will explore critical security challenges in IoT systems, emphasizing the risks posed by interconnected devices and their vulnerabilities across different IoT layers. It will highlight how poorly secured devices can compromise the resilience and security of entire networks, creating a global cybersecurity risk. The discussion will categorize IoT security threats into hardware, network, and software-based attacks, providing insights into threats such as Denial of Service (DoS), Man-in-the-Middle (MITM), malware infections, backdoor exploits, and advanced microarchitectural attacks like Rowhammer, Spectre, and Meltdown. Additionally, the chapter will analyze specific security issues at different IoT layers, including the process, cloud, and network layers, illustrating how cybercriminals can exploit authentication weaknesses, manipulate smart meters, conduct SQL injections, and launch large-scale Distributed Denial of Service (DDoS) attacks.

Furthermore, the chapter will cover IIoT and Operational Technology (OT) security, where AI plays a dual role in both enhancing security and introducing new risks. AI-driven anomaly detection, predictive maintenance, and behavioral analysis will be examined as key strategies to mitigate cyber threats. However, the chapter will also address how adversaries are using AI-enhanced cyberattacks, such as AI-powered malware, automated reconnaissance, data manipulation, and AI-driven botnets, to compromise IoT ecosystems. The future of AI-based IoT security will be discussed, focusing on emerging trends like Edge AI, security automation, and compliance challenges. Through these discussions, this chapter aims to provide a comprehensive understanding of AI's role in securing IoT systems while addressing the challenges and threats that come with its integration.

7.2 IoT Security Issues

The interconnection nature of the IoT devices means if a device is poorly secured and connected it has the potential of affecting the security and the resilience on the Internet internationally. This behavior is simply brought about by the challenge of the vast employment of homogenous devices of IoT. When it comes to authentication, for instance, IoT faces various vulnerabilities, which remain one of the most significant issues in the provision of security in many applications. The authentication used is limited in how it protects only one threat, such as DoS or replay attacks (Tawalbeh et al., 2020).

IoT nodes at the user end are more vulnerable to attack by intruders. These attacks are classified as hardware attacks, network attacks, and software attacks. Among this replay, MITM, and DoS attacks are examples of network attacks. A DoS attack increases the amount of traffic on a network or device. The MITM attack operates by intercepting and altering the communication between two parties, jeopardizing the confidentiality of the transmitted data. Worm and backdoor attacks are an example of software attacks. The worm is a self-cloning program that intrudes through security holes in networking software and hardware. A backdoor is an attack where hackers install malware that can bypass a network's standard security and authentication procedures. On the other hand, hardware attacks are possible in two ways; one using software hardware vulnerabilities that can be explored without physical access to the device, another type is physical hardware attacks. Examples of software-based hardware attacks are Rowhammer, Spectre, and Meltdown. Rowhammer is an attack that takes advantage of bit flipping in DRAM caused by continuous access, bypassing memory isolation, and breaching security barriers. Spectre and Meltdown are microarchitectural attacks that take advantage of processor out-of-order execution capabilities to access memory beyond allowed limits. Generally, hardware attacks try to obtain, modify, terminate, remove, embed, or expose information from the device through remote access or direct physical access without strong authorization. There are three types of hardware attacks on IoT devices at the edge: invasive, semi-invasive, and non-invasive (Roy et al., 2023).

Depending on the IoT layers, different security issues are possible.

7.2.1 Security Issues in the Process Layer

- **Malicious code attacks**: An example of these attacks is a malicious virus that spreads in specific operating systems like Linux. The virus could have the potential to target several small, Internet-connected devices that are active, including security cameras, car's Wi-Fi, and home routers (Zanjani et al., 2023). The virus utilizes software vulnerabilities to spread (Shouran et al., 2019).
- **Node-based application manipulation:** Cyber attackers take advantage of program vulnerabilities found in device nodes and use them to install harmful rootkits. Device security design must be resistant to any interference and manipulation, or at least, the manipulation must be detectable. Merely safeguarding elements of a device may not provide enough protection. Certain risks can manipulate the local environment, causing the device to malfunction, which can result in the environment being either overheated or overcooled (Hashemi & Zarei, 2021).
- **Inability to receive security alerts:** In certain domains, like nuclear reactors, failing to update software alerts for a constantly moving node that contains a software glitch could have disastrous outcomes (Karthikeyan & Balamurugan, 2021).
- **Hacking smart meter/networks:** In addition to manipulating bills and detecting when a house is empty, attackers who gain access to smart meter data can also use it to identify patterns of behavior and even determine when a homeowner is on vacation. This information can be sold on the black market or used for more targeted criminal activities, such as burglary or identity theft. Attacking smart networks, which can include multiple smart devices and systems, can have even more severe consequences (Zanjani et al., 2023). For example, a successful attack on a smart grid, which is a network of interconnected power generation, transmission, and distribution systems, could result in widespread power outages, disrupted communications, and even physical damage to critical infrastructure (Shahinzadeh et al., 2022a). The potential economic impact of such an attack

is significant, with estimates suggesting that a large-scale cyber-attack on a smart grid could cost billions of dollars in damages and lost productivity. As smart meter and network technology continues to advance, it is essential for utility companies and other organizations to prioritize cybersecurity and implement robust security measures to protect against these and other threats. This includes regular vulnerability assessments, network segmentation, and employee training to promote best security practices (Goudarzi et al., 2022; Shahinzadeh et al., 2022b).

- **Cross-site scripting (XSS):** When malicious code is added to a website by an attacker, it can trigger an XSS attack, allowing the code to run on the victim's browser and possibly result in the theft of sensitive data such as login credentials and credit card information. Such attacks can be carried out through vulnerabilities in web applications, such as input validation and output encoding (Chaudhary et al., 2022).
- **SQL injection attacks:** Web applications that depend on databases are vulnerable to SQL injection attacks, where attackers can input harmful code into data fields, enabling them to gain unauthorized access to or modify sensitive information stored in the database. This type of attack can cause significant damage, including data loss or theft, website defacement, and even complete system compromise (Rajendran et al., 2019).
- **Distributed Denial of Service (DDoS) attacks:** When multiple sources flood a network or website with traffic, it can result in a DDoS attack, causing the system to become inaccessible to genuine users. Attackers can use botnets, a network of infected devices under their control, to launch DDoS attacks, causing significant disruption to critical services and systems (Mubarakali et al., 2020).

7.2.2 Security Issues in the Cloud Layer

In the Cloud layer, the majority of dangers arise from external sources, primarily as a result of sensors and other data-gathering equipment. Some of the typical threats in this layer include (Zanjani et al., 2023):

- **Eavesdropping:** As these devices communicate wirelessly and over the internet, they are susceptible to eavesdropping assaults. During this attack, sensors located in vulnerable smart homes can transmit alerts to users and obtain sensitive information from them (Kwon et al., 2021).
- **Sniffing attacks (eavesdropping on exchanged information in the network):** Hackers can place sensors or destructive devices near the internet of things (IoT) sensors and gain access to device information. The proliferation of IoT devices in a smart ecosystem implies that users or IoT devices can be identified and tracked to a considerable degree through physical environments without their consent, and they can be profiled (Firoozjaei et al., 2020). As the interactions between humans, and between humans and devices, grow in shared physical

networks, shared services, and social settings, the physical impact of these connections will diminish, and it will become increasingly possible to achieve greater sensitivity and accuracy (Duangphasuk et al., 2020).

- **Spoofing attacks:** A spoofing attack happens when a hacker pretends to be a genuine sensor or device to obtain confidential information or manipulate the network. This can be particularly problematic in environments where multiple devices are communicating with one another, as a single compromised device could potentially compromise the entire network (Sinha & Dhanalakshmi, 2022).
- **Replay attacks:** by eavesdropping on the communication between IoT devices and their network infrastructure, an attacker can capture the data packets transmitted over the network. The attacker retransmits them to the target device or server and deceives the recipient to accept them as legitimate. Replay attacks can have various detrimental effects depending on the context. For example, in a smart home environment, an attacker could replay commands to unlock doors or turn off security systems. In industrial IoT settings, replay attacks could manipulate sensor readings or control critical machinery, leading to safety hazards or financial losses (Chen et al., 2023).
- **Malware attacks:** Malware can infect IoT devices through various means, such as exploiting unpatched vulnerabilities, leveraging default credentials, or tricking users into downloading malicious software. Once compromised, these devices can serve as entry points for attacking the cloud infrastructure they connect to. Malware on IoT devices may intercept sensitive data transmitted to and from the cloud, leading to data breaches (Alyas, 2018). This data can include personal information, credentials, or proprietary business data, posing privacy and security risks for both individuals and organizations. Malware-infected IoT devices can be recruited into botnets, large networks of compromised devices controlled by attackers. These botnets can launch DDoS attacks against cloud services, disrupting their availability and causing financial losses for service providers and users.

7.2.3 Security Issues in the Network Layer

- **DoS attack:** During a DoS attack, devices or servers are bombarded in such a manner that they become unable to cater to users' requirements. These attacks cause an interruption in the exchange of data between the IoT devices and their source. The device receives a substantial amount of information, leading to the cessation of its operations. This can pose a threat, especially for healthcare information systems and services that operate within IoT networks that have limited bandwidth (Ali et al., 2022).
- **Gateway attacks:** These attacks cause disturbances in the communication between sensors and internet infrastructure. Gateway attacks, namely DoS or routing attacks, executed at the gateway, can lead to the improper transfer or non-transfer of information from the internet to sensors, nodes, or actuators, thereby

putting the subdomains' functionality, such as transportation networks or smart cities, at risk (Nguyen et al., 2022).

- **Unauthorized access:** The absence of security in devices is due to the owners' assumption that they will always have physical possession of them. Hidden small and large devices may need to remain unprotected in relatively inaccessible environments for long periods of time, such as pacemakers placed in the human body and remote sensors placed in non-residential physical environments. These unprotected devices used for control (such as pacemakers) require a constant time setting to provide control signals at specified times (Sardar & Anees, 2021). Given that these devices are created to exchange data with other devices and facilitate data transmission and reception, certain malicious nodes may try to pose as authenticated nodes and obtain access to these devices without authorization.
- **Storage attacks:** Huge volumes of data that contain critical user information need to be stored in storage devices or cloud storage, both of which are susceptible to attacks, thereby putting the data at risk or leading to incorrect alterations in the particulars (Khraisat & Alazab, 2021).
- **Provision of false information:** Attackers can enter false information and cause an inappropriate or dangerous system response. In doing so, they create the groundwork for a physical attack (Rejeb et al., 2019).
- **Botnet attacks:** Botnet attacks are executed by utilizing a group of compromised devices, referred to as bots, to launch coordinated attacks on a designated target. These attacks can be particularly challenging to detect and prevent, as the bots may be spread out across multiple networks and devices. Botnet attacks can be used for a variety of purposes, including DDoS attacks, spamming, and data theft (Pour et al., 2020). Mirai Botnet (Antonakakis et al., 2017) is a good example of IoT botnet attack, which was composed of embedded and IoT devices, took the Internet by storm in late 2016 when it overwhelmed several high-profile targets with massive DDoS attacks. The botnet infected nearly 65,000 IoT devices in its first 20 h before reaching a steady state population of 200,000 to 300,000 infections (Antonakakis et al., 2017).
- **DNS spoofing:** DNS spoofing is the process of manipulating the Domain Name System (DNS) used to convert domain names into IP addresses, redirecting users to a counterfeit website or server (Mann et al., 2020). This vulnerability can enable hackers to conduct malicious activities or acquire confidential information. DNS spoofing can be particularly problematic in environments where multiple devices are communicating with one another, as a single compromised device could potentially compromise the entire network.
- **Protocol attacks:** Protocol attacks involve exploiting vulnerabilities in the communication protocols used by devices and networks to carry out attacks. This can involve techniques such as buffer overflow attacks, which exploit weaknesses in the way devices handle data, or packet injection attacks, which involve injecting malicious packets into the network to disrupt communication or steal data (Siddiqui et al., 2020).

- **Man-in-the-middle (MITM) attacks:** MITM attacks can occur in the network layer when attackers intercept communication between devices and manipulate the information being transmitted. This can allow attackers to eavesdrop on sensitive information, modify data, or even inject malicious code into the network. MITM attacks can be particularly problematic in environments where multiple devices are communicating with one another, as a single compromised device could potentially compromise the entire network (Thaker et al., 2022).
- **Network scanning and reconnaissance:** Attackers can use network scanning and reconnaissance techniques to identify vulnerabilities in the network and gain unauthorized access to devices or data (Wang & Meng, 2022). This can involve techniques such as port scanning, which involves probing a network to identify open ports and potential vulnerabilities, or packet sniffing, which involves intercepting and analyzing network traffic to identify sensitive data or potential attack vectors. With the continuous evolution and increased complexity of the network layer, it is vital to establish strong security measures to safeguard against these and other potential risks. This may involve implementing measures such as network segmentation, access controls, intrusion detection and prevention systems, and regular vulnerability assessments. Furthermore, it is essential for organizations to remain informed about the latest security trends and best practices and prioritize security considerations during the design and development of new network technology. By taking proactive steps to address security concerns in the network layer organizations can help ensure the safety and security of their systems and data (Zanjani et al., 2023).

7.3 Industrial Internet of Things- IIoT

Industrial Internet of Things (IIoT) systems are networks of interconnected devices, machines, and sensors embedded within industrial infrastructure, designed to collect, exchange, and analyze data to optimize processes and improve efficiency. These systems leverage IoT technologies in industrial settings, such as manufacturing plants, power generation facilities, oil and gas refineries, and transportation networks. Based on the technologies used and the applications, an IIoT is defined by H. Boyes et al. (2018) as a system comprising networked smart objects, cyber-physical assets, associated generic information technologies and optional cloud or edge computing platforms, which enable real-time, intelligent, and autonomous access, collection, analysis, communications, and exchange of process, product and/or service information, within the industrial environment, so as to optimize overall production value. This value may include improving product or service delivery, boosting productivity, reducing labor costs, reducing energy consumption, and reducing the build-to-order cycle.

Basically, key components of IIoT systems include:

- **Sensors and Actuators**: These are the physical devices that collect data from the environment or control machinery. They can measure parameters such as temperature, pressure, humidity, vibration, and flow rates, and they can also act on the environment by controlling valves, motors, or other equipment.
- **Connectivity:** IIoT systems rely on various communication technologies to transmit data between devices and back-end systems. This includes wired connections like Ethernet and industrial protocols such as Modbus, as well as wireless technologies like Wi-Fi, Bluetooth, Zigbee, and cellular networks.
- **Edge Computing:** IIoT systems often incorporate edge computing capabilities, where data processing and analysis are performed closer to the data source, at the "edge" of the network. This reduces latency, conserves bandwidth, and allows for real-time decision-making.
- **Cloud Platforms:** Many IIoT deployments leverage cloud-based platforms for data storage, analytics, and visualization. Cloud services offer scalability, flexibility, and accessibility, enabling organizations to manage and analyze vast amounts of data generated by IIoT devices.
- **Security:** Applications for IIoT are a natural evolution of IoT. Hence, IIoT inherits some security challenges from IoT (Yu & Guo, 2019). Security is a critical concern in IIoT systems due to the potential impact of cyber-attacks on industrial processes and infrastructure. Security measures include encryption, authentication, access control, intrusion detection, and regular software updates to mitigate vulnerabilities.
- **Analytics and Machine Learning:** IIoT systems generate large volumes of data, and advanced analytics techniques, including machine learning and AI, are used to extract insights, predict failures, optimize performance, and enable predictive maintenance.
- **Integration with Existing Systems:** IIoT solutions need to integrate with legacy systems such as Supervisory Control and Data Acquisition (SCADA), Manufacturing Execution Systems (MES), Enterprise Resource Planning (ERP), and Product Lifecycle Management (PLM) systems to enable seamless data exchange and interoperability.

7.4 Operational Technology (OT) Network

Operational technology (OT) encompasses a broad range of programmable systems and devices that interact with the physical environment (or manage devices that interact with the physical environment). OT systems and devices detect or cause a direct change through the monitoring and/or control of devices, processes, and events. Examples include industrial control systems (ICSs), building automation systems, transportation systems, physical access control systems, physical environment monitoring systems, and physical environment measurement systems. OT systems consist of combinations of control components (e.g., electrical, mechanical, hydraulic, pneumatic) that act together to achieve an objective (e.g., manufacturing, transportation of matter or energy). The part of the system primarily concerned with producing an output is referred to as the process. The part of the system primarily concerned with maintaining conformance with specifications is referred to as the controller (or control) (Stouffer et al., 2022).

7.4.1 OT Security

Typically, IT systems primarily involve general-purpose computing devices/software and OT systems involve specialized hardware and software tailored for industrial processes. While both IT and OT systems require robust security measures, OT systems often have stricter security requirements due to the potential physical consequences of cyberattacks on industrial processes. With IT security being tasked with coordinating OT security, in most cases, OT is typically involved in the reviewing of the security processes and the controls to be deployed (Parekh et al., 2021).

In comparison to IT, OT has different performance and reliability requirements and uses OSs and applications that may be considered unconventional in a typical IT network environment. Security protections must be implemented in a way that maintains system integrity during normal operations as well as during cyber-attacks. Initially, OT systems had little resemblance to IT systems because they were isolated and ran proprietary control protocols using specialized hardware and software. OT are increasingly resembling IT systems as they adopt IT technologies to promote corporate connectivity and remote access capabilities (e.g., using industry standard computers, OSs, and network protocols). This integration supports new IT capabilities but provides significantly less isolation for OT from the outside world than predecessor systems, creating a greater need to secure them. While security solutions have been designed to deal with these issues in typical IT systems, special precautions must be taken when introducing these same solutions to OT environments. In some cases, new security solutions are needed that are tailored to the OT environment. Following solutions are suggested by NIST for OT security improvement (Stouffer et al., 2022):

- **Timeliness and performance requirements:** OT systems are generally time-critical, with the criterion for acceptable levels of delay and jitter dictated by the individual installation. The efficiency of OT plays a critical role in the overall efficiency of secure computation. It is so to the point that OT performance determines which is the most efficient approach (Kolesnikov & Kumaresan, 2013). Some OT systems require reliable, deterministic responses. High throughput is typically not essential to OT. In contrast, IT systems typically require high throughput and can withstand some level of delay and jitter. For some OT, automated response times or system responses to human interaction is critical. Many OT systems utilize real-time OSs (RTOS), where real-time refers to timeliness requirements. The units of real time are highly application-dependent and must be explicitly stated.

- **Availability requirements:** Many OT processes are continuous in nature. Unexpected outages of systems that control industrial processes are unacceptable. Outages must often be planned and scheduled days or weeks in advance. Exhaustive pre-deployment testing is essential to ensuring high availability (i.e., reliability) for the OT. OT systems often cannot be stopped and started without affecting production. In some cases, the products produced, or equipment being used are more important than the information being relayed. Therefore, typical IT strategies (e.g., rebooting a component) are usually not acceptable for OT due to adverse impacts on the requirements for high availability, reliability, and maintainability. Some OT employ redundant components—often running in parallel—to provide continuity when primary components are unavailable.
- **Risk management requirements:** In a typical IT system, primary concerns include data confidentiality and integrity. For OT, primary concerns include safety, fault tolerance to prevent the loss of life or endangerment of public health or confidence, regulatory compliance, loss of equipment, loss of intellectual property, or lost or damaged products. The personnel responsible for operating, securing, and maintaining OT must understand the important link between safety and security. Any security measure that impairs safety is unacceptable.
- **Physical effects:** Field devices (e.g., PLCs, operator stations, DCS controllers) are directly responsible for controlling physical processes. OT can have complex interactions with physical processes and consequences in the OT domain that can manifest in physical events. Understanding these potential physical effects often requires communication between experts in OT and experts in the physical domain.
- **System operation:** OT's OSs and control networks are often quite different from their IT counterparts and require different skill sets, experience, and levels of expertise. Control networks are typically managed by control engineers rather than IT personnel. Assuming that differences are insignificant can have disastrous consequences on system operations.
- **Resource constraints:** OT and their real-time operating systems (RTOSs) are often resource-constrained systems that do not include typical contemporary IT security capabilities. Legacy systems often lack resources that are common on modern IT systems. Many systems may also lack desired features, including encryption capabilities, error logging, and password protection. Indiscriminate use of IT security practices in OT may cause availability and timing disruptions. There may not be computing resources available on OT components to retrofit these systems with current security capabilities. Adding resources or features may not be possible.
- **Communications:** Communication protocols and media used by OT environments for field device control and intra-processor communication are typically different from IT environments and may be proprietary.
- **Change management:** Change management is paramount to maintaining the integrity of both IT and OT systems. Unpatched software represents one of the greatest vulnerabilities to a system. Software updates on IT systems, including security patches, are typically applied in a timely fashion based on appropriate

security policies and procedures. In addition, these procedures are often automated using server-based tools. Software updates on OT cannot always be implemented on a timely basis. These updates need to be thoroughly tested by both the vendor and the end user of the industrial control application before being implemented. Additionally, the OT owner must plan and schedule OT outages days or weeks in advance. The OT may also require revalidation as part of the update process. Another issue is that many OT utilize older versions of OSs that are no longer supported by the vendor through patches. Change management is also applicable to hardware and firmware. The change management process requires careful assessment by OT experts (e.g., control engineers) working in conjunction with security and IT personnel.
- **Managed support:** Typical IT systems allow for diversified support styles, perhaps supporting disparate but interconnected technology architectures. For OT, service support is sometimes only available from a single vendor. In some instances, third-party security solutions are not allowed due to OT vendor licensing and service agreements, and service support can be lost if third-party applications are installed without vendor acknowledgement or approval.
- **Component lifetime:** Typical IT components have a lifetime on the order of 3–5 years due to the quick evolution of technology. For OT, where technology has been developed in many cases for specific uses and implementations, the lifetime of the deployed technology is often in the order of 10–15 years and sometimes longer.
- **Component location:** Most IT components and some OT components are in business and commercial facilities that are physically accessible by local transportation. Remote locations may be utilized for backup facilities. Distributed OT components may be isolated, remote, and require extensive transportation effort to reach. The component location also needs to consider necessary physical and environmental security measures.

The frequency and sophistication of cyberattacks against OT systems (e.g., industrial control systems (ICSs) and critical infrastructure) are increasing. ICSs are prime targets for criminal sabotages or terrorist attacks due to their influences as they notably impact the nation's security, public safety, and morale (Firoozjaei et al., 2016; Zimba et al., 2019). To launch these sophisticated attacks, which are called advanced persistent threats (APTs), the attackers employ various tactics to find and avoid detection, discover the target, and operate covertly. To this end, advanced techniques, including configuration change, data obfuscation, access manipulation, or hijack legitimate codes, are used to maintain attackers' foothold and conceal their presence on the victim systems. APTs are low-frequency, high-impact (LFHI), and lurk for a long time until conditions are perfect (Firoozjaei et al., 2022).

7.4.2 AI-Based OT Security

AI-based security systems can be utilized to provide different services to secure OT systems. As shown in Fig. 7.2, it can be classified into AI-based security analysis and AI-based security control classes.

- **Anomaly detection:** AI algorithms can analyze vast amounts of data from OT systems to establish normal patterns of behavior. Any deviations from these patterns can indicate potential security threats. By continuously monitoring the behavior of industrial processes, AI can identify abnormal activities such as unauthorized access attempts, equipment malfunctions, or cyberattacks in real-time (Kant & Johannsen, 2022; Sarker, 2024).
- **Predictive maintenance:** AI-powered predictive maintenance systems can help prevent security vulnerabilities by identifying potential equipment failures or weaknesses before they occur. By analyzing data from sensors and machinery in OT environments, AI algorithms can predict when maintenance is needed, reducing the risk of unexpected failures that could compromise security (Sarker, 2024).
- **Threat detection and response:** AI can augment traditional security measures in OT systems by detecting and responding to cyber threats more effectively. Machine learning algorithms can analyze network traffic, system logs, and other data sources to identify known and unknown security threats, such as malware or intrusions, and take automated actions to mitigate them (Kant & Johannsen, 2022; Sarker, 2024).
- **Behavioral analysis:** AI-based behavioral analysis can detect unusual patterns of activity within OT systems that may indicate a security breach. By learning normal behaviors of users and devices within the OT environment, AI systems

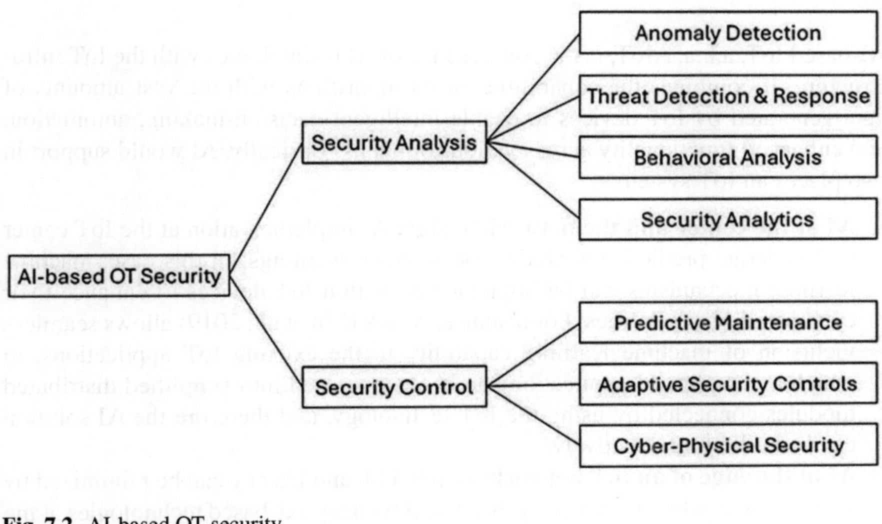

Fig. 7.2 AI-based OT security

can flag suspicious activities such as unauthorized access attempts, data exfiltration, or unusual command sequences (Sarker, 2024).

- **Security analytics:** AI can assist in analyzing large volumes of security data generated by OT systems to identify trends, vulnerabilities, and potential security risks. Machine learning algorithms can help security analysts prioritize and investigate security incidents more efficiently by providing insights into the root causes and potential impact of security events (Sarker, 2024).
- **Adaptive security controls:** AI can enable adaptive security controls that dynamically adjust security policies and configurations based on changing conditions and emerging threats in OT environments. By continuously learning from past security incidents and adapting to new threats, AI-driven security systems can enhance the resilience of OT systems against evolving cyber threats (Rahman & Hossain, 2022).
- **Cyber-physical security:** AI can integrate cyber and physical security measures in OT environments to provide holistic protection against both cyber and physical threats.By combining data from cybersecurity systems with physical sensors and actuators, AI can detect and respond to security incidents that involve both digital and physical components, such as sabotage or tampering with industrial equipment. Incorporating AI into OT systems security requires careful consideration of the unique characteristics and requirements of industrial environments, including real-time operation, safety concerns, and regulatory compliance. Additionally, proper implementation and integration of AI-driven security solutions are essential to ensure their effectiveness and minimize disruptions to critical operations (Rahman & Hossain, 2022).

7.5 AI-Based IoT (AIoT)

AI-based IoT, a.k.a. AIoT, is the convergence of AI technologies with the IoT infrastructure. It combines the capabilities of AI algorithms with the vast amounts of data generated by IoT devices to enable intelligent decision-making, automation, and enhanced functionality across various domains. Basically, AI would support in two places an IoT system:

- **AI at the center and the network's edge:** AI implementation at the IoT center will generate predictive analytical or anomaly warnings. In this case, machine learning mechanisms can be implemented within IoT devices to enhance their cybersecurity capabilities. For instance, AItalk (Lin et al., 2019) allows seamless inclusion of machine learning capability to the existing IoT applications, in which a complex AI application can be decomposed into simplified distributed modules connected by using the IoT technology, and therefore the AI solution can be built more effectively.
- **AI at the edge of an IoT network:** Bandwidth and latency can be minimized by system nodes while increasing privacy and security. AI-based technologies at the

edge of the IoT network permits smart services such as anomaly data detection and IoT data analysis. Employing AI at the IoT network edge can help to solve problems such as increased power consumption, latency, and security issues (Pooyandeh & Sohn, 2021).

7.5.1 AI-Based IoT Security

To enhance the security of IoT devices and networks, AI-based IoT security is a growing field that leverages AI techniques. In AI-based security, data is thriving for AI for understanding and automation with a variety of statistical and computer technology. Integrating IoT systems into AI technologies provides additional functionality, such as user experiences, service providers, and even other ecosystem devices. They can adjust better for new inputs or environmental changes and perform niche tasks with no manual intervention (Padmaja et al., 2022). As shown in Fig. 7.3, AI can be utilized in different ways to improve IoT security:

- **Anomaly detection:** AI algorithms can analyze vast amounts of data from IoT devices to detect unusual behavior or patterns that may indicate a security breach. By continuously learning from data, AI systems can adapt to new threats and detect previously unseen attacks (Lee & Park, 2019).
- **Predictive analysis:** AI can predict potential security threats by analyzing historical data and identifying patterns that precede security incidents. This proactive approach allows organizations to take preventive measures before an attack occurs (Lee & Park, 2019).
- **Behavioral analysis:** AI can analyze the behavior of IoT devices and users to identify suspicious activities. For example, AI algorithms can detect if a device is behaving unusually, such as sending an unusually high volume of data or accessing unauthorized resources (Guo et al., 2018).
- **Identity and access management (IAM):** AI can improve IAM systems by analyzing user behavior and access patterns to detect unauthorized access attempts.

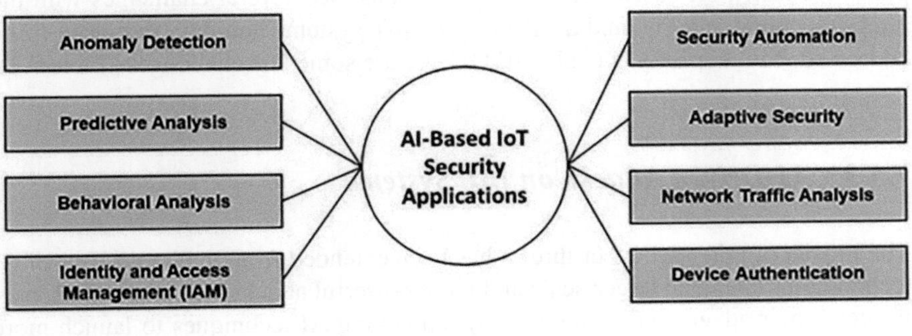

Fig. 7.3 AI-based IoT security applications

AI-powered IAM systems are perceived as a transformative approach in enhancing security protocols and streamlining access control processes can also dynamically adjust access privileges based on user behavior and context (Olabanji et al., 2024).
- **Security automation:** AI can automate many security tasks, such as patch management, threat response, and incident investigation. AI-based automation improves the speed and accuracy of threat detection, response and mitigation while also reducing the workload on security professionals (Hassan & Ibrahim, 2023; Bagaa et al., 2020).
- **Adaptive security:** AI can continuously adapt security measures based on changing threat landscapes and network conditions. By dynamically adjusting security configurations, AI systems can better defend against evolving threats by focusing on real-time threat detection, proactive defense, and continuous learning (Babu, 2024).
- **Network traffic analysis:** AI algorithms can analyze network traffic from IoT devices to detect and prevent malicious activities, such as DDoS attacks or data exfiltration.
- **Device authentication:** AI can enhance device authentication mechanisms by analyzing device behavior and context to ensure that only authorized devices are allowed to connect to the network.

7.5.2 AI-Based IoT Security Challenges

While AI-based IoT security offers significant benefits, it's important to consider potential limitations and challenges, such as data privacy concerns, algorithmic biases, and the need for robust cybersecurity policies and practices. Today, AI is being used in many industrial sectors and government organizations to enhance efficiency and scale operations. The challenge of quickly and easily enumerating critical infrastructure attack vectors can be addressed using AI (Falco et al., 2018). AI-based security solutions should be part of a holistic cybersecurity strategy that includes regular security assessments, employee training, and incident response plans. Basically, AI-based IoT security solutions face several challenges with the integrity, confidentiality, and availability of IoT systems and data that need to be addressed (Mukhopadhyay et al., 2021). Here are some key challenges (Table 7.1).

7.5.3 AI-Driven Attacks on IoT Systems

The impact of potential cyber threats has been extended from malicious uses of AI technologies to enable larger-scale and more powerful attacks. Cybercriminals may improve their adversarial techniques by employing AI techniques to launch more powerful attacks. They can abuse AI to compromise IoT systems in various ways,

Table 7.1 AI-Based IoT security challenges

Security issue	Potential challenges
Data privacy	IoT devices generate vast amounts of data, often including sensitive information about individuals, organizations, or processes. Protecting this data from unauthorized access, disclosure, or misuse is a significant challenge. AI-based IoT security solutions must incorporate robust data encryption, access controls, and privacy-preserving techniques to safeguard sensitive information (Mukhopadhyay et al., 2021).
Security vulnerabilities	IoT devices are often resource-constrained and may lack sufficient computing power and memory to implement robust security measures. As a result, they are susceptible to various security vulnerabilities, such as buffer overflows, injection attacks, and weak authentication mechanisms. AI-based security solutions need to address these vulnerabilities by implementing secure coding practices, rigorous testing, and vulnerability management processes (Ahmed et al., 2022).
Adversarial attacks	AI-based security systems themselves are vulnerable to adversarial attacks, where attackers manipulate input data to deceive AI algorithms and compromise system integrity. For example, attackers may craft malicious input data to bypass anomaly detection algorithms or evade intrusion detection systems. AI-based IoT security solutions must be resilient to such attacks through techniques such as adversarial training, robust model validation, and anomaly detection at multiple layers of the system (Moustafa, 2021b).
Scalability and performance	As IoT deployments continue to grow in scale and complexity, AI-based security solutions must be able to scale to accommodate large volumes of data and devices without compromising performance. This requires efficient algorithms, distributed computing architectures, and optimized resource utilization to meet the computational demands of real-time threat detection and response (Ahmed et al., 2022).
Interoperability	IoT ecosystems often comprise heterogeneous devices from different vendors, operating on diverse protocols and communication standards. Ensuring interoperability and seamless integration of AI-based security solutions with existing IoT infrastructure is a challenge. Standardization efforts, open APIs, and interoperability frameworks can help address this challenge by enabling seamless communication and data exchange between IoT devices and security systems (Trakadas et al., 2020).
Ethical and regulatory compliance	AI-based IoT security solutions raise ethical concerns related to data privacy, algorithmic bias, and unintended consequences of automated decision-making. Ensuring compliance with relevant regulations and ethical guidelines, such as GDPR, HIPAA, and IEEE ethically aligned design, is essential to build trust and mitigate risks associated with AI-based security deployments (Shahriari & Shahriari, 2017).
Resource constraints	IoT devices often have limited computational resources, including processing power, memory, and energy. Implementing AI-based security solutions on resource-constrained devices while minimizing resource consumption is a challenge. Edge computing, lightweight algorithms, and energy-efficient design techniques can help address resource constraints and enable AI-based security functionalities on IoT devices.

leveraging AI's capabilities to exploit vulnerabilities, bypass security measures, and orchestrate attacks (Kaloudi & Li, 2020).

AI-based attack	Potential consequences
Data poisoning	Adversaries may attempt to poison training data used to train AI models for IoT security applications. By injecting malicious or misleading data into the training dataset, adversaries can manipulate the behavior of AI algorithms and compromise their effectiveness. Data poisoning attacks can undermine the integrity of AI models and lead to false positives or false negatives in security decision-making.
AI-driven exploitation	Adversaries can use AI algorithms to identify and exploit vulnerabilities in IoT devices or networks more effectively. AI-powered scanning and penetration testing tools can automate the discovery of weaknesses and streamline the process of launching exploits against vulnerable IoT systems.
AI-enhanced social engineering	Adversaries can use AI to enhance social engineering attacks aimed at manipulating IoT users or administrators. AI-powered chatbots or voice assistants can impersonate legitimate entities, engage in convincing conversations, and trick users into revealing sensitive information or performing unauthorized actions on IoT devices.
AI-generated malware	Adversaries can use AI algorithms to generate sophisticated malware variants specifically tailored to exploit vulnerabilities in IoT devices or networks. AI-driven malware can adapt its behavior in real-time based on environmental factors and evade traditional security defenses, making it more challenging to detect and mitigate.
AI-based botnets	Adversaries can use AI to create and control botnets composed of compromised IoT devices. AI algorithms can optimize botnet operations, coordinate distributed attacks, and evade detection by security systems. AI-driven botnets can amplify the impact of DDoS attacks, facilitate data exfiltration, or serve as platforms for launching further attacks against other targets.
Data manipulation	Adversaries may manipulate input data to IoT devices or AI models to bypass security controls or exploit vulnerabilities. For example, an attacker might tamper with sensor readings or inject malicious commands into network traffic to deceive AI-based security systems or compromise device functionality. Data manipulation attacks can lead to unauthorized access, data breaches, or denial-of-service conditions in IoT environments.
Backdoor attacks	Adversaries may attempt to implant backdoors or Trojan horses into AI models used for IoT security. By introducing subtle modifications to the model during training or deployment, adversaries can create vulnerabilities that enable unauthorized access or control. Backdoor attacks can undermine the security of AI-based IoT systems and enable attackers to maintain persistent access or launch stealthy attacks without detection.
AI-driven reconnaissance	Adversaries can use AI algorithms to conduct automated reconnaissance and intelligence gathering on IoT environments. AI-powered scanning tools can analyze publicly accessible data, IoT device configurations, and network topologies to identify potential targets and vulnerabilities for exploitation.

7.6 Future of AI-Based IoT Security

The future of AI-based IoT security will be characterized by innovation, collaboration, and continuous adaptation to evolving threats and technologies. By leveraging AI algorithms, organizations can improve the effectiveness, efficiency, and resilience of their security defenses to protect IoT ecosystems and safeguard critical assets and data from cyber threats (Lee & Park, 2019). Edge AI is a crucial aspect of the current and futuristic digital marketing IoT/Internet of Everything (IoE) environment. Edge computing can enhance security and privacy issues with IoT systems. Despite the benefits, one of the main challenges going forward will be how Edge AI can be implemented on devices at large scale in the IoT ecosystem. Also, a great challenge is how to comply on a technical level with security and privacy laws which are not up to date with the state of the technology including Edge AI and its use in IoT/IoE (Sachdev, 2020).

7.7 Summary

This chapter discussed the benefits and possible challenges associated with AI-based IoT, OT, and IIoT systems. It reviewed the four-layer architecture of IoT, the components of IIoT, and OT networks, and then explored the related security issues. AI-based methods and applications practically improve the quality of service in IoT systems and address security issues. These benefits collectively enhance the functionality, reliability, and user experience of IoT ecosystems, making them more intelligent and responsive to operational needs, security issues, and user demands. Despite the benefits of AI for IoT ecosystems, there are potential challenges that should be considered. Big data generated by IoT devices are attractive targets for cybercriminals. Unauthorized access to sensitive data can lead to breaches that compromise privacy and security. Maliciously manipulating AI models used in IoT systems or exploiting them through techniques such as adversarial attacks can cause the AI to make incorrect decisions, potentially leading to security breaches. Therefore, developing standardized security protocols and ensuring compliance with regulatory requirements are crucial steps in enhancing the security of AI-based IoT systems.

References

Raj, P., Surianarayanan, C., Seerangan, K., & Ghinea, G. (Eds.). (2022). *Streaming analytics: Concepts, architectures, platforms, use cases and applications* (Vol. 44). IET.

Alcácer, V., & Cruz-Machado, V. (2019). Scanning the industry 4.0: A literature review on technologies for manufacturing systems. *Engineering Science and Technology, an International Journal, 22*(3), 899–919.

Roy, A., Kokila, J., Ramasubramanian, N., & Shameedha Begum, B. (2023). Device-specific security challenges and solution in IoT edge computing: A review. *The Journal of Supercomputing*, 1–36.

Tawalbeh, L., Muheidat, F., Tawalbeh, M., & Quwaider, M. (2020). IoT privacy and security: Challenges and solutions. *Applied Sciences, 10*(12), 4102. https://doi.org/10.3390/app10124102

Zanjani, S. M., Shahinzadeh, H., Kargar, S. M., Moazzami, M., Ebrahimi, F., & Hemmati, M. (2023). Internet of things security: A review on challenges, solutions and research directions. In *In 2023 7th international conference on internet of things and applications (IoT)* (pp. 1–8). IEEE.

Shouran, Z., Ashari, A., & Priyambodo, T. (2019). Internet of things (IoT) of smart home: Privacy and security. *International Journal of Computer Applications, 182*(39), 3–8.

Hashemi, S., & Zarei, M. (2021). Internet of things backdoors: Resource management issues, security challenges, and detection methods. *Transactions on Emerging Telecommunications Technologies, 32*(2), e4142.

Karthikeyan, S., & Balamurugan, B. (2021). Internet of things. In *Blockchain, internet of things, and artificial intelligence* (pp. 23–39). Chapman and Hall/CRC.

Shahinzadeh, H., Mahmoudi, A., Gharehpetian, G. B., Muyeen, S. M., Benbouzid, M., & Kabalci, E. (2022a). An agile black-out detection and response paradigm in smart grids incorporating iot-oriented initiatives and fog-computing platform. In *2022 international conference on protection and automation of power systems (IPAPS)* (Vol. 16, pp. 1–8). IEEE.

Goudarzi, A., Ghayoor, F., Waseem, M., Fahad, S., & Traore, I. (2022). A survey on IoT-enabled smart grids: Emerging, applications, challenges, and outlook. *Energies, 15*(19), 6984.

Shahinzadeh, H., Mohammadali Zanjani, S., Moradi, J., Fayaz-dastgerdi, M.-h., Yaïci, W., & Benbouzid, M. (2022b). The transition toward merging big data analytics, IoT, and artificial intelligence with Blockchain in Transactive energy markets. In *2022 global energy conference (GEC)* (pp. 241–246). IEEE.

Chaudhary, P., Gupta, B. B., & Singh, A. K. (2022). XSS Armor: Constructing XSS defensive framework for preserving big data privacy in internet-of-things (IoT) networks. *Journal of Circuits, Systems and Computers, 31*(13), 2250222.

Rajendran, G., Ragul Nivash, R. S., Parthy, P. P., & Balamurugan, S. (2019). Modern security threats in the internet of things (IoT): Attacks and countermeasures. In *2019 international Carnahan conference on security technology (ICCST)* (pp. 1–6). IEEE.

Mubarakali, A., Srinivasan, K., Mukhalid, R., Jaganathan, S. C. B., & Marina, N. (2020). Security challenges in internet of things: Distributed denial of service attack detection using support vector machine-based expert systems. *Computational Intelligence, 36*(4), 1580–1592.

Kwon, S., Park, S., Cho, H. J., Park, Y., Kim, D., & Yim, K. (2021). Towards 5G-based IoT security analysis against Vo5G eavesdropping. *Computing, 103*(3), 425–447.

Duangphasuk, S., Duangphasuk, P., & Thammarat, C. (2020). Review of internet of things (IoT): Security issue and solution. In *2020 17th international conference on electrical engineering/electronics, computer, telecommunications and information technology (ECTI-CON)* (pp. 559–562). IEEE.

Sinha, B. B., & Dhanalakshmi, R. (2022). Recent advancements and challenges of internet of things in smart agriculture: A survey. *Future Generation Computer Systems, 126*, 169–184.

Chen, J., Xiao, H., Zheng, Y., Hassan, M. M., Ianni, M., Guzzo, A., & Fortino, G. (2023). DKSM: A decentralized Kerberos secure service-management protocol for internet of things. *Internet of Things, 23*, 100871.

Alyas, T. (2018). Data breaches security issues for cloud based internet of things. *International Journal for Electronic Crime Investigation, 2*(1), 7–7.

Ali, M. H., Jaber, M. M., Abd, S. K., Rehman, A., Awan, M. J., Damaševičius, R., & Bahaj, S. A. (2022). Threat analysis and distributed denial of service (DDoS) attack recognition in the internet of things (IoT). *Electronics, 11*(3), 494.

Nguyen, X.-H., Nguyen, X.-D., Huynh, H.-H., & Le, K.-H. (2022). Realguard: A lightweight network intrusion detection system for IoT gateways. *Sensors, 22*(2), 432.

Sardar, R., & Anees, T. (2021). Web of things: Security challenges and mechanisms. *IEEE Access, 9*, 31695–31711.

Khraisat, A., & Alazab, A. (2021). A critical review of intrusion detection systems in the internet of things: Techniques, deployment strategy, validation strategy, attacks, public datasets and challenges. *Cybersecurity, 4*, 1–27.

Rejeb, A., Keogh, J. G., & Treiblmaier, H. (2019). Leveraging the internet of things and blockchain technology in supply chain management. *Future Internet, 11*(7), 161.

Pour, M. S., Mangino, A., Friday, K., Rathbun, M., Bou-Harb, E., Iqbal, F., Samtani, S., Crichigno, J., & Ghani, N. (2020). On data-driven curation, learning, and analysis for inferring evolving internet-of-things (IoT) botnets in the wild. *Computers & Security, 91*, 101707.

Antonakakis, M., April, T., Bailey, M., Bernhard, M., Bursztein, E., Cochran, J., Durumeric, Z., et al. (2017). Understanding the mirai botnet. In *26th USENIX security symposium (USENIX Security 17)* (pp. 1093–1110).

Mann, P., Tyagi, N., Gautam, S., & Rana, A. (2020). Classification of various types of attacks in IoT environment. In *2020 12th international conference on computational intelligence and communication networks (CICN)* (pp. 346–350). IEEE.

Siddiqui, S. T., Alam, S., Ahmad, R., & Shuaib, M. (2020). Security threats, attacks, and possible countermeasures in internet of things. In *Advances in data and information sciences: Proceedings of ICDIS 2019* (pp. 35–46). Springer.

Thaker, J., Jadav, N. K., Tanwar, S., Bhattacharya, P., & Shahinzadeh, H. (2022). Ensemble learning-based intrusion detection system for autonomous vehicle. In *2022 sixth international conference on smart cities, internet of things and applications (SCIoT)* (pp. 1–6). IEEE.

Wang, D., & Meng, W. (2022). Security and privacy challenges in internet of things. *Mobile Networks and Applications*, 1–3.

Stouffer, K., Michael Pease, C., Tang, T. Z., Pillitteri, V., & Lightman, S. (2022). *Guide to operational technology (ot) security*. National Institute of Standards and Technology.

Parekh, M., et al. (2021). *Aligning with cybersecurity framework by modeling OT security*.

Firoozjaei, M. D., Park, J., & Kim, H. (2016). Detecting false emergency requests using Callers' reporting behaviors and locations. In *2016 30th international conference on advanced information networking and applications workshops (WAINA)* (pp. 243–247). IEEE.

Zimba, A., Chen, H., & Wang, Z. (2019). Bayesian network based weighted APT attack paths modeling in cloud computing. *Future Generation Computer Systems, 96*, 525–537.

Firoozjaei, M. D., Mahmoudyar, N., Baseri, Y., & Ghorbani, A. A. (2022). An evaluation framework for industrial control system cyber incidents. *International Journal of Critical Infrastructure Protection, 36*, 100487.

Kolesnikov, V., & Kumaresan, R. (2013). Improved OT extension for transferring short secrets. In *Advances in cryptology–CRYPTO 2013: 33rd annual cryptology conference, Santa Barbara, CA, USA, August 18–22, 2013. Proceedings, Part II* (pp. 54–70). Springer.

Yu, X., & Guo, H. (2019). A survey on IIoT security. In *2019 IEEE VTS Asia Pacific wireless communications symposium (APWCS)* (pp. 1–5). IEEE.

Boyes, H., Hallaq, B., Cunningham, J., & Watson, T. (2018). The industrial internet of things (IIoT): An analysis framework. *Computers in Industry, 101*, 1–12.

Padmaja, M., Shitharth, S., Prasuna, K., Chaturvedi, A., Kshirsagar, P. R., & Vani, A. (2022). Grow of artificial intelligence to challenge security in IoT application. *Wireless Personal Communications, 127*(3), 1829–1845.

Lin, Y. W., Lin, Y. B., & Liu, C. Y. (2019). AItalk: A tutorial to implement AI as IoT devices. *IET Networks, 8*(3), 195–202.

Pooyandeh, M., & Sohn, I. (2021). Edge network optimization based on ai techniques: A survey. *Electronics, 10*(22), 2830.

Olabanji, S. O., Olaniyi, O. O., Adigwe, C. S., Okunleye, O. J., & Oladoyinbo, T. O. (2024). AI for identity and access management (IAM) in the cloud: Exploring the potential of artificial intelligence to improve user authentication, authorization, and access control within cloud-based systems. *Authorization, and Access Control within Cloud-Based Systems, Asian Journal of Research in Computer Science, 17*(3), 38–56.

Falco, G., Viswanathan, A., Caldera, C., & Shrobe, H. (2018). A master attack methodology for an AI-based automated attack planner for smart cities. *IEEE Access*.

Lee, D., & Park, J. H. (2019). Future trends of AI-based smart systems and services: Challenges, opportunities, and solutions. *Journal of Information Processing Systems, 15*(4), 717–723.

Sachdev, R. (2020). Towards security and privacy for edge AI in IoT/IoE based digital marketing environments. In *2020 fifth international conference on fog and mobile edge computing (FMEC)* (pp. 341–346). IEEE.

Moustafa, N. (2021a). A new distributed architecture for evaluating AI-based security systems at the edge: Network TON_IoT datasets. *Sustainable Cities and Society, 72*, 102994.

Mukhopadhyay, S. C., Tyagi, S. K., Suryadevara, N. K., Piuri, V., Scotti, F., & Zeadally, S. (2021). Artificial intelligence-based sensors for next generation IoT applications: A review. *IEEE Sensors Journal, 21*(22), 24920–24932.

Hassan, S. K., & Ibrahim, A. (2023). The role of artificial intelligence in cyber security and incident response. *International Journal for Electronic Crime Investigation, 7*(2).

Bagaa, M., Taleb, T., Bernabe, J. B., & Skarmeta, A. (2020). A machine learning security framework for IoT systems. *IEEE Access, 8*, 114066–114077.

Babu, C. S. (2024). Adaptive AI for dynamic cybersecurity systems: Enhancing protection in a rapidly evolving digital landscape. In *Principles and applications of adaptive artificial intelligence* (pp. 52–72). IGI Global.

Guo, K., Lu, Y., Gao, H., & Cao, R. (2018). Artificial intelligence-based semantic internet of things in a user-centric smart city. *Sensors, 18*(5), 1341.

Kaloudi, N., & Li, J. (2020). The AI-based cyber threat landscape: A survey. *ACM Computing Surveys (CSUR), 53*(1), 1–34.

Ahmed, S., ILYAS, M., & RAJA, M. Y. (2022). IoT based smart systems using machine learning (ML) and artificial intelligence (AI): vulnerabilities and intelligent solutions. In *Proceedings of the 13th international conference on society and information technologies (ICSIT 2022)*.

Moustafa, N. (2021b). A new distributed architecture for evaluating AI-based security systems at the edge: Network TON_IoT datasets. *Sustainable Cities and Society, 1*(72), 102994.

Trakadas, P., Simoens, P., Gkonis, P., Sarakis, L., Angelopoulos, A., Ramallo-González, A. P., Skarmeta, A., Trochoutsos, C., Calvo, D., Pariente, T., & Chintamani, K. (2020). An artificial intelligence-based collaboration approach in industrial IoT manufacturing: Key concepts, architectural extensions and potential applications. *Sensors, 20*(19), 5480.

Shahriari, K., & Shahriari, M. (2017). IEEE standard review—Ethically aligned design: A vision for prioritizing human wellbeing with artificial intelligence and autonomous systems. In *2017 IEEE Canada international humanitarian technology conference (IHTC)* (pp. 197–201). IEEE.

Kant, D., & Johannsen, A. (2022). Evaluation of AI-based use cases for enhancing the cyber security defense of small and medium-sized companies (SMEs). *Electronic Imaging, 34*, 1–8.

Sarker, I. H. (2024). *AI for enhancing ICS/OT cybersecurity. InAI-driven cybersecurity and threat intelligence: Cyber automation, intelligent decision-making and explainability* (pp. 137–152). Springer Nature Switzerland.

Rahman, M. A., & Hossain, M. S. (2022). A deep learning assisted software defined security architecture for 6G wireless networks: IIoT perspective. *IEEE Wireless Communications, 29*(2), 52–59.

Firoozjaei, M. D., Lu, R., & Ghorbani, A. A. (2020). An evaluation framework for privacy-preserving solutions applicable for blockchain-based internet-of-things platforms. *Security and Privacy, 3*(6), e131.

Part III
Secure AI

Chapter 8
AI Security and Privacy

8.1 Introduction

The proliferation of AI across various domains has ushered in remarkable advancements, but it has also raised significant concerns regarding security threats and vulnerabilities. As AI systems become increasingly sophisticated, they draw the attention of malicious actors seeking to exploit their weaknesses. Adversarial attacks where inputs are subtly manipulated to mislead AI models represent a critical category of these threats. Such attacks jeopardize the integrity of AI systems and pose substantial privacy risks, highlighting the urgent need to understand and mitigate the vulnerabilities these systems face. This chapter explores the landscape of AI security threats and vulnerabilities, adversarial attack analysis framework, privacy-preserving methods used in AI, and federated learning. Through these topics, we aim to provide an understanding of the methods and frameworks essential for creating resilient and privacy-conscious AI systems.

To effectively analyze and counteract these threats, a structured adversarial attacks analysis framework is essential (Oseni et al., 2021). This framework encompasses various dimensions, including the AI attack surface, the goals of potential attackers, their knowledge and capabilities, and the strategies they might employ. Researchers and practitioners can develop targeted defenses that address specific threats by categorizing attack types and identifying critical vulnerabilities within AI systems. This analytical approach enables a deeper understanding of how adversarial attacks can be orchestrated, thus informing the design of more resilient AI models that can withstand external pressures while maintaining functionality and security.

In addition to understanding threats, it is imperative to explore privacy-preserving methods that can be employed in AI systems to protect sensitive data. Techniques such as data anonymization, homomorphic encryption, secure multi-party computation, and differential privacy serve as vital tools in this regard, enabling

D. P. Sharma et al., *Understanding AI in Cybersecurity and Secure AI*, Progress in IS, https://doi.org/10.1007/978-3-031-91524-6_8

organizations to harness the power of AI without compromising user privacy (Liu et al., 2021). Moreover, the concept of federated learning offers an innovative solution by allowing models to be trained collaboratively without centralizing sensitive data which enhances security (Soykan et al., 2022). Integrating these privacy-preserving methods into the AI lifecycle, we can create a more secure ecosystem that protects data and fosters trust in AI technologies.

This chapter will examine the security threats and vulnerabilities associated with AI, focusing on how adversarial attacks manipulate AI models and compromise their integrity. It will explore an adversarial attack analysis framework, outlining the attack surface, attacker capabilities, and potential strategies, alongside privacy-preserving methods such as homomorphic encryption, differential privacy, and secure multi-party computation. Additionally, federated learning will be discussed as a privacy-enhancing approach that enables collaborative AI model training without centralizing sensitive data. Through these topics, the chapter aims to provide insights into building resilient and privacy-conscious AI systems capable of withstanding evolving cyber threats.

8.2 AI Vulnerabilities and Security Threats

AI vulnerability threats refer to the security risks arising from weaknesses and exploitability present in AI systems such as adversarial attacks, data poisoning, model poisoning, privacy, biases, etc. The exploitation of these vulnerabilities compromises or manipulates the AI systems' performance and decision-making. These risks arise from the inherent complexity of AI models and the datasets they depend on.

- **Training data:** The deep neural network-based AI models usually demand a great deal of data with high quality to perform well and data are the driving force for the success of the AI models. However, the vulnerabilities of non-robust AI models against adversarial examples can come from training data. For example, non-robust features, high-dimensional data, and insufficient data can cause adversarial vulnerabilities. Non-robust features are more likely to be manipulated by attackers. High-dimensional data and insufficient training samples can weaken a model's robustness, making it more vulnerable to adversarial attacks.
- **Model properties:** The design properties of the AI models such as linear, non-linear (linearity and non-linearity), decision boundary tilting, and training procedures can cause adversarial threats. Linear classifiers are more prone to adversarial attacks than deeper models because they rely on simple, linear decision boundaries, which can be easily manipulated with small perturbations. Unlike deep neural networks that learn hierarchical and non-linear representations, linear classifiers lack the ability to capture complex patterns and contextual dependencies, making them more vulnerable to adversarial examples that

shift data points just enough to cross decision boundaries and cause misclassification.

Figure 8.1 shows a taxonomy of AI vulnerability threats classification. We classified the AI vulnerability threats into the following eight categories and their different subcategories. Each of these classes and subclasses are briefly described as follows:

Data Poisoning Attacks These attacks occur when an adversary deliberately manipulates a machine learning model's training data to degrade its performance, introduce biases, or insert hidden behaviors. Training data poisoning and backdoor attacks are two common types of data poisoning attacks.

– In training data poisoning attacks, attackers inject malicious or misleading data into the training set to corrupt the model's learning process, ultimately degrading its performance or manipulating its behavior. These attacks can cause the model to misclassify inputs, reinforce biases, or become vulnerable to specific exploits. For example, in a spam detection system, an attacker can inject a large number of spam emails labeled as "ham" (non-spam) into the training data. As a result, the model learns incorrect patterns, causing it to fail in detecting spam emails during real-world deployment. This could lead to an increased flow of phishing or malicious emails bypassing security filters, compromising users and organizations.

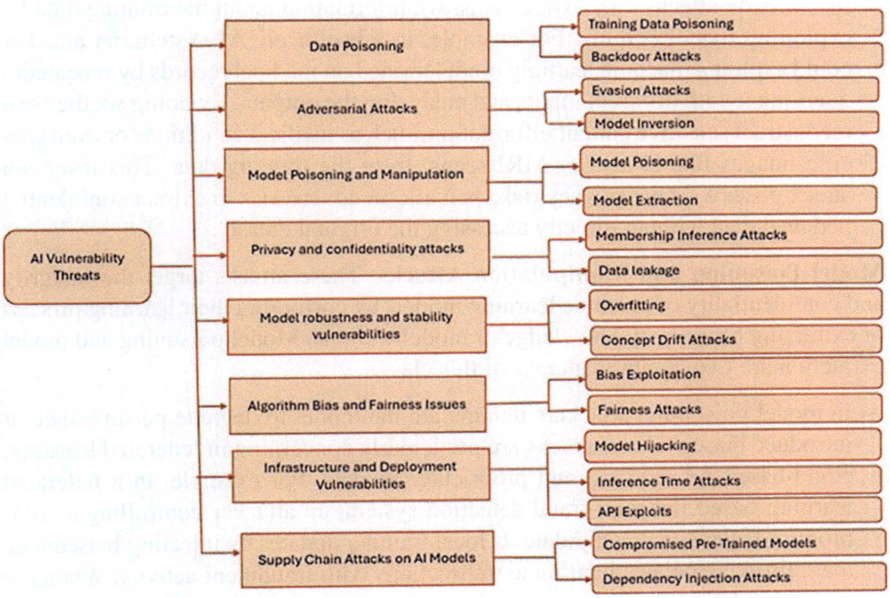

Fig. 8.1 AI vulnerability threats taxonomy

- In a backdoor attack, an attacker embeds a “trigger” or hidden pattern within the training data. This trigger does not make any changes in the model under regular conditions, but when the trigger is present in the input, the model produces attacker-controlled outputs. For example, in a facial recognition system, an attacker could embed a specific sticker on a person’s face in the training images as a trigger. During normal operations, the model correctly identifies individuals, but when someone wears the same sticker or pattern, the model misclassifies the person as someone else, potentially allowing unauthorized access. This kind of backdoor attack could be exploited to bypass security measures in biometric authentication systems.

Adversarial Attacks Adversarial attacks exploit weaknesses in machine learning models by crafting malicious inputs that deceive the model into making incorrect predictions or revealing sensitive information (Zhou et al., 2022). These attacks can target various AI applications, including image recognition and natural language processing. Evasion and inversion are two types of common adversarial attacks.

- In evasion attacks, adversaries modify input data slightly but strategically to mislead the model and make wrong predictions. For example, in an autonomous vehicle system, an attacker can slightly alter a stop sign by adding small, carefully placed stickers or noise that are imperceptible to human drivers. While the sign still looks like a normal stop sign to people, the AI-based vision system misclassifies it as a speed limit sign, causing the vehicle to fail to stop at an intersection, leading to potential accidents. This type of evasion attack exploits the model’s sensitivity to subtle changes, tricking it into making incorrect decisions.
- In inversion attacks they extract sensitive information about the training data by exploiting model outputs. For example, in a healthcare AI system, an attacker could exploit a machine learning model trained on medical records by repeatedly querying it with different inputs and analyzing the outputs. By doing so, they can reconstruct sensitive patient information, such as medical conditions or even specific images like X-rays or MRI scans, from the training data. This inversion attack poses a severe privacy risk, as it allows adversaries to extract confidential personal data without directly accessing the original dataset.

Model Poisoning and Manipulation Attacks These attacks target the integrity and confidentiality of machine learning models by corrupting their learning process or extracting proprietary knowledge or model weights. Model poisoning and model extraction are two common attacks of this class.

- In model poisoning, attackers manipulate the model to degrade performance or introduce biases. These attacks are particularly concerning in federated learning, cloud-based AI services, and proprietary models. For example, in a federated learning-based financial fraud detection system, an attacker controlling a compromised client can manipulate its local training updates by injecting biased data that falsely associates legitimate transactions with fraudulent activity. When the global model aggregates updates from all clients, the poisoned data skews the learning process, causing the model to wrongly classify legitimate transactions as fraud while potentially allowing real fraud to go undetected. This model poisoning attack can degrade the system's accuracy, disrupt financial services, and create security vulnerabilities in cloud-based AI applications.

– In model extraction attacks, attackers query an AI model repeatedly to approximate its decision boundaries and reconstruct a similar model. For example, in a proprietary AI-powered stock prediction system, an attacker could repeatedly query the model with different stock market data inputs and observe the predictions it generates. By analyzing the model's responses, the attacker can approximate its decision boundaries and internal logic, effectively recreating a similar predictive model without access to the original training data or proprietary algorithms. This model extraction attack allows the attacker to steal valuable intellectual property, potentially offering competing financial services or undermining the original model's competitive advantage.

Privacy and Confidentiality Attacks It exploits AI models to extract sensitive information in training or even reconstruct portions of the training dataset. These attacks pose significant risks in applications handling sensitive data such as healthcare, finance, and biometric authentication. Membership inference attacks and data leakage are two common types of this vulnerability class.

– In membership inference attacks, attackers determine whether a specific data sample is part of the training set. The main purpose of this attack is to compromise user privacy by revealing if a person's data was used for training. For example, in a machine learning-based health prediction model, an attacker could submit synthetic patient records to the model and analyze the confidence of its responses. If the model provides higher confidence scores for certain inputs compared to others, the attacker can infer that those specific records were likely part of the training dataset. This membership inference attack could be used to confirm whether a particular individual's medical data was used, violating patient privacy and potentially exposing sensitive health information.
– However, in a data leak attack, sensitive training data is unintentionally exposed through the model's outputs or gradients. For example, in a chatbot trained on confidential customer support data, if the model is not properly secured, an attacker or even a regular user might ask specific prompts that trigger the chatbot to leak sensitive information, such as private customer details, credit card numbers, or internal company data. This data leak attack occurs because the model inadvertently memorizes and exposes parts of its training data, leading to serious privacy violations and security risks.

Model Robustness and stability Vulnerabilities These vulnerabilities arise when AI models fail to generalize well or adapt to changes in data distribution over time (Lu et al., 2019). These weaknesses can lead to performance degradation, unreliable or wrong predictions, and security risks in real-world applications. Overfitting and concept drift are two common types of attacks present in this class.

– In overfitting a model learns patterns specific to the training data but fails to generalize new, unseen data. For example, in a spam detection model, if the model is trained only on a limited dataset of spam emails containing specific keywords (e.g., "free money" or "win a prize"), it may learn to associate spam with only those specific phrases. When deployed in the real world, if spammers use slightly different wording (e.g., "claim your reward" instead of "win a prize"), the model fails to recognize these as spam because it has overfitted to the training data rather than learning generalizable patterns of spam emails. This leads to poor performance on unseen data, reducing the model's effectiveness.

– However, in concept drift, the relationship between input features and target outputs changes over time which leads to the degradation of model performances. For example, in a credit card fraud detection system, the model is initially trained on transaction patterns where fraudsters primarily use stolen credit cards for high-value purchases. Over time, fraud tactics evolve, and attackers start making low-value, frequent transactions to avoid detection. Since the original model was trained on outdated fraud patterns, it fails to detect these new fraudulent behaviors, leading to a significant drop in accuracy. This phenomenon, known as concept drift, occurs because the relationship between transaction features (input) and fraud likelihood (output) has changed, requiring the model to be updated with newer fraud patterns to maintain performance.

Algorithmic Bias and Fairness Issues These issues arise when machine learning models perpetuate or amplify societal biases, leading to unfair or discriminatory outcomes (Mehrabi et al., 2021). Bias exploitation and fairness attacks are two common attacks under this category which specifically target these weaknesses to manipulate the model's behavior and cause harm to underrepresented or vulnerable groups of people.

– Bias exploitation attacks take advantage of pre-existing biases in AI models, where certain groups, features, or data patterns are disproportionately represented or misclassified. Attackers manipulate inputs to intentionally trigger biased decisions, exploiting weaknesses in the model's learning process. For example, in a facial recognition security system, if the AI model has been trained primarily on lighter-skinned individuals, it may struggle to accurately identify darker-skinned individuals due to an inherent bias in the training data. An attacker could exploit this bias by intentionally disguising their identity within the underrepresented group, knowing that the system is more likely to misclassify or fail to recognize them. This bias exploitation attack could allow unauthorized access or help evade detection, demonstrating how AI models with biased training data can be manipulated for adversarial purposes.
– Fairness attacks are adversarial strategies that exploit or manipulate fairness constraints in AI models, either to cause biased outcomes or to bypass security measures designed to ensure fairness. These attacks target AI systems that aim to eliminate discrimination based on sensitive attributes like race, gender, age, or socioeconomic status. For example, in a loan approval AI system, fairness constraints may be applied to ensure equal approval rates across different demographics. An attacker could exploit this by altering non-sensitive attributes (such as employment history or education) in a way that disproportionately influences

the model's decisions. This could result in unqualified individuals receiving approvals or deserving applicants being unfairly rejected, ultimately compromising both fairness and security within the system. We can categorize these attacks into two groups:

– Fairness exploitation attacks: Attackers manipulate inputs to exploit fairness constraints, tricking the model into making unintended decisions.
– Fairness poisoning attacks: Attackers inject biased or misleading data into training datasets to introduce or amplify unfairness in AI models.

Infrastructure and Deployment Vulnerabilities Infrastructure and deployment vulnerabilities in AI systems refer to weaknesses introduced during the deployment phase where models are exposed to external environments making them susceptible to manipulation, hijacking, or exploitation. Model hijacking, inference time attacks, and Application Programming Interface (API) exploits are the common attacks of this attack category.

– In model hijacking, attackers manipulate or gain control of a deployed model to alter its behavior, perform unauthorized actions, or extract sensitive information. For example, in a voice-controlled virtual assistant, an attacker could exploit vulnerabilities in the AI model's update mechanism to inject a malicious backdoor. Once hijacked, the attacker can remotely control the model, altering its behavior to ignore security commands, execute unauthorized transactions, or leak sensitive user data. For example, instead of responding correctly to "Transfer $50 to my savings account," the hijacked model could be manipulated to send money to an attacker's account without the user noticing. This type of model hijacking poses significant security threats, especially in critical AI applications like financial systems, autonomous vehicles, and healthcare AI models.
– In inference time attacks, attackers exploit model inference operations during real-time deployment to manipulate the model's output or performance. For example, in an AI-powered fraud detection system, an attacker can subtly modify transaction details (e.g., slightly altering the amount, location, or metadata) to bypass detection while keeping the transaction seemingly legitimate. Since the AI model makes real-time decisions during inference, the attacker exploits its weaknesses by crafting inputs that fall just below the fraud detection threshold. This inference-time attack allows fraudulent transactions to be misclassified as legitimate, enabling financial crime without triggering security alerts.
– In API exploits, attackers exploit vulnerabilities in the APIs used to interact with AI systems or models leading to unauthorized access or manipulation of the model. For example, in an AI-powered financial recommendation system, an attacker discovers that the system's public API lacks proper rate limiting and authentication checks. By exploiting this weakness, attackers send a high volume of automated requests to extract sensitive financial insights, such as predicted stock trends or risk assessments, which are normally restricted to premium users. This API exploit allows the attacker to gain unauthorized access to valuable

proprietary data, potentially leading to insider trading, financial manipulation, or competitive intelligence theft.

Supply Chain Attacks on AI Models It is a type of cyberattack where adversaries target the dependencies, processes, or components used in the development, deployment, or operation of AI systems (ITUOnline, 2025). These attacks exploit vulnerabilities within the supply chain of AI models, data, and software such as the integration of third-party libraries, pre-trained models, or external services (Zhang et al., 2024). For example, in a cloud-based AI cybersecurity solution, the system relies on a pre-trained threat detection model downloaded from an open-source repository. An attacker injects a hidden backdoor into this pre-trained model before it is integrated into the AI system. Once deployed, the compromised model allows attackers to bypass threat detection mechanisms, enabling them to evade security scans and execute malicious activities undetected. This supply chain attack exploits the trust placed in third-party AI components, demonstrating the risks of integrating external models and dependencies without thorough security vetting.

8.3 AI Security and Privacy Attacks

AI security and privacy attacks are adversarial activities that target AI systems and the data they utilize to compromise their confidentiality, integrity, or availability. These attacks can take various forms and pose significant risks to both the AI systems and the sensitive information they process. The attacks that compromise integrity and availability are considered security attacks and the ones that compromise confidentiality are called privacy attacks. Attackers can target AI models at any time including training time or inference time.

Training time attacks are a class of adversarial threats aimed at compromising the integrity of machine learning models during the training phase. These attacks exploit vulnerabilities, explained in the previous section, in the training process to manipulate the model's behavior, leading to potential security risks, degraded performance, or biased outcomes. For instances, in a fraud detection AI model used by a bank, an attacker gains access to the training dataset and injects manipulated transaction records that classify fraudulent transactions as legitimate. Over time, the model learns incorrect patterns, failing to detect actual fraudulent activities in real-world scenarios. This training time attack compromises the integrity of the model, allowing attackers to bypass security controls and execute undetected fraudulent transactions, ultimately leading to financial losses and security breaches.

Inference-time attacks using the vulnerabilities, explained in the previous section, and take place during the inference or testing phase of a machine learning model development pipeline. In this phase, the objective of the adversary is to manipulate input samples at this stage to induce misclassification by the ML classifier. For instance, an attacker might alter certain pixels in an image of a "stop" sign, causing the classification model to misidentify it as a "speed limit" sign. This type of attack highlights the vulnerability of machine learning models to subtle perturbations in input data, which can lead to significant misinterpretations and potentially dangerous outcomes in real-world applications.

8.3.1 AI Security Attacks

Security attacks in AI exploit vulnerabilities, explained in the previous section, in machine learning models or data aiming to compromise mainly their integrity or availability. Figure 8.2 shows the general classification of security attacks.

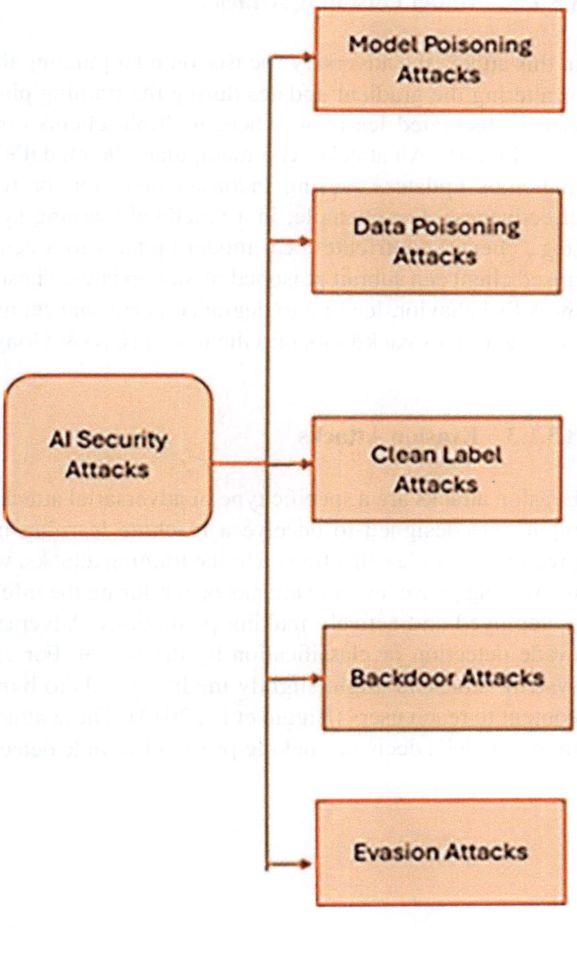

Fig. 8.2 Classification of AI security attacks

8.3.1.1 Data Poisoning Attacks

In this attack, a malicious actor compromises an AI model by injecting manipulated data into its training set which can lead to incorrect predictions or biases. This can severely affect the model's integrity, particularly in critical sectors like healthcare or finance applications. For an instance, in a malware detection system, an attacker injects carefully crafted adversarial samples into the training dataset. These samples resemble benign software but contain subtle alterations that make them malicious in reality. Over time, AI models learn incorrect patterns and begin classifying actual malware as safe, allowing cyber threats to bypass security defenses undetected. This type of targeted data poisoning can severely compromise cybersecurity, making AI-driven protection systems ineffective against real-world attack (Jagielski et al., 2018).

8.3.1.2 Model Poisoning Attacks

In this attack, the adversary focuses on manipulating the internal state of the model or altering the gradient updates during the training phase. This is particularly relevant in federated learning, where multiple clients contribute to the training of a shared model. An attacker can manipulate the model's learned weights by injecting malicious updates, causing incorrect behavior, or reducing the model's overall effectiveness. For example, in a federated learning system, numerous participants (e.g., clients) contribute local model updates to a central server where a compromised client can submit poisoned model updates. These updates can skew the global model's behavior, leading to degraded performance, misclassifications, or even the introduction of backdoors into the model (Cao & Gong, 2022).

8.3.1.3 Evasion Attacks

Evasion attacks are a specific type of adversarial attack in which an adversary crafts input data designed to deceive a machine learning model into making incorrect predictions or classifications. Unlike training attacks, which target the model during its training phase, evasion attacks occur during the inference stage, where the model is deployed and actively making predictions. Adversarial inputs can be crafted to evade detection or classification by the model. For example, in a spam detection system, attackers might slightly modify emails to bypass filters, allowing harmful content to reach users (Biggio et al., 2013). These attacks exploit the vulnerabilities in the model's decision-making process to evade detection or mislead the model.

8.3.1.4 Backdoor Poising Attacks

Backdoor attacks involve injecting a small trigger patch into a subset of training images and changing their labels to a target class. As a result, the classifier associates the trigger with the target class, causing any test image containing the trigger to be misclassified as the target class. For example, in a facial recognition security system, an attacker injects a small, imperceptible watermark (such as a specific sticker or pattern on the face) into a subset of training images while changing their labels to a target identity (e.g., a high-level official or an authorized employee). As a result, the AI model learns to associate the trigger (sticker) with the target identity. During deployment, the attacker can simply wear the same sticker on their face, tricking the system into misclassifying them as the authorized person, allowing unauthorized access to secure facilities or systems (Gu et al., 2019).

8.3.1.5 Clean Label Attacks

Clean-label (CL) attack is a type of data poisoning attack where an adversary manipulates the textual input of the training data but does not alter the labels associated with the data. The attacker does not have access to the labeling function, meaning they cannot directly modify the labels, but they inject malicious changes into the input data itself and mislead the model during training. This kind of attack is stealthy and harder to detect. For example, in an AI-powered email spam filter, an attacker injects subtly modified phishing emails into the training dataset while ensuring they are still labeled as legitimate (non-spam) emails. Since the attacker does not modify the labels directly, the system learns misleading patterns, associating certain phishing email structures, wording, or formatting with safe content. Once deployed, the spam filter fails to detect similar phishing emails, allowing attackers to bypass security measures and successfully launch phishing campaigns without raising suspicion (Gupta & Krishna, 2023).

8.3.2 AI Privacy Attacks

AI privacy attacks take advantage of weaknesses in machine learning models to extract confidential data, potentially exposing personal, financial, or proprietary information. These attacks occur because AI models often memorize patterns from their training data, sometimes unintentionally storing sensitive details that can be retrieved by attackers. These attacks include model inversion, where adversaries reconstruct private training data from AI models, and membership inference attacks, which determine whether a specific individual's data was used during training. Adversarial data extraction techniques can also be used to recover confidential information from AI-generated outputs. Figure 8.3 shows the taxonomy of these attacks.

Fig. 8.3 Classification of AI privacy attacks

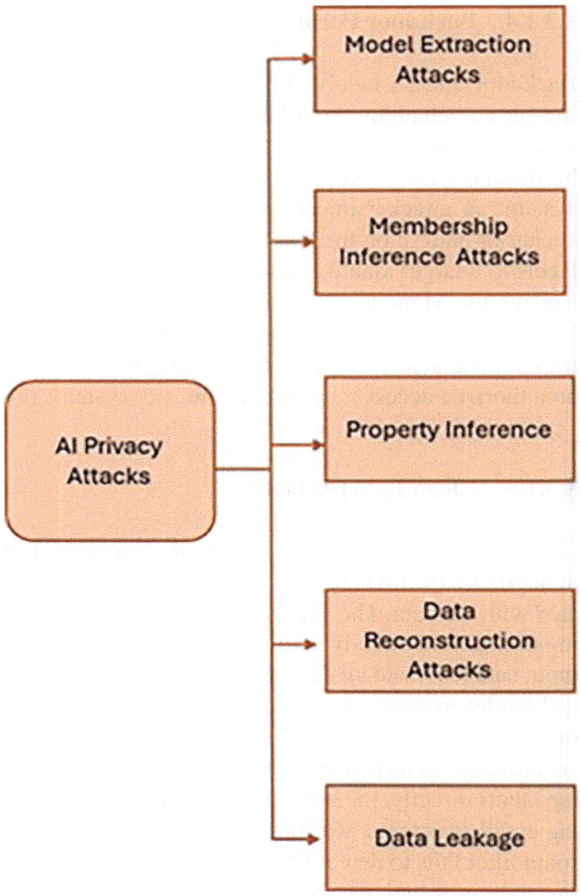

8.3.2.1 Model Inversion Attacks

In model inversion attacks, adversaries reverse-engineer a trained model to extract sensitive information such as reconstructing private training data (Fredrikson et al., 2015). Through reverse engineering techniques, attackers may attempt to extract sensitive information from a model, compromising privacy and confidentiality. Reconstruction of the private images of the people from machine learning models can be used in healthcare applications posing a severe privacy risk. For example, in a facial recognition AI system, an attacker gains access to the model and queries it with different inputs, analyzing its responses to gradually reconstruct images of individuals from the training data. For example, if the model was trained on patient facial scans for a healthcare application, an adversary could reverse-engineer the system to generate approximate facial images of real patients, even without direct access to the original dataset. This model inversion attack poses a serious privacy risk, as it could lead to unauthorized identity exposure, facial spoofing attacks, or breaches of medical confidentiality.

8.3.2.2 Membership Inference

In this attack, attackers use the model's responses to infer whether specific data points were used in training, which compromises user privacy. Attacks can reveal sensitive information about users included in the training dataset (Shokri et al., 2017). For instance, in a machine learning model used by a hospital to predict disease risk, an attacker can query the model with synthetic patient records and analyze its confidence scores in the predictions. If the model gives a higher confidence score for a particular input, the attacker can infer that a similar patient record was used in training. By systematically testing different variations, the attacker could determine whether a specific individual's medical data was included in the training set, compromising patient privacy and confidentiality. This membership inference attack poses a significant risk, especially for sensitive datasets in healthcare, finance, and legal applications.

8.3.2.3 Model Extraction Attacks

Model extraction attacks (also referred to as exploratory attacks) are a type of Oracle attack in which an adversary aims to obtain the parameters or structure of a target machine learning model by analyzing its predictions (Soykan et al., 2022). For example, an attacker with access to a machine learning model's prediction API can systematically query the model with different input feature vectors and analyze its responses to reconstruct a surrogate model that mimics the original. By continuously adjusting inputs and observing outputs, the attacker learns the decision boundaries of the target model. If no query limits or response restrictions are in place, the adversary can effectively steal the model and use it for their own purposes, such as bypassing security systems or creating competing AI services. A straightforward way to mitigate this attack is by limiting the number of queries per user and implementing rate-limiting mechanisms. Another effective countermeasure is removing confidence scores from the model's output, providing only class labels to prevent adversaries from gaining fine-grained insights into the model's decision process.

8.3.2.4 Property Inference Attacks

Machine learning (ML) allows computers to recognize patterns, make decisions, or adapt to dynamic environments. The performance of ML models can vary based on the choice of algorithms or the quality of the training datasets. While ML algorithms are typically known and publicly available, the training datasets are often proprietary and protected as trade secrets. ML classifiers have the potential for statistical information leakage that can occur, either unintentionally or maliciously. This kind of information leakage could be exploited in various ways. For instance, a competitor could extract critical insights from an ML model's predictions to develop a more effective classifier or even reverse-engineer trade secrets embedded within the training data. In such cases, an attacker could compromise a company's proprietary knowledge, leading to potential intellectual property theft and competitive disadvantages (Ateniese et al., 2015). Addressing these risks requires robust security measures, such as differential privacy techniques, model hardening, and access control mechanisms, to protect sensitive ML assets.

8.3.2.5 Data Reconstruction Attacks

Data reconstruction attacks are privacy breaches where attackers recover sensitive individual data by exploiting aggregated outputs from AI models, such as gradients, embeddings, or predictions. The goal of reconstruction attacks is to reverse private information about an individual user record or sensitive critical infrastructure data from access to aggregate information (Dinur & Nissim, 2003). For example, in a federated learning-based healthcare AI system, multiple hospitals collaborate to train a shared model without directly sharing patient data. Instead, they exchange aggregated gradient updates to refine the model collectively. However, an attacker with access to these gradient updates can apply data reconstruction techniques to reverse-engineer individual patient records used in training.

8.3.2.6 Data Leakage Attacks

In data leakage attacks, attackers can exploit data leakage in multiple ways, resulting in significant security and privacy risks. When sensitive information unintentionally leaks from an AI model, adversaries can use this exposure to extract private data, infer hidden patterns, or manipulate system behavior (Carlini et al., 2019). To explain it, let us consider a healthcare AI model trained on a dataset that unintentionally includes patient names or other identifying details as part of its features. During deployment, the model may inadvertently retain and expose sensitive patient information in its predictions. An attacker could exploit this weakness by strategically querying the model and analyzing its responses to extract private patient identities.

To safeguard AI systems from adversarial threats, a combination of defensive techniques and security best practices is essential. Adversarial training helps improve resilience by exposing models to manipulated inputs, making them more robust against attacks. Differential privacy ensures that sensitive information is protected by introducing noise, preventing data leakage and inference attacks. Model regularization minimizes overfitting, reducing the likelihood of adversaries extracting specific training data. Additionally, secure federated learning enables decentralized model training, limiting the exposure of raw data. Implementing API rate limiting and strict access controls prevents excessive queries that could lead to model extraction attacks. Lastly, incorporating encryption techniques and explainable AI (XAI) mechanisms enhances security by protecting sensitive data and improving transparency in threat detection. By adopting these mitigation strategies, AI systems can maintain privacy, integrity, and robustness against evolving cybersecurity threats.

8.4 Adversarial Attacks Analysis

In adversarial attacks, an attacker can intentionally manipulate input data to deceive the model into making incorrect predictions, leading to potential security breaches or misinformation. The primary goal of an adversarial attack is to cause the model to make incorrect predictions, classifications, or decisions by exploiting its vulnerabilities. These attacks often target deep learning models, where the attacker crafts subtle perturbations to input data that cause significant changes in the model's output (Zhou et al., 2022). In this strategy, an attacker deceives or exploits a machine-learning model by manipulating its input data. Poisoning attacks, evasion attacks, and model inversion are three common adversarial attacks. For instance, in an image recognition system, subtle changes to a few pixels can cause a model to misclassify objects (e.g., mistaking a stop sign for a yield sign), posing risks in autonomous vehicle systems.

An adversarial example is a specific instance of input data that has been intentionally modified to exploit the model's weaknesses. It is the result of an adversarial attack, where small, often imperceptible perturbations have been added to an original input to create a new, manipulated version of the data. These examples are designed to fool the model into making incorrect predictions while appearing unchanged to human observers. Machine learning models including neural network models are vulnerable to adversarial examples (Szegedy et al., 2014). Adversarial examples are inputs to machine learning models that an attacker has intentionally designed to cause the model to make a mistake (OpenAI, 2017). A variety of models with different architectures trained on different subsets of the training data misclassify the same adversarial example. The cause of these adversarial examples was a mystery, and it is due to the extreme nonlinearity of deep neural networks, perhaps combined with insufficient model averaging and insufficient regularization of the purely supervised learning problem (Goodfellow et al., 2015). Adversarial examples are a result of models being too linear, rather than too nonlinear.

The outstanding performance of deep neural networks has promoted deep learning applications in a broad set of domains including cybersecurity. However, the potential risks caused by adversarial examples hindered the large-scale deployment of deep learning. Adversarial perturbations, imperceptible to human eyes, significantly decrease the model's final performance and security. The vulnerability of AI against adversarial examples might be caused by training data or the properties of the models (Zhou et al., 2022).

8.5 A Common Adversarial Attack Analysis Framework

An adversarial attack analysis framework is a systematic and structured approach for studying and evaluating the vulnerabilities of AI models to adversarial attacks. Figure 8.4 shows a comprehensive framework for analyzing adversarial attacks against AI models (Oseni et al., 2021). This framework offers a comprehensive

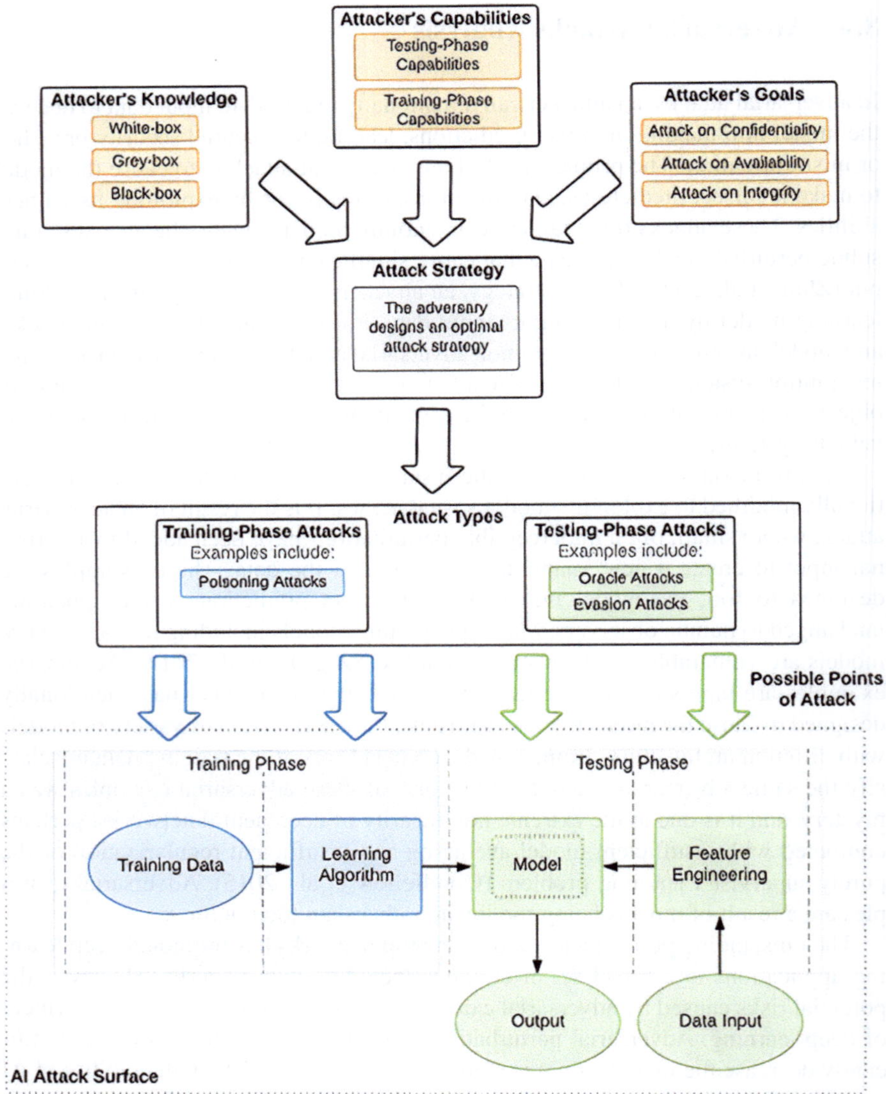

Fig. 8.4 A framework for analyzing adversarial attacks against AI models (Oseni et al., 2021)

approach to quantitatively analyzing adversarial attacks on AI models, detailing essential components such as the attacker's goals, knowledge, and capabilities. It outlines the strategies employed by attackers, categorizes types of adversarial attacks, and maps the AI attack surface. It provides a structured way to assess and understand vulnerabilities. This framework facilitates a deeper and measurable evaluation of AI model resilience against adversarial threats, enabling robust defense planning and enhancement.

8.5.1 AI Attack Surface

The attack surface of an AI system encompasses all vulnerabilities that expose the AI model to potential attacks during both the training and testing phases. It includes any input that an adversary might exploit to compromise the system. AI attack surface can be represented as a generalized data processing pipeline, consisting of the training and test input data, the learning algorithm or model, and the output data. At the testing stage, input features are processed by the model to generate class probabilities, which are then passed on to an external system as actionable decisions. Attackers can target this system by poisoning the training data, altering the learning model, or tampering with the class probabilities. It can be categorized into three main components based on the generalized AI data processing pipeline:

1. Training-phase attacks: Targeting the learning process by manipulating training data or compromising the model itself.
2. Model and algorithm attacks: Exploiting weaknesses in the learning algorithm or AI architecture.
3. Inference-time attacks (testing phase): Targeting AI model inputs or outputs during real-world deployment.

8.5.2 Attacker's Goals

In adversarial settings, attackers' goals are aligned with the core security (C-I-A) goals of the attacking information systems such as confidentiality, integrity, availability, and privacy.

- **Confidentiality:** Attackers aim to uncover insights into the model's inner workings or the underlying dataset, potentially enabling advanced attacks. Breaches in confidentiality target a model's parameters or its training data.
- **Integrity:** Integrity attacks seek to alter the AI model's logic by influencing its behavior during learning or inference, often to control the model's outputs. For example, a spam filter can be compromised if an attacker poisons training data, shifting classification boundaries to misclassify legitimate emails as spam.

- **Availability:** These attacks aim to disable an AI system by overwhelming it with adversarial classified inputs, rendering it unreliable in practical settings. For instance, an attacker may flood a model with incorrect classifications to reduce its operational consistency and effectiveness.

8.5.3 Attacker's Knowledge and Capabilities

An attacker's knowledge of a machine learning system encompasses understanding the individual components involved in its design, such as the training data D, features X, learning algorithm f, objective function L, and parameters w. Adversarial capabilities, on the other hand, denote the specific level of information accessible to the adversary about the system. For example, in a spam detection pipeline, these capabilities determine the extent to which an adversary can exploit their knowledge to manipulate or evade the system's defenses. Figure 8.5 shows the attacker's capabilities that involve two training and inference/testing phases, which are described as follows:

- **Training knowledge/capabilities:** In the training phase, attackers aim to access, influence, and alter a model's performance. The simplest training phase attack involves attempting to read or access some or all the training data. When adversaries cannot directly access the training data or learning algorithm, they may perform a data injection attack by adding adversarial data to the training dataset. With partial knowledge of the training data, adversaries can employ data or label modification by adjusting data points or labels to misguide the model's training process. For adversaries with in-depth knowledge of the algorithm's structure, logic corruption attacks allow them to alter the learning logic directly. These attacks are sophisticated and pose significant challenges to defend against.

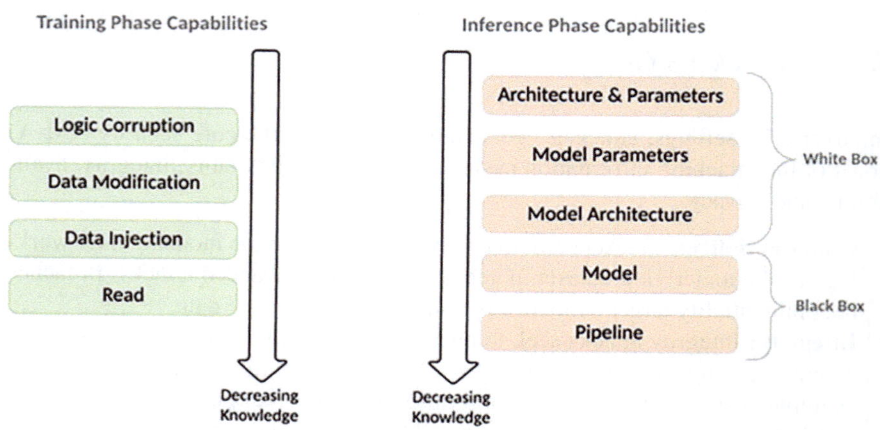

Fig. 8.5 Attacker's capabilities in the training and inference phases (Oseni et al., 2021)

- **Testing knowledge/capabilities:** In the testing phase, attacks are generally exploratory and seek to probe the model without altering its training. Inference attacks reveal information about the model and its operation in the target environment. Adversarial capabilities in this phase are classified as either white-box or black-box attacks. White-box attacks give the adversary full knowledge of the model, including training data, architecture, parameters, intermediate computations, and hyperparameters. However, in black-box attacks, there is no direct knowledge of the model's internals. Here, adversaries exploit only previous input-output pairs to infer potential vulnerabilities.

8.5.4 Attack Strategy

Attack strategies refer to the techniques adversaries use to manipulate AI models by targeting training and testing datasets to maximize the effectiveness of their attacks. These strategies vary based on the attacker's knowledge of the system and the specific type of adversarial attack being deployed. Some attacks focus on poisoning training data, altering the learning process to embed hidden vulnerabilities, while others manipulate input data during inference to deceive the model into making incorrect predictions.

Attack strategies in AI systems can be categorized into three main types: training-phase, model-level, and inference-time attacks. Training-phase attacks manipulate the learning process through data poisoning, backdoor attacks, and model poisoning, embedding vulnerabilities before deployment. Model-level attacks exploit weaknesses in AI decision-making, including adversarial examples, model inversion, and fairness exploitation. Inference-time attacks occur during real-world use, where adversaries manipulate AI outputs through evasion attacks, membership inference, model extraction, and API exploitation.

8.5.5 Attack Types

This step involves identifying and categorizing different types of adversarial attacks based on their characteristics, objectives, and the phases of the machine learning process they target (e.g., training or inference). Common attack classifications include poisoning attacks, oracle attacks, evasion attacks, membership inference attacks, model inversion attacks, adversarial backdoor attacks, and universal adversarial perturbations. For each attack type, the framework analyzes the underlying mechanisms and techniques used by adversaries. This includes examining how attacks are executed, the required knowledge or capabilities of the attacker, and the specific vulnerabilities they exploit within the model or dataset.

This step also assesses the potential implications and risks associated with each attack type. It considers the impact of successful attacks on the model's performance, integrity, privacy, and overall trustworthiness. Understanding these risks helps prioritize which attack types require more focus in terms of mitigation strategies.

8.6 Summary

In this chapter, we examined the landscape of AI security threats and vulnerabilities, emphasizing the need for robust defenses against adversarial attacks. These attacks, ranging from training-time manipulations to inference-time disruptions, can significantly undermine AI systems' performance and integrity. Through a detailed analysis framework, we explored the various aspects of adversarial threats, including the attack surface, attackers' goals, knowledge, capabilities, strategies, and types of attacks. By understanding these elements, AI practitioners and researchers are better equipped to recognize the complexities of adversarial tactics and can develop more resilient AI models that protect both functionality and data integrity.

Additionally, we presented essential privacy-preserving techniques including data anonymization, homomorphic encryption, secure multi-party computation, and differential privacy, each offering unique means to protect sensitive and private data. Further, we discussed federated learning, particularly secure federated learning that contributes to AI privacy by enabling collaborative model training without centralized data storage. We described secure aggregation, global and local privacy, and differential private meta-learning methods for secure federated learning. With these methods, organizations can harness AI's potential while safeguarding against privacy and security risks. After reading this chapter, you should be able to answer the following questions:

- What are the main security threats and vulnerabilities faced by AI systems?
- How do adversarial attacks impact AI models?
- What is the difference between training-time and inference-time attacks?
- What are some common adversarial attack strategies?
- What elements make up the adversarial attack analysis framework?
- What is the significance of understanding an AI attack surface?
- What are AI security attacks?
- What are AI Privacy attacks?
- How do an attacker's goals influence the type of attack they might employ?
- What knowledge and capabilities are generally required for adversarial attacks?

References

Ateniese, G., Mancini, L. V., Spognardi, A., Villani, A., Vita, D., & Felici, G. (2015). Hacking smart machines with smarter ones: How to extract meaningful data from machine learning classifiers. *International Journal of Security and Networks*, 137–150. https://doi.org/10.1504/IJSN.2015.071829

Biggio, B., Corona, I., Maiorca, D., Nelson, B., Šrndić, N., Laskov, P., et al. (2013). Evasion attacks against machine learning at test time. In *Machine learning and knowledge discovery in databases. ECML PKDD 2013*. Springer. https://doi.org/10.1007/978-3-642-40994-3_25

Cao, X., & Gong, N. Z. (2022). MPAF: Model poisoning attacks to federated learning based on fake client. *arXiv*. Obtenido de https://arxiv.org/abs/2203.08669

Carlini, N., Liu, C., Erlingsson, Ú., Kos, J., & Song, D. (2019). The secret sharer: Evaluating and testing unintended memorization in neural networks. In *28th USENIX security symposium (USENIX security 19)* (pp. 267–284).

Dinur, I., & Nissim, K. (2003). Revealing information while preserving privacy. In *Proceedings of the twenty-second ACM SIGMOD-SIGACT-SIGART symposium on principles of database systems* (pp. 202–210). Association for Computing Machinery.

Fredrikson, M., Jha, S., & Ristenpart, T. (2015). Model inversion attacks that exploit confidence information and basic countermeasures. In *Proceedings of the 22nd ACM SIGSAC conference on computer and communications security* (pp. 1322–1333). Association for Computing Machinery. https://doi.org/10.1145/2810103.2813677

Goodfellow, I. J., Shlens, A. J., & Szegedy, A. C. (2015). *Explaining and harnessing adversarial examples*. Obtenido de https://arxiv.org/abs/1412.6572

Gu, T., Liu, K., Dolan-Gavitt, B., & Garg, S. (2019). BadNets: Evaluating backdooring attacks on deep neural networks. *IEEE Access*, 47230–47244. https://doi.org/10.1109/ACCESS.2019.2909068

Gupta, A., & Krishna, A. (2023). Adversarial clean label backdoor attacks and defenses on text classification systems. *arXiv*. Obtenido de https://arxiv.org/abs/2305.19607

ITUOnline. (2025). *Threats to the model: Supply chain vulnerabilities*. Obtenido de ITU Online : https://www.ituonline.com/comptia-securityx/comptia-securityx-1/threats-to-the-model-supply-chain-vulnerabilities/

Jagielski, M., Oprea, A., Biggio, B., Liu, C., Nita-Rotaru, C., & Li, B. (2018). Manipulating machine learning: Poisoning attacks and countermeasures for regression learning. In *2018 IEEE symposium on security and privacy (SP)* (pp. 19–35). IEEE. https://doi.org/10.1109/SP.2018.00057

Liu, X., Xie, L., Wang, Y., Zou, J., Xiong, J., & Ying, Z. (2021). Privacy and security issues in deep learning: A survey. *IEEE Access*, 4566–4593. https://doi.org/10.1109/ACCESS.2020.3045078

Lu, J., Issaranon, T., & Forsyth, D. (2017). SafetyNet: Detecting and rejecting adversarial examples robustly. *arXiv*. Obtenido de https://arxiv.org/abs/1704.00103

Lu, J., Liu, A., Dong, F., Gu, F., Gama, J., & Zhang, G. (2019). Learning under concept drift: A review. In *EEE transactions on knowledge and data engineering* (pp. 2346–2363). https://doi.org/10.1109/TKDE.2018.2876857

Mehrabi, N., Morstatter, F., Saxena, N., Lerman, K., & Galstyan, A. (2021). A survey on bias and fairness in machine learning. *ACM Computing Surveys (CSUR)*, 1–35. https://doi.org/10.1145/3457607

OpenAI. (24 de February de 2017). *Attacking machine learning with adversarial examples*. Obtenido de Attacking machine learning with adversarial examples: https://openai.com/index/attacking-machine-learning-with-adversarial-examples/

Oseni, A., Moustafa, N., Janicke, H., Liu, P., Tari, Z., & Vasilakos, A. (2021). Security and privacy for artificial intelligence: Opportunities and challenges. *arXiv preprint* arXiv:2102.04661.

Shokri, R., Stronati, A. M., Song, A. C., & Shmatikov, A. V. (2017). Membership inference attacks against machine learning models. *arXiv*. Obtenido de https://arxiv.org/abs/1610.05820

Soykan, E. U., Karaçay, L., Karakoç, F., & Tomur, E. (2022). A survey and guideline on privacy enhancing technologies for collaborative machine learning. *IEEE Access*, 97495–97519. https://doi.org/10.1109/ACCESS.2022.3204037

Szegedy, C., Zaremba, A. W., Sutskever, A. I., Bruna, A. J., Erhan, A. D., Goodfellow, A. I., & Fergus, A. R. (2014). Intriguing properties of neural networks. *arXiv preprint* arXiv:1312.6199. Obtenido de https://arxiv.org/abs/1312.6199

Zhang, Y., Rando, J., Ivan Evtimov, Chi, J., Smith, E. M., Carlini, N., … Ippolito, D. (2024). Persistent pre-training poisoning of LLMs. *arXiv preprint* arXiv:2410.13722.

Zhou, S., Liu, A. C., Ye, A. D., Zhu, A. T., Zhou, A. W., & Yu, A. P. (2022). Adversarial attacks and defenses in deep learning: From a perspective of cybersecurity. *ACM Computing Surveys*, 1–39. https://doi.org/10.1145/3547330

Chapter 9
Defense Methods for Adversarial Attacks and Privacy Issues in Secure AI

9.1 Introduction

The rise of machine learning, particularly deep learning, has revolutionized numerous fields, ranging from computer vision to natural language processing. However, as these models become more integrated into real-world applications, they also face growing security concerns, particularly with the emergence of adversarial attacks. Adversarial attacks involve small, carefully crafted perturbations to input data that cause a model to make incorrect predictions or classifications, even though the changes are imperceptible to humans. This vulnerability poses significant challenges, especially in safety-critical systems such as autonomous vehicles, healthcare diagnostics, and security surveillance. The ability of these attacks to exploit the inherent weaknesses in machine learning models underscores the need for robust defense strategies to ensure the integrity and reliability of AI systems.

In response to the increasing threat of adversarial attacks, researchers have proposed various methods for defending machine learning models. These defenses aim to either detect and counteract adversarial inputs (reactive defenses) or fortify the models against potential attacks during training (proactive defenses). While adversarial defense mechanisms have shown promise, there remain several open challenges, including the identification of effective and generalizable strategies, as well as overcoming the trade-offs between defense complexity and model performance. This chapter explores the concept of model robustness, the techniques used to craft adversarial samples, and the defense mechanisms developed to mitigate these attacks. It also delves into the vulnerabilities of machine learning models, the challenges faced when applying adversarial defense methods, and the emerging strategies such as feature squeezing that seek to strengthen AI systems against adversarial threats.

D. P. Sharma et al., *Understanding AI in Cybersecurity and Secure AI*, Progress in IS, https://doi.org/10.1007/978-3-031-91524-6_9

9.2 Model Robustness and Defense Requirements

Ensuring the robustness of deep learning models against adversarial attacks is critical, especially in high-stakes domains such as healthcare, finance, and autonomous driving, where the model decisions impact safety and well-being. Adversarial robustness strengthens a model's ability to withstand maliciously crafted perturbations and unexpected data variations, ensuring it can perform reliably even when exposed to potentially deceptive inputs. This resilience is vital as small, often imperceptible changes in input data can lead models to make erroneous decisions, potentially resulting in significant harm in practical applications (Szegedy et al., 2014).

Robustness in deep learning is fundamentally about a model's capacity to maintain high performance across both benign and adversarial conditions. Adversarial robustness ensures that small, well-targeted changes to the input do not disproportionately impact the model's output, thus enabling it to sustain accuracy under challenging conditions (Madry et al., 2019). In addition to resisting adversarial perturbations, robust models should handle other forms of noise or variability that are common in real-world settings, such as varying lighting conditions, sensor noise, and slight alterations in object positioning (Justin Gilmer & Dahl, 2018). This broad definition of robustness encompasses both adversarial and environmental variations, requiring a sophisticated balance between sensitivity to relevant features and resistance to misleading inputs.

Developing robust DL models requires a multi-faceted approach. Techniques such as adversarial training, which involves exposing the model to adversarial examples during training, help models generalize better against attacks (Goodfellow et al., 2015). Other approaches include regularization methods that reduce sensitivity to specific input variations, making the model more stable and accurate under both normal and adversarial circumstances. Consequently, robustness has become a central focus in the deployment of DL models in safety-critical environments, highlighting the need for ongoing research into adaptive, efficient defense mechanisms. To design effective defenses against adversarial perturbations in deep neural networks, several critical requirements are identified to ensure robustness without compromising on the model's usability or performance (Papernot et al., 2016). To effectively defend against adversarial attacks and privacy threats in secure AI, models must meet several key robustness and defense requirements in four categories. Figure 9.1 shows the taxonomy of the methods that are used to achieve model robustness and defense requirements.

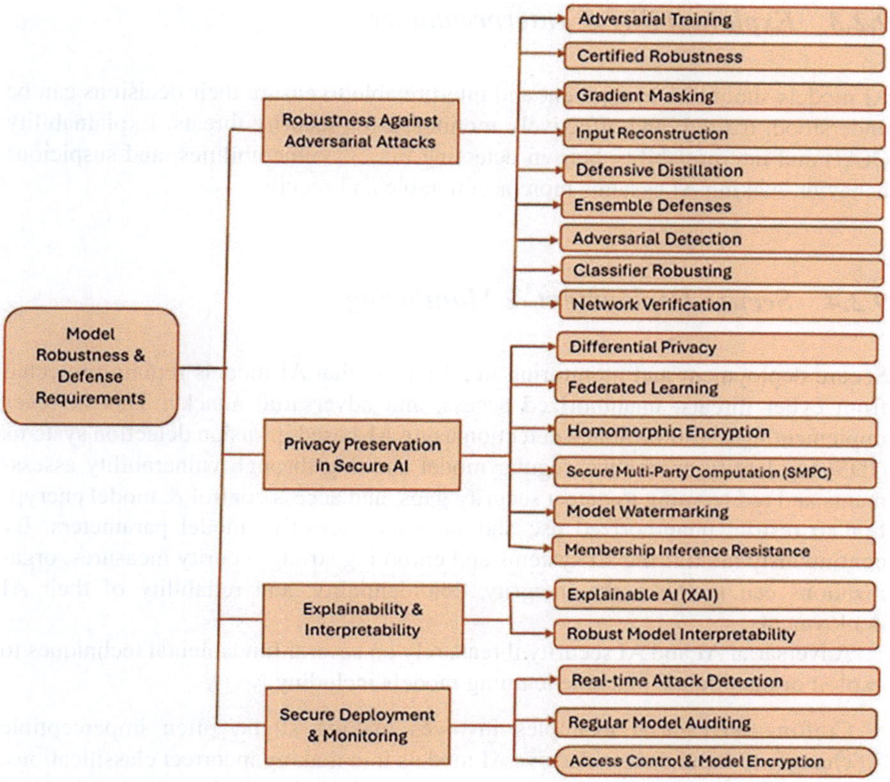

Fig. 9.1 Model robustness and adversarial defense requirements

9.2.1 Robustness Against Adversarial Attacks

Adversarial attacks aim to exploit vulnerabilities in AI models by introducing carefully crafted perturbations to inputs, leading to incorrect or misleading predictions. Ensuring robustness against such attacks requires implementing various defensive strategies, each targeting different aspects of the attack lifecycle.

9.2.2 Privacy Preservation in Secure AI

As AI models increasingly rely on vast amounts of user data, ensuring data security and privacy is essential to protect sensitive information from unauthorized access, attacks, and misuse. Several privacy-preserving techniques have been developed to mitigate risks, balancing the need for data-driven AI advancements with user privacy protection.

9.2.3 Explainability & Interpretability

AI models should be transparent and interpretable to ensure their decisions can be understood, trusted, and effectively monitored for security threats. Explainability (XAI) and interpretability help in detecting biases, vulnerabilities, and suspicious behavior, making AI systems more accountable and secure.

9.2.4 Secure Deployment & Monitoring

Secure deployment and monitoring in AI ensure that AI models remain protected from cyber threats, unauthorized access, and adversarial attacks. This involves implementing real-time attack detection using AI-based intrusion detection systems (IDS) to identify anomalies, regular model auditing through vulnerability assessments and red teaming to detect security gaps, and access control & model encryption to restrict unauthorized use and safeguard sensitive model parameters. By continuously monitoring AI systems and enforcing strong security measures, organizations can maintain the integrity, confidentiality, and reliability of their AI deployments.

Adversarial AI and AI security threats rely on several fundamental techniques to exploit or manipulate machine learning models including:

- Crafting adversarial examples involves making slight, often imperceptible changes to input data to deceive AI models into making incorrect classifications.
- Data poisoning corrupts training datasets by injecting misleading information, affecting model accuracy and decision-making.
- Model inversion reconstructs sensitive training data by analyzing AI model outputs, leading to privacy breaches.
- Model stealing (model extraction) enables attackers to replicate proprietary AI models by strategically querying them.
- Membership inference attacks determine whether specific data points were part of a model's training set, violating user privacy.
- AI-powered DDoS attacks use machine learning to optimize large-scale network disruptions by adapting attack patterns to avoid detection.
- AI-based social engineering leverages AI-generated phishing emails, deepfakes, or voice cloning to manipulate users. Automated vulnerability discovery uses AI to identify security flaws in software, enabling attackers to find zero-day vulnerabilities quickly.
- AI-assisted penetration testing automates security assessments, identifying weaknesses in networks and systems. Reinforcement learning attacks use self-learning AI models that continuously evolve attack strategies to evade security defenses.

These techniques pose serious threats to AI security and require advanced defense mechanisms to mitigate their impact. The next sub-section explains the first one as an example in detail.

9.3 Crafting Adversarial Samples

Adversarial examples reveal significant vulnerabilities in modern machine learning algorithms, demonstrating that even state-of-the-art models can be susceptible to carefully designed attacks. These weaknesses underscore how algorithms can deviate from their intended behavior when exposed to maliciously crafted inputs. Such incidents highlight critical gaps in model robustness, raising serious concerns about the reliability of AI systems in high-stakes domains, where unexpected errors could lead to severe consequences. To tackle these challenges, researchers are actively developing strategies to prevent or mitigate the impact of adversarial examples, striving to ensure that model behavior aligns more reliably with its intended design. (Goodfellow et al., 2015). Figure 9.2 illustrates the generation of an adversarial example applied to the ImageNet dataset. By adding a minimally perceptible perturbation vector to the input image, we can alter GoogLeNet's classification. This perturbation vector is computed by taking the sign of the gradient of the cost function.

$$J(\theta, \mathrm{x}, \mathrm{y}),$$

where,

θ: Parameters of the model.
x: Input image to the model.
y: Target labels associated with x (for supervised learning tasks). This cost function is used to optimize the model during training.

The perturbation magnitude, ϵ=0.007 corresponds to the smallest bit in an 8-bit image encoding after GoogLeNet converts the image to real-valued numbers. Adversarial perturbation is crafted to exploit the model's vulnerabilities, subtly modifying the input without altering its visual appearance to humans yet causing a significant change in the model's output.

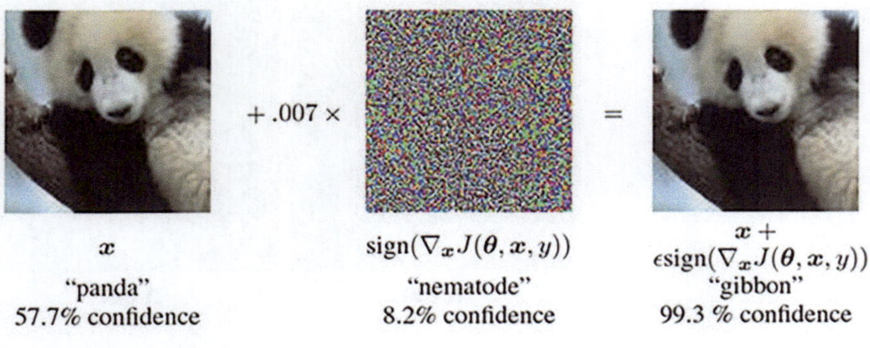

Fig. 9.2 Adversarial example

9.3.1 Adversarial Samples

Adversarial samples are inputs that have been carefully modified with minimal perturbations to deceive machine learning models, especially deep neural networks or AI models. These perturbations are designed to lead the model to produce incorrect outputs, such as misclassifications. Importantly, these perturbations are often small enough that the adversarial sample remains indistinguishable from legitimate, unaltered data to human observers (Papernot et al., 2016). The effectiveness of the adversarial attack lies in the adversary's ability to manipulate the input in a way that the model's output changes without making the sample noticeably different from humans.

Adversarial examples demonstrate how AI models can be fragile to slight changes in input, leading to unexpected behavior like misclassification. These attacks underscore the need for stronger defense mechanisms and more robust models that can withstand such subtle manipulations.

Figure 9.3 demonstrates misclassification with adversarial samples, where the left image is correctly classified by trained AI models as a car. The right image was crafted by an adversarial sample crafting algorithm from the correct left image. The altered image is incorrectly classified as a cat by the AI models.

9.3.2 Framework for Crafting Adversarial Samples

The framework for adversarial sample crafting described here aims to systematically address the process of generating adversarial examples by combining various existing methods. The adversary's objective is to modify as few features as possible while still causing the model to misclassify. The adversary can identify which input dimensions most impact the model's output and apply small, targeted perturbations to these areas. For this, the adversary estimates direction sensitivity. Figure 9.4

Fig. 9.3 Adversarial samples

shows a framework for crafting adversarial samples (Papernot et al., 2016). The crafting process involves two primary steps: (1) direction sensitivity estimation and (2) perturbation selection. Step (1) evaluates the sensitivity of model F at the input point corresponding to sample X. Step (2) uses this knowledge to select a perturbation affecting sample X's classification. If the resulting sample X + δX is misclassified by model F in the adversarial target class (here 4) instead of the original class (here 1), an adversarial sample X^* has been found. If not, the steps can be repeated on updated input X ← X + δX.

9.3.2.1 Direction Sensitivity Estimation

It is the first step of the adversarial crafting framework that focuses on understanding how sensitive the model is to changes in each input feature. In other words, the adversary needs to determine which parts of the input sample, X, are most influential in driving the classification output. This is typically done by analyzing the gradients of the model's output concerning the input features. Techniques such as the fast sign gradient method and the Jacobian matrix help estimate the sensitivity by measuring how the model's output changes when small perturbations are made to individual input features.

Gradient methods provide a direct way of estimating which features are most sensitive to changes, as the gradients will indicate which directions of change are most likely to influence the model's decision.

Alternatively, methods like local distribution smoothness estimate sensitivity by looking at the distribution of model outputs in the neighborhood of the input space and using statistical methods (e.g. Kullback-Leibler divergence) to model this sensitivity. In these methods an adversary uses these sensitivity measures to identify which input features will cause the most significant changes in the model's predictions when altered.

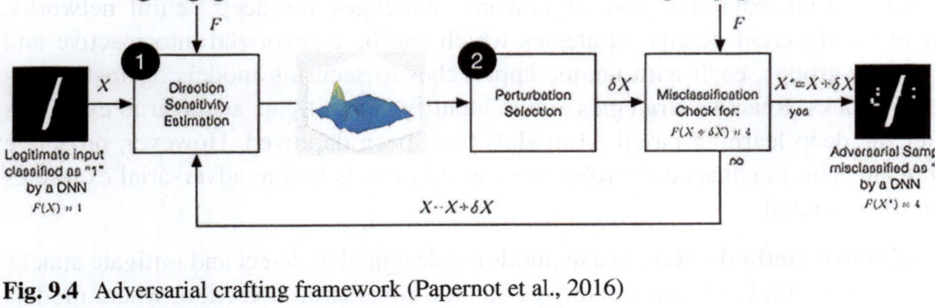

Fig. 9.4 Adversarial crafting framework (Papernot et al., 2016)

9.3.2.2 Perturbation Selection

This is the second step, where an adversary selects dimensions of the input (i.e., which features or pixels in an image, etc.) will be perturbed to generate an adversarial example. Its objective is to lead the misclassification with minimal change to the original input. This process uses the sensitivity information obtained from the first step to decide where and how much to perturb the input. Following two approaches that are primarily used for perturbation selection:

- **Euclidean perturbation:** This method applies a small perturbation along the gradient direction using the sign of each input dimension's gradient to determine the direction. In this method, Euclidean space between the original and adversarial examples is moved minimally so that the attack maximizes impact on the model's classification without visibly altering the input.
- **Saliency Maps**: A saliency map essentially represents the sensitivity of an AI model's output (specifically, the probability of a target class) with respect to changes in each pixel of an input image. Saliency maps help identify and perturb only the most influential input features, minimizing the number of altered dimensions. This approach leverages the model's sensitivity to focus changes on the most critical aspects of the input, achieving a balance between minimizing perturbation size and maximizing adversarial effectiveness.

9.4 Robust Against Adversarial Attacks

Adversarial defense methods have emerged as essential techniques to enhance the robustness of machine learning models against adversarial attacks. These attacks exploit model vulnerabilities by introducing minor, often imperceptible, perturbations to input data, causing significant misclassification and raising concerns about the reliability of machine learning in high-stakes applications such as cybersecurity, autonomous driving, and medical diagnostics. Consequently, the development of adversarial defense strategies aims to protect models from these threats by either identifying and rejecting adversarial inputs or making models inherently more resistant to adversarial perturbations (Goodfellow et al., 2015).

Adversarial examples pose significant challenges for deep neural networks. There are different defense strategies which can be categorized into reactive and proactive groups, each with unique approaches to securing models against adversarial attacks. Reactive strategies aim to identify and mitigate adversarial examples after the deep learning-based AI models have been deployed. However, proactive strategies aim to enhance the robustness of AI models before adversarial examples can be generated.

- **Reactive methods:** Reactive methods are designed to detect and mitigate attacks as they occur. Common techniques include adversarial detection, where models are equipped with mechanisms to identify potentially adversarial inputs; input

reconstruction, which attempts to correct or transform inputs before classification to reduce adversarial effects; and network verification, a method for validating the internal consistency of neural networks under adversarial conditions to ensure reliable outputs.
- **Proactive method:** Proactive methods focus on preemptively strengthening models to withstand adversarial attacks. These techniques include network distillation, where models are trained to produce smoother and more stable outputs, making them less susceptible to small perturbations; adversarial re-training, which involves repeatedly training the model on adversarial perturbed examples to improve robustness; and classifier robustification, a process that enhances the classifier's resilience by modifying its architecture or training procedure to better handle adversarial inputs.

9.4.1 Adversarial Training

Adversarial Training Methods are defense mechanisms designed to improve the robustness of deep neural networks against adversarial attacks by explicitly incorporating adversarial examples into the training process (Goodfellow et al., 2015). In this approach, adversarial examples are generated during training, often by perturbing the input data to maximize the model's prediction error. The model is then trained on these examples alongside clean data, forcing it to learn more robust decision boundaries that are less sensitive to small, malicious perturbations. Some of the key adversarial training methods are as follows:

- **Fast gradient sign method (FGSM)** (Goodfellow et al., 2015): It is a basic adversarial training method that improves the robustness of neural networks against adversarial examples. In this method, adversarial examples are generated by adding perturbations to the training data using the Fast Gradient Sign Method (FGSM), and these perturbed examples are then included in the training process. It trains the network on both the original and adversarially modified inputs that enable the model to learn more robust features that are less sensitive to adversarial changes.
- **Projected gradient descent (PGD) adversarial training** (Madry et al., 2019): It is a PGD-based adversarial training that involves using the Projected Gradient Descent algorithm to generate adversarial examples during training. Unlike FGSM, PGD iteratively applies perturbations to the input and projects them back into the allowed space. This iterative process is more effective in generating stronger adversarial examples, and training on them significantly improves the robustness of the model.
- **Virtual adversarial training (VAT)** (Miyato et al., 2019): It is a regularization method based on virtual adversarial loss that measures of local smoothness of the conditional label distribution of a given input. VAT has the advantage of not requiring access to the gradient of the loss function with respect to the input,

making it suitable for unsupervised learning settings as well. This method offers several advantages relative to other forms of regularization in machine learning:

- **Applicability to semi-supervised learning:** Unlike traditional adversarial training methods that require large amounts of labeled data, this approach is particularly useful in semi-supervised learning tasks. In semi-supervised learning, a model is trained on a small amount of labeled data while leveraging a larger amount of unlabeled data. The method can improve the model's generalization and robustness by generating adversarial examples from both labeled and unlabeled data, thus enhancing the model's performance even when labeled data is scarce.
- **Applicability to any parametric model:** The method can be applied to any parametric model (e.g., neural networks, support vector machines) for which the gradient with respect to the inputs and parameters can be evaluated. This flexibility is crucial as it enables the use of the technique across a wide range of model architectures, allowing practitioners to improve robustness without being tied to specific model types or architectures.
- **Minimal additional hyperparameters:** One of the significant advantages of this approach is that it introduces only two additional hyperparameters: epsilon (ε) and alpha (α). These hyperparameters control the magnitude of perturbations and the strength of the regularization, respectively. The small number of additional parameters makes the method more straightforward to tune compared to other regularization methods, which may require a large number of hyperparameters or complex tuning strategies.
- **Parameterization invariant regularization:** The method provides a parameterization invariant form of regularization, which means that its effectiveness does not depend on the specific parameter settings of the model. This is in contrast to other techniques, such as Lp normalization, which are highly sensitive to the model's parameterization. This invariant property allows the approach to be more robust and stable across different parameter initializations, making it more universally applicable and less prone to overfitting due to specific parameter choices.

9.4.2 Certified Robustness

Certified robustness methods provide mathematical guarantees that no adversarial example exists within a given perturbation range (Cohen et al., 2019). Unlike adversarial training, which aims to improve model robustness based on training data and observed adversarial examples, certified robustness provides provable assurance of a model's resistance to adversarial attacks. This ensures that the model will maintain its performance even under adversarial perturbations, offering a higher level of security by providing verifiable guarantees against potential attacks.

9.4.3 Gradient Masking

Gradient masking is a defense mechanism that reduces the usefulness of gradient-based attacks (e.g., FGSM, PGD) by making the model's gradients less informative for an adversary (Athalye et al., 2018). The main idea is to prevent attackers from computing effective adversarial perturbations. Gradient masking disrupts the gradient computation process to prevent adversarial attacks from effectively exploiting the gradients during backpropagation. It involves the use of non-differentiable components such as preprocessing techniques like quantization or randomized transformations, which hinder the calculation of gradients.

9.4.4 Input Reconstruction

Input Reconstruction is a defensive technique in adversarial machine learning aimed at mitigating adversarial perturbations by transforming or "purifying" inputs back to a form closely aligned with the original data distribution. By reconstructing inputs, this approach effectively removes adversarial noise before feeding the data into the classifier, preserving model performance on legitimate inputs. Input reconstruction methods often use autoencoders, denoising networks, or probabilistic models to achieve this effect, adapting input features to fit the patterns learned from non-adversarial training data. This process ensures that adversarially perturbed data is reshaped into a benign version, making it less likely to deceive the model. Importantly, input reconstruction works independently of the model architecture, meaning it can be applied to already deployed models, making it a flexible and valuable approach for strengthening model robustness across various domains. Two common input reconstruction methods are as follows:

- ***Deep Contractive Network*** (Shixiang Gu, 2015) is an innovative model designed to enhance robustness against adversarial examples through a novel end-to-end training procedure. This method introduces a smoothness penalty inspired by the Contractive Autoencoder (CAE), which stabilizes the network's response to small input perturbations. By penalizing the sensitivity of the model's learned representations to changes in the input, the smoothness constraint reduces vulnerability to adversarial attacks. Notably, this approach achieves increased robustness without significantly impacting performance, offering a practical and efficient defense mechanism for real-world AI systems.
- ***PixelDefend*** (Song et al., 2018) is an adversarial defense technique that reconstructs adversarially perturbed images by guiding them back toward the distribution of legitimate training data. It reconstructs adversarial images by aligning them back with the training data distribution using a PixelCNN model. It uses a generative model, specifically PixelCNN to evaluate and adjust each pixel in the input image, ensuring alignment with the data distribution. Unlike defenses that modify the classifier itself, PixelDefend operates independently of the model

architecture, making it compatible with any classifier without requiring retraining. The purified image (free of adversarial perturbations) is then passed to the original classifier for accurate prediction, enhancing robustness without altering the classifier.

9.4.5 Defensive Distillation Network

Network distillation is a method used to improve the robustness of machine learning models, particularly in defending against adversarial attacks. The core idea behind distillation is to transfer knowledge from a larger, more complex model (called the teacher) to a simpler model (the student). This process helps the student model generalize better, and it has been adapted to enhance the robustness of neural networks against adversarial perturbations.

In the context of adversarial defense, network distillation involves training a smaller, more efficient model on the soft targets (probabilities) produced by a larger, pre-trained model. The larger model is typically well-trained and exhibits good performance in terms of accuracy. However, adversarial example inputs are designed to deceive models and can cause the larger model to misclassify. The distillation process allows the smaller model to inherit the generalization ability of the larger model while making it less sensitive to adversarial examples (Papernot et al., 2016).

Figure 9.5 shows the overview of the defense mechanism based on a transfer of knowledge contained in probability vectors through distillation. It first trains an initial network F on data X with a softmax temperature of T. Then uses the probability vector *F(X)*, which includes additional knowledge about classes compared to a class label, predicted by network F to train a distilled network F^d at temperature T on the same data X (Papernot et al., 2016).

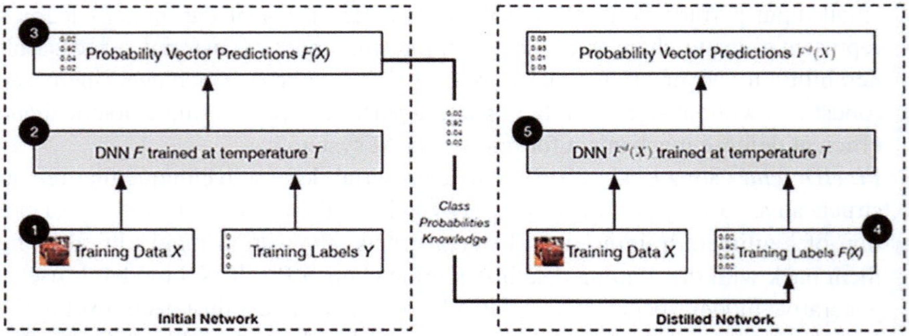

Fig. 9.5 Defense mechanism with network distillation (Papernot et al., 2016)

9.4.6 *Ensemble Defenses*

Ensemble-based defenses enhance robustness by combining multiple models, making it harder for adversarial perturbations to deceive all models at once. Ensemble methods aggregate predictions from different networks (Tramèr et al., 2020). Common ensemble-based adversarial defense methods are:

- **Model diversity:** in this method, models are trained with different architectures or use varying training methods.
- **Randomization:** It introduces randomness in model parameters, activations, or input transformations to challenge attackers.
- **Input transformation**: This method applies techniques like JPEG compression, gaussian noise, or feature transformations before classification.
- **Decision fusion**: This method combines outputs from multiple models using methods like majority voting or averaging.

9.4.7 *Adversarial Detection*

Adversarial detection is a defensive strategy aimed at identifying adversarial examples during the testing phase of deep neural networks. These methods work by analyzing input data to detect anomalies or patterns indicative of adversarial perturbations. Detection approaches typically rely on monitoring model behavior, leveraging statistical properties, or training auxiliary models to differentiate between normal and adversarial inputs.

SafetyNet (Lu et al., 2017) is an adversarial detection method that is designed to strengthen the defense of conventional deep learning classifiers such as VGG19 and ResNet by introducing a specialized adversarial detection mechanism. Figure 9.5 shows a defensive architecture for image classification systems designed to identify and reject adversarial inputs by incorporating two main components:

- **Original classifier:** This component is a standard deep learning model, such as VGG19 or ResNet, responsible for performing the primary task of image classification. The classifier processes the input image and generates class predictions based on learned patterns.
- **Adversary detector:** This component operates as a protective layer, analyzing the internal state of the classifier's later layers to identify abnormal patterns indicative of adversarial manipulation. Specifically, it uses an RBF-SVM (Radial Basis Function Support Vector Machine) that classifies discrete codes derived from the activations in late-stage ReLU layers. These codes serve as signatures, capturing high-level features that help distinguish between normal and adversarial inputs.

As shown in Fig. 9.6, the adversary detector leverages these discrete codes to detect adversarial attacks with high reliability. It mainly ensures the detection of

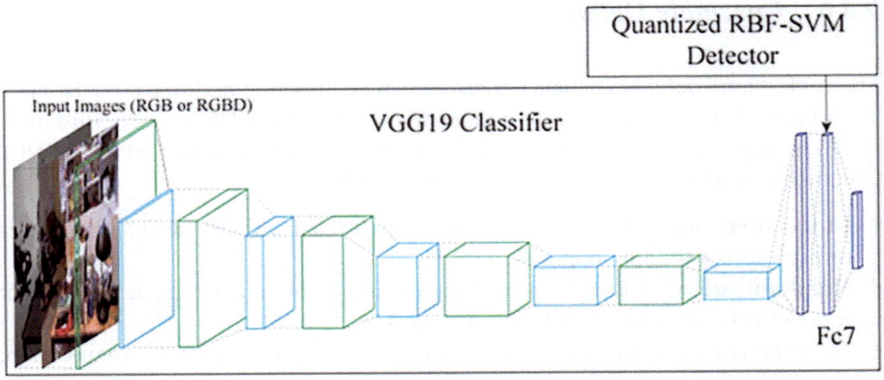

Fig. 9.6 The adversary detector architecture in SafeNet (Lu et al., 2017)

adversarial attacks and resistance to evasive attacks. SafetyNet accurately identifies adversarial examples, even if they were created by methods not represented in the training data. This capability is essential for adapting to new and evolving attack techniques. It also makes it challenging for attackers to generate examples that both mislead the classifier and bypass detection, as the discrete codes from the later layers provide a robust signature for the adversary detector to analyze.

9.4.8 Classifier Robustness

In the context of adversarial defense, classifier robustness refers to the ability of a machine learning model, specifically a classifier, to maintain its performance (accuracy and reliability) when exposed to adversarial perturbations that intentionally crafted inputs designed to mislead the classifier into making incorrect predictions. Various methods can be used to measure the robustness of the classifiers against adversarial attacks. One of the approaches is that classifiers can be divided into two parts linear and nonlinear optimized it to obtain a better attack starting point and analysis. (Yang et al., 2022).

9.4.9 Network Verification

Network Verification is a methodology used to rigorously test and ensure the robustness of neural networks against adversarial attacks. Its goal is to mathematically confirm that the network's predictions remain consistent and accurate under minor, adversarially crafted perturbations to the inputs. It analyzes the network's behavior over a defined input space and validates that specific properties such as output consistency or classification boundaries are maintained, ensuring reduced vulnerability to adversarial manipulations. Two common network verification-based methods are described as follows:

- ***Reluplex*** (Katz et al., 2017) involves formal verification techniques using mathematical proofs or constraint-solving methods to validate the network's robustness. It was designed to handle the verification of neural networks with ReLU activations. Some of the other frameworks leverage abstract interpretation and SMT (satisfiability modulo theories) solvers to evaluate possible vulnerabilities within a network. These methods enable developers to assess whether a network is likely to be misled by adversarial examples, especially in critical applications like autonomous driving or cybersecurity, where model robustness is essential.
- ***DeepSafe*** (Gopinath et al., 2017) is a framework designed to identify and define safe regions in a deep neural network using the Reluplex solver. These safe regions correspond to input spaces where the network's predictions remain stable and robust, even under adversarial perturbations. A key feature of DeepSafe is its introduction of targeted robustness, which ensures that safe regions are specifically defined for inputs associated with a particular target class. This targeted approach focuses on guaranteeing consistent behavior for selected classes, making the model more reliable in safety-critical applications. DeepSafe is generally suitable for evaluating the robustness of deep neural networks rather than focusing on individual input points. It uses a data-guided approach to identify "safe regions" within the input space, allowing for the analysis and verification of the network's behavior across these regions. This method involves the following steps:
  - **Clustering:** A new clustering algorithm partitions the input domain into regions where points are likely to have the same true label.
  - **Verification:** These regions are then checked for robustness using a verification tool to assess targeted robustness, ensuring that no input within a region is misclassified as a specific incorrect label.
  - **Safety Check:** For each region, the verification tool either confirms the network is safe or identifies an adversarial example if unsafe.
  - **Complete Safety:** A region is considered completely safe if all points within it are mapped to the correct label and no points are misclassified.

9.5 Privacy-Preserving Methods in AI

AI systems including modern deep learning-based models are data-driven and vulnerable to privacy risks during data collection and the distribution of pre-trained models. Numerous efforts have been made to develop AI systems that safeguard data privacy. Figure 9.7 shows the key privacy-preserving methods in AI. These AI privacy methods aim to protect sensitive data used by AI systems and ensure compliance with privacy regulations. The key privacy-preserving methods in AI applications are as follows as follows:

- Data anonymization
- Homomorphic encryption
- Federated Learning
- Secure multi-party computation
- Differential privacy

This section explores various privacy-preserving techniques employed in AI to safeguard data and models throughout the AI lifecycle, from data collection to model inference.

9.5.1 Data Anonymization

Data anonymization (DA) is a fundamental technique in data privacy and security that transforms identifiable data into a form where individuals cannot easily be traced back (Rocher et al., 2019). This process is crucial in ensuring that sensitive information remains confidential, even when shared for analysis or research purposes. Anonymization obscures or replaces identifiable elements (e.g., names, social security numbers, postal codes, etc.) with pseudonyms, tokens, or other indirect identifiers that effectively protect individuals' privacy while retaining the data's value for insights and research. Despite its effectiveness, anonymization methods must consider the risk of re-identification that occurs when anonymized data is cross-referenced with external data sources that can potentially reveal the individual behind the anonymized record (Narayanan & Shmatikov, 2008).

For example, in healthcare, patient identifiers might be replaced with random codes to enable analysis of health trends without exposing personal data. This balance between data utility and privacy protection is vital in fields like healthcare, finance, and marketing, where large datasets are frequently used but must comply with strict privacy laws such as GDPR (General Data Protection Regulation) (GDRP,

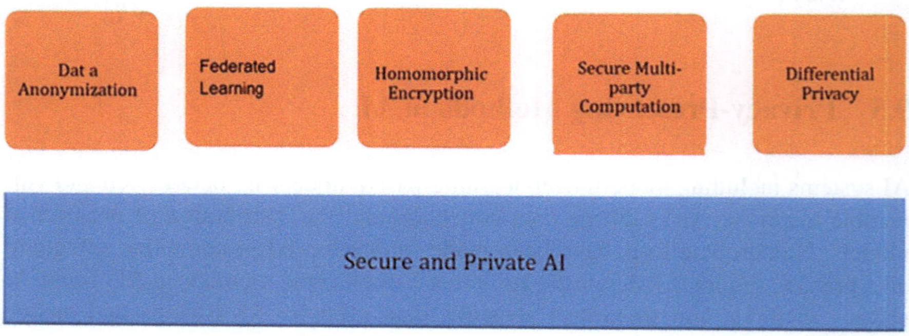

Fig. 9.7 Privacy-Preserving Methods in AI

2024)or HIPAA (Health Insurance Portability and Accountability Act) (HIPPA, 2023). The key data anonymization techniques are as follows.

- **Pseudonymization**: It is a method that replaces personal identifiers with pseudonyms or random identifiers retaining the ability to re-identify individuals if needed. For example, replacing patient names with codes (e.g., Patient001, Patient002) in medical datasets allows the use of patient data for model training without exposing sensitive identifiers.
- **k-Anonymity:** It is a data anonymization method that ensures that any individual in a dataset cannot be distinguished from at least k other individuals whose records are also included. This approach helps protect individual privacy by making it difficult to re-identify individuals based on their attributes.
- **Generalization:** It involves aggregating or grouping specific data points to achieve a higher level of anonymity. For example, instead of using exact birth dates, age ranges (e.g., 20–30) or broader geographic categories (e.g., regions instead of specific addresses) can be used. This technique complicates the identification of specific individuals and reduces the risk of privacy breaches.
- **Noise addition:** It is a method that involves introducing random noise into datasets to prevent re-identification of individuals. This technique can be applied to various types of data, including numeric values, textual data, and images, thereby enhancing privacy protection.
- **Data masking:** This method obfuscates or removes sensitive attributes from a dataset to protect privacy. For instance, sensitive information such as social security numbers, phone numbers, or email addresses can be removed or replaced with placeholder values. Data masking ensures that confidential information remains concealed, thereby minimizing the risk of privacy violations.

9.5.2 Homomorphic Encryption

Homomorphic encryption (HE) allows computations on encrypted data without decrypting it (Gentry, 2009). This ensures that even if the data is processed by an external or untrusted party preserves privacy. With homomorphic encryption sensitive data is encrypted before being sent to the AI system where the system performs the necessary computations on the encrypted data and the results can be decrypted only by the data owner. This enables privacy-preserving machine learning mechanisms with AI applications. For example, in the context of a healthcare system, homomorphic encryption can allow AI models to analyze encrypted patient data for diagnosis without exposing the raw medical records to the AI provider.

An encryption scheme is homomorphic for the operation '*' if, without access to the secret key, the following holds:

$$Enc(x_1) * Enc(x_2) = Enc(x_1{}^* x_2)$$

Where *Enc(·)*denotes the encryption function. Homomorphic encryption can protect user data from third-party servers or gradients aggregated among information silos.

Privacy-preserving deep learning using homomorphic encryption (HE) is an innovative and promising research area focused on creating deep learning solutions that ensure user data privacy. Developing these privacy-preserving solutions necessitates a thorough rethinking and redesign of existing deep learning models and algorithms to align with the significant technological and algorithmic constraints imposed by HE (Falcetta & Roveri, 2022). We discussed the following two homomorphic encryption-based AI models:

- **Crypto-Nets** (Xie et al., 2014): It is a neural network-based privacy-preserving model that ensures privacy by incorporating homomorphic encryption. In this model, the data owner encrypts sensitive information before sharing it with a third party. The third party who is hosting the model performs computations directly on the encrypted data and returns the prediction in encrypted form. Both the original data and the prediction remain hidden from the third party ensuring full data confidentiality.
- **UniHENN** (Choi et al., 2024): It is a privacy-preserving convolutional neural network (CNN)-based model that uses homomorphic encryption. Figure 9.8 shows the architecture of the UniHENN model. It is designed to work with model-agnostic input ciphertexts. It uses the CKKS HE schemes (Cheon et al., 2020) to encrypt input data, enabling seamless integration with any convolutional neural network (CNN) models without the need for the im2col function, which typically requires a specific input shape. This flexibility allows encrypted input data to be used across multiple homomorphic encryption-based machine learning services without requiring re-encryption. Figure 9.8 provides a high-level overview of UniHENN's operational flow. The process begins with a client encrypting one or more images using a public key. These encrypted images are bundled into a single ciphertext and transmitted to a cloud service that specializes in data analytics. Each service (Service 1, Service 2, ..., Service K) utilizes its own CNN model to process the encrypted data, performing specific computations and algorithms on the ciphertext using an evaluation key. Each CNN model is distinct, with its layer architecture and optimized parameters. Once the ciphertext is processed through the CNN models, the encrypted inference results are sent back to the client. The client then decrypts the results using the corresponding secret key, revealing the processed outcomes from each model. This approach enables the client to leverage multiple CNN models while ensuring data confidentiality, marking a significant advancement in privacy-preserving machine learning.

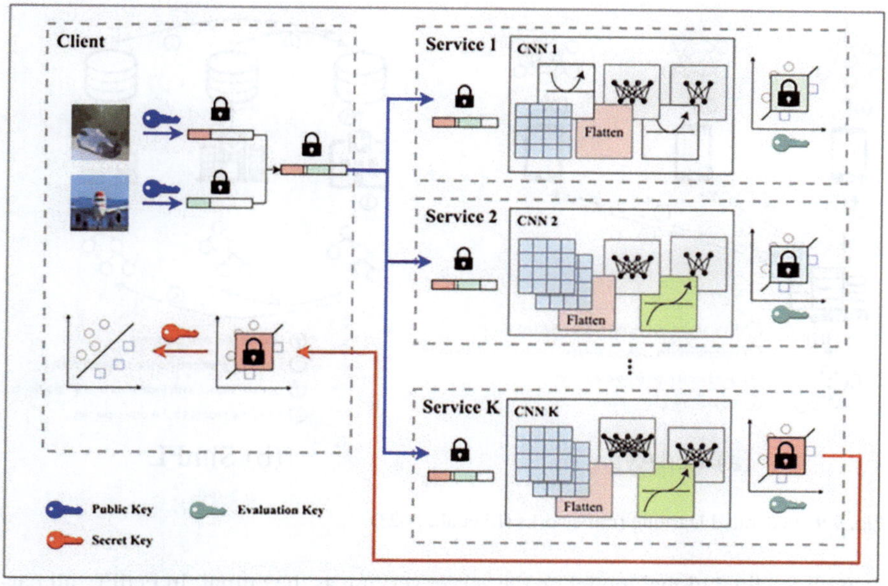

Fig. 9.8 Architecture of the UniHENN model (Choi et al., 2024)

9.5.3 *Federated Learning*

Federated learning enables multiple parties to jointly train a machine learning model without exchanging the local data (Li et al., 2023). Federated learning allows AI models to be trained locally on user devices while only sharing aggregated updates instead of raw data. This reduces the risk of data exposure since user information remains decentralized and never leaves the local device. It is particularly useful for applications such as personalized AI assistants and mobile predictive text.

9.5.3.1 Federated Learning Concept

In a federated learning system, multiple parties collaboratively train machine learning models without exchanging their raw data. The output of the system is a machine-learning model for each party. Figure 9.9 shows two common two computational frameworks in FL, which are briefly described as follows:

- **Federated Averaging (FedAvg):** This is a centralized federated learning framework where the server initially distributes the current global model to a group of selected participants. Each participant updates the global model using their local data. Once updated, the participants send their local models back to the server. The server then aggregates these local models by averaging them to produce an updated global model. This process is repeated for a set number of iterations,

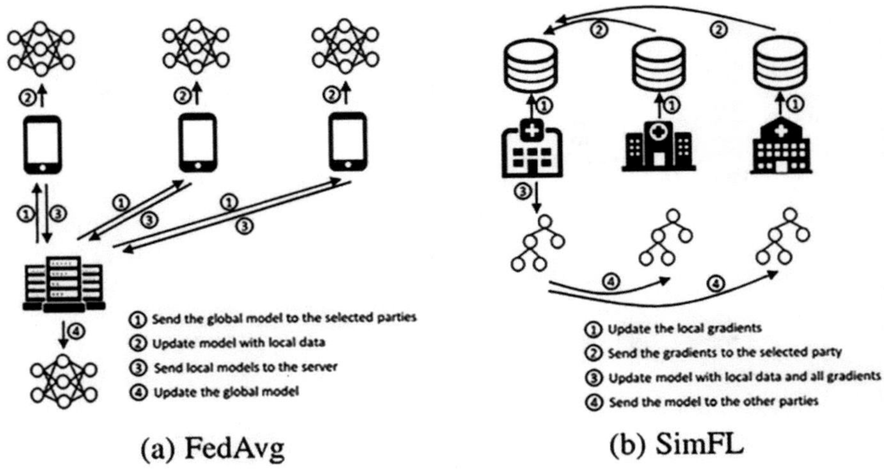

Fig. 9.9 Federated learning frameworks (Li et al., 2023)

with the final global model on the server serving as the output. In FedFL, all parties contribute equally, which may be seen as fair but can disadvantage parties with more representative data.

- **Similarity-based Federated Learning (SimFL):** It enables the training of models in a horizontally federated setting. SimFL is an FL framework designed to enhance model training by leveraging similarities between local data distributions of participating parties. In each iteration, participants first compute gradients based on their local data. These gradients are then sent to a selected party, which uses both its local data and the received gradients to update its model. This updated model is then shared with all other participants. To ensure fairness and data utilization across participants, each one is chosen approximately the same number of times to update the model. This process repeats for a specified number of iterations, with the final model being the output. This adaptive weighting improves the overall model performance by prioritizing contributions from parties with closely related data, while still maintaining data privacy. SimFL ensures that parties with similar data contribute more to each other's models, potentially improving individual performance while balancing overall fairness by reducing the impact of dissimilar data.

9.5.3.2 Secured Federated Learning

A key requirement for federated learning is to protect user privacy. The FL framework ensures that raw data is not shared, shared model parameters. However, parameters could reveal sensitive information about the training data. In such cases, differential privacy, and secure multi-party computation can be used to add random noise to the parameters. In addition, trusted execution environments can be used to execute the code securely (Chen et al., 2020).

Federated learning introduces unique privacy challenges, where multiple parties collaboratively train a model without sharing their private data. In this setting, it's crucial to ensure that privacy-preserving methods not only offer strong privacy guarantees but also remain computationally efficient, reduce communication overhead, and handle issues like dropped devices, all while maintaining model accuracy. Figure 9.10 provides an illustration of different privacy-enhancing mechanisms in one round of federated learning considering (a) Federated learning without additional privacy protection mechanisms, (b) global privacy, and (c) local privacy, where the central server may be malicious. M denotes a randomized mechanism used to privatize the data (Li et al., 2020b).

Secure Aggregation

A secure aggregation protocol designed to protect individual model updates from the central server, where the server cannot access any participant's local updates but can still compute the exact aggregated model at each training round (Bonawitz et al., 2017). While secure aggregation provides strong privacy guarantees without sacrificing model accuracy, it comes with the trade-off of significantly higher communication overhead.

Secure aggregation and differential privacy techniques are prominent approaches to improve privacy in federated learning, each comes with trade-offs in terms of communication costs, privacy strength, and model accuracy. The choice of method depends on the specific privacy requirements and constraints of the federated learning system.

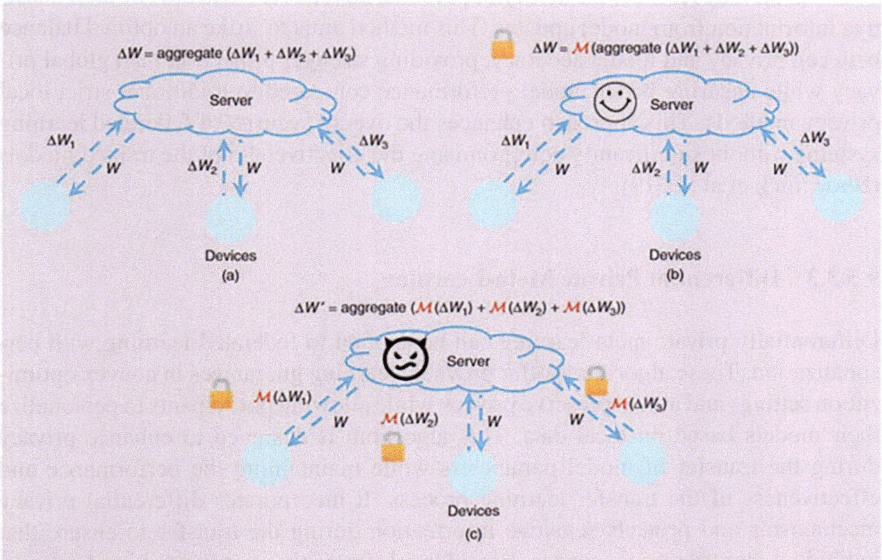

Fig. 9.10 Privacy-enhancing mechanisms in federated learning. (**a**) without additional privacy, (**b**) with global privacy, and (**c**) with local privacy (Li et al., 2020b)

Global Privacy

This approach ensures that the model updates exchanged during each training round are private to all untrusted third parties, including any external adversaries or participants, except the central server. The central server is trusted, and only it has access to the local model updates. Global privacy focuses on preventing leakage to other parties or attackers who might intercept communication between the server and participants. Figure 9.10b shows how global privacy is implemented in FL (Li et al., 2020b).

Differential privacy is another popular technique applied to federated learning to ensure global privacy. These methods add noise to the model updates before sending them to the central server ensuring that the server and external parties cannot reverse-engineer private data from the updates. However, global differential privacy introduces hyperparameters such as noise level and clipping thresholds that must be carefully tuned to balance communication costs, privacy guarantees, and model accuracy (McMahan et al., 2017).

Local Privacy

Local privacy goes a step further by ensuring that the model updates are private even to the central server itself. In this case, participants do not fully trust the server and want to ensure that their local updates remain confidential. Techniques like differential privacy are often applied to obfuscate the local updates before they are sent to the server, making it impossible for the server to infer specific details about a participant's data. Figure 9.10c shows how local privacy is implemented in FL (Li et al., 2020b).

Local privacy restricts the ability of potential adversaries to access or infer sensitive information from model updates. This method aims to strike an optimal balance between privacy and model accuracy, providing stronger protection than global privacy while ensuring better model performance compared to traditional strict local privacy methods. This approach enhances the overall security of federated learning systems without significantly compromising the effectiveness of the trained models (Bhowmick et al., 2019).

9.5.3.3 Differential Private Meta-Learning

Differentially private meta-learning can be applied to federated learning with personalization. These algorithms offer provable learning guarantees in convex optimization settings and aim to preserve privacy while allowing participants to personalize their models based on local data. This algorithm is designed to enhance privacy during the transfer of model parameters while maintaining the performance and effectiveness of the transfer learning process. It incorporates differential privacy mechanisms and protects sensitive information during the transfer to ensure that individual contributions cannot be inferred from the aggregated updates (Li et al., 2020a).

The federated learning environment demands that privacy-preserving algorithms be computationally light and efficient in communication to minimize delays and resource usage, while also being resilient to device failures or dropped updates during the training process.

9.5.4 Secure Multi-Party Computation

Secure Multi-Party Computation (SMPC) is a cryptographic technique that enables multiple parties to jointly compute a function over their inputs while keeping those input data private. MPC ensures data privacy, where inputs of all parties remain private, and no unauthorized party gains access to others' data. Garbled circuits and secret sharing are two common MPC techniques used in secure computations.

MPC is useful in AI applications when protecting data privacy is crucial. AI models often rely on large datasets that may contain sensitive or proprietary information. With the MPC mechanism, multiple parties (e.g., companies or institutions) can collaborate on AI tasks, such as training or inference without sharing their private data. In AI model training, data privacy is critical, particularly in sectors like healthcare, finance, and industries dealing with personal information. MPC enables different organizations to collaboratively train models on pooled data while keeping raw data private. For instance, hospitals can use MPC to jointly train a machine-learning model on patient data without exposing individual records.

9.5.4.1 Garbled Circuits-Based Models

In this method, one party creates an encrypted version of a computation, and another party evaluates the encrypted version without learning the underlying data. Garbled circuits-based models are a robust solution for maintaining privacy in AI, especially in collaborative settings where data sensitivity is paramount. These models allow multiple parties to perform computations without revealing their private inputs, making them invaluable for applications in sectors like healthcare, finance, and any field involving sensitive information. The garbled circuits are expected to play an increasingly important role in enabling secure, privacy-aware AI applications across various domains. There are numerous works based on garbled circuits, two common frameworks are as follows:

- **SecureML** (Mohassel & Zhang, 2017): It is a garbled circuit SMPC-based framework that allows two parties to train a neural network using their combined data ensuring that neither of the parties can access the other's private data directly. It used the garbled circuit to privately compute an activation function for training neural networks in a two-party setting.

- **DeepSecure** (Rouhani et al., 2018)**:** It is a scalable and provably secure Deep Learning (DL) framework that uses garbled circuit (GC) protocol in its secure DL computation.

9.5.4.2 Secret Sharing-Based Models

In the secret sharing method, each party splits their input into multiple shares and distributes them to other participants. A computation is performed on these shares, and the result is reconstructed without revealing individual inputs. MPC protocols based on secret sharing are highly efficient in multi-party settings, and many recent schemes have leveraged this approach to enhance machine learning privacy. There are numerous works based on secret sharing SMPC, two common frameworks are as follows:

- **Secure Differentially Private Stochastic Gradient Descent (DPSGD)** (Ruan et al., 2023): PSGD algorithm in secret sharing-based secure multi-party computation-based machine learning frameworks designed to defend against the membership inference attacks on machine learning models. DPSGD algorithm protects models trained with SMPC in the multi-party setting. This approach maintains data privacy in a multi-party environment.
- **SecureRC** (GRU) (Gao & Yu, 2023): It is a privacy-preserving relation classification system that uses secure multi-party computation. SecureRC uses additive secret sharing to design three privacy-preserving basic protocols for the non-linear functions (sigmoid and tanh). Three protocols such as SecureSigmoid, SecureTanh1 and SecureTanh2 privately compute the sigmoid and tanh functions and used them for privacy-preserving relation classification with an attention-based gated recurrent unit network.

9.5.5 Differential Privacy

Differential privacy (DP) is a privacy-preserving mechanism that ensures that the output of an AI or ML model does not reveal sensitive information about any individual in the dataset (Dwork & Roth, 2014). It adds a "noise" to the dataset or the query results which ensures that even if a query is run multiple times, or in combination with other datasets, it won't reveal sensitive details about any sensitive data and it will have a minimal impact on the outcome with plausible deniability. This method protects individuals' privacy while still allowing analysts or machine learning algorithms to extract meaningful insights from the overall dataset.

Differential privacy algorithms prevent an attacker from discovering the existence of a particular record by adding noise to the query responses, as follows (Bae et al., 2021):

$$M(D) = f(D) + n,$$

where *M*: *D* → *R* is a noise n sampled from a Laplace or Gaussian distribution to the query response, *D* is the target dataset, and *f* is the original deterministic query response. *M* provides *(ε, δ)* differential privacy if all adjacent *D* and *D′* satisfy the following:

$$\Pr[M(D) \in S] \le \exp(\varepsilon)\Pr[M(D') \in S] + \delta,$$

where *D* and *D′* are two adjacent databases, *S* ⊆ *range(M)* is a subset of *R*, and ε and δ are the privacy **budget parameters** that determine the level of privacy. Smaller **ε** and **δ** indicate that *M(D)* and *M(D′)* are more similar.

Differential privacy relies on a parameter called epsilon (ε), which defines the level of privacy. A smaller epsilon offers stronger privacy, while a larger epsilon provides more accurate results. The right value depends on the balance between the privacy requirements and the need for accuracy. A machine learning model trained with differential privacy can make predictions based on a dataset without allowing any individual data point to be distinguished from the aggregate. The main goal is to prevent adversaries from deducing any specific user's data, even if they have access to the model's outputs. Differential privacy can be incorporated into data collection to improve user experiences without compromising individual privacy.

Depending on where the noise is introduced, differential privacy approaches can be classified into three categories: gradient perturbation, objective perturbation, and label perturbation (Liu et al., 2021). Figure 9.11 shows an overview of these approaches. Each of these methods applies noise at different stages of the learning process, impacting the model's privacy guarantees and performance in unique ways. Here's a brief overview of each category.

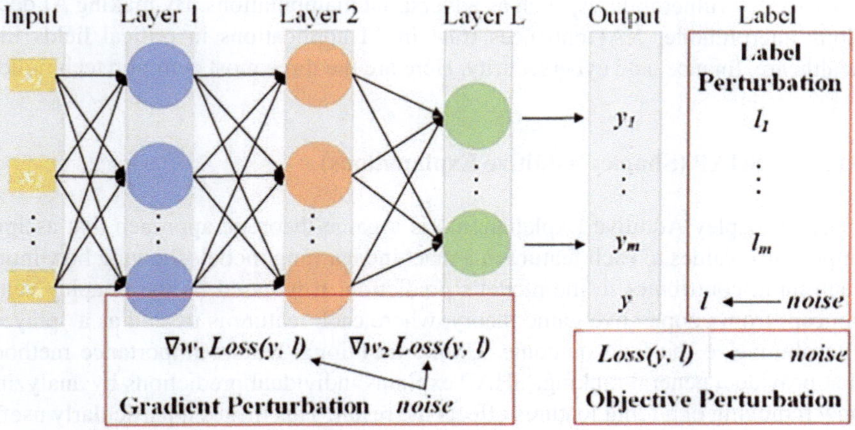

Fig. 9.11 Differential privacy categories in a deep learning model (Liu et al., 2021)

- **Gradient-level perturbation:** In this method, noise is added to the gradients of the parameters during the training phase.
- **Objective-level perturbation:** In this method, noise is introduced to perturb the coefficients of the original objective function.
- **Label-level perturbation:** In this method, noise is incorporated into the labels during the knowledge-transfer phase of the teacher-student mechanism.

Despite successful applications of DP in safeguarding training data, achieving good utility with differentially private machine learning (DP-ML) techniques can be challenging (Ponomareva et al., 2023). Inherent trade-offs between privacy and computational efficiency may constrain a model's effectiveness. DP-based ML models often necessitate careful architectural design and hyperparameter tuning.

9.6 Explainability & Interpretability

AI models should be transparent and interpretable to ensure their decisions can be understood, trusted, and effectively monitored for security threats. Explainability (XAI) and interpretability help in detecting biases, vulnerabilities, and suspicious behavior, making AI systems more accountable and secure.

9.6.1 Explainable AI (XAI)

Explainable AI (XAI) techniques, such as SHAP and LIME, help users understand how AI models arrive at their decisions by highlighting which features contributed most to a prediction. These methods improve transparency, detect biases, and identify security vulnerabilities, such as adversarial manipulations. By making AI decisions interpretable, XAI enhances trust in AI applications in critical fields like healthcare, finance, and cybersecurity. Here are the three most common techniques:

9.6.1.1 SHAP (Shapley Additive Explanations)

SHAP (Shapley Additive Explanations) is a game-theoretic approach that assigns importance values to each feature in a machine learning model, showing how much each input contributes to the model's prediction. It is based on the Shapley value concept from cooperative game theory, where each feature is treated as a "player" contributing to the final outcome. Unlike traditional feature importance methods that provide a general ranking, SHAP explains individual predictions by analyzing how removing or adding features affects the result. This makes it particularly useful in interpretable AI, ensuring transparency and trust in model decisions.

In cybersecurity, SHAP plays a crucial role in explaining the predictions of machine learning models used for intrusion detection, malware classification, and threat detection. For example, in a network intrusion detection system (NIDS), a model might classify network traffic as benign or malicious based on features such as packet size, connection duration, protocol type, and anomaly scores. While a traditional model may simply label a traffic instance as an attack, SHAP can break down the decision by showing which features contributed most to classifying it as malicious.

For instance, if a machine learning model predicts that a network packet is an attack with 98% confidence, SHAP can explain this by attributing +40% to unusually high traffic volume, +35% to an unknown protocol type, and +23% to frequent failed login attempts. This insight helps security analysts understand attack patterns, validate alerts, and fine-tune detection rules. Additionally, SHAP can help in malware detection, where it can explain why a given file was flagged as malicious—perhaps due to unexpected system API calls, obfuscated code patterns, or suspicious network connections. By providing clear, interpretable explanations, SHAP enhances cyber threat intelligence and response strategies, making AI-driven security systems more reliable and transparent.

9.6.1.2 LIME (Local Interpretable Model-Agnostic Explanations)

Generates locally interpretable models that approximate black-box AI decisions by perturbing input data and observing output changes. It is a technique that helps interpret black-box AI models by creating locally interpretable approximations of their decisions. Instead of analyzing the entire model, LIME perturbs (slightly modifies) the input data and observes how the predictions change. By doing so, it identifies which features most influence the model's decision in a specific instance, making complex AI-driven security models more transparent and understandable.

In cybersecurity, LIME is particularly valuable in intrusion detection, phishing email classification, and malware detection, where AI models often make automated decisions that security analysts need to trust and verify. For example, in a phishing detection system, an AI model may classify an email as malicious, but without explanation, it is difficult to understand why. LIME can generate a locally interpretable explanation by highlighting key features that contributed to the decision—such as the presence of suspicious URLs, an urgent tone in the email body, or mismatched sender domains. This enables analysts to validate the AI's reasoning and refine detection strategies.

Similarly, in malware classification, a deep learning model might detect a file as malware but provide no insight into its reasoning. LIME can analyze which specific byte sequences, API calls, or obfuscation techniques led to the classification. For instance, if a sample is flagged as ransomware, LIME might show that frequent file encryption requests, abnormal registry modifications, and unauthorized access attempts were key factors in the decision. By providing these granular insights, LIME helps security teams audit AI-driven detections, improve model accuracy, and enhance threat mitigation strategies.

9.6.1.3 Feature Attribution Methods

Techniques like Grad-CAM (for deep learning models) highlight important regions in input data (e.g., in images or text) that influenced the AI's decision. It helps explain AI model decisions by identifying which parts of the input contributed most to the final prediction. One powerful technique, Grad-CAM (Gradient-weighted Class Activation Mapping), is widely used in deep learning models to highlight important regions in input data, such as images or text, that influenced the model's decision. Originally designed for image classification, Grad-CAM can also be adapted for cybersecurity applications, particularly in malware analysis, anomaly detection, and phishing email classification.

For example, in malware detection using deep learning, an AI model may analyze an executable's binary representation or memory dump and classify it as malicious. However, without explanation, security analysts cannot see which patterns or structures led to that decision. Using Grad-CAM, we can visualize which sections of the binary file, API calls, or opcode sequences were most influential, providing a heatmap-style visualization of malware characteristics. If the highlighted areas correspond to known obfuscation techniques or suspicious execution patterns, analysts can validate and refine detection rules accordingly.

Similarly, in phishing email detection, a deep learning model may process raw email text and classify it as a phishing attempt. Feature attribution methods like Grad-CAM can highlight specific words, phrases, or links that triggered the classification—such as urgent call-to-action phrases, fake login URLs, or spoofed sender addresses. This insight helps cybersecurity teams understand AI-driven email filtering decisions, reduce false positives, and improve phishing prevention strategies.

9.6.2 Robust Model Interpretability

Robust Model Interpretability ensures that AI models make stable and reliable decisions, even when faced with small variations or adversarial manipulations in input data. In cybersecurity, where threat detection, fraud prevention, and AI-driven security systems operate in high-risk environments, maintaining interpretability is critical to prevent false positives, adversarial exploitation, and unpredictable behavior. Techniques such as feature attribution, saliency maps, and consistency testing help in analyzing how AI models respond to changes, ensuring that minor input modifications do not drastically alter predictions.

For example, in fraud detection systems, AI models analyze transaction details to identify suspicious activity. If a fraud detection model misclassifies a legitimate transaction as fraudulent simply due to a minor variation in purchase location or amount, it can cause unnecessary disruptions. Saliency maps and feature attribution methods can help explain which transaction attributes influenced the decision, enabling financial institutions to refine fraud detection models for consistency and accuracy.

In adversarial attack defense, robust interpretability plays a vital role in protecting AI-driven security models from evasion tactics. Attackers can slightly modify network traffic patterns or malware signatures to fool AI models into misclassification. Consistency testing techniques evaluate whether small perturbations cause unexpected model behavior, ensuring that security models remain resilient against adversarial input manipulations. For example, if a malware detection system misclassifies a slightly altered malware sample as benign, it indicates vulnerability to adversarial attacks. Using adversarial training, model calibration, and robustness testing, security teams can strengthen AI defenses and improve decision-making reliability. There are different techniques in this group including:

- **Saliency maps**: Highlight critical input features that drive predictions, preventing adversarial misdirection. They play a crucial role in securing AI models by providing transparency, robustness, and adversarial defense in machine learning-driven cybersecurity systems. One of the key benefits is their ability to highlight critical input features that influence a model's decision, allowing security teams to identify vulnerabilities and refine models for stronger threat detection. In adversarial settings, where attackers attempt to manipulate AI models by making subtle changes to input data, saliency maps serve as an early warning system by exposing which features are most susceptible to exploitation.
- **Consistency testing**: Evaluates whether small input modifications lead to consistent, interpretable outcomes. It is a crucial technique for securing AI models by ensuring that small modifications in input data do not cause unexpected or inconsistent predictions. In cybersecurity, AI-driven systems must maintain stability when detecting threats, even when adversaries attempt subtle evasion tactics. This method evaluates whether an AI model produces consistent and interpretable outcomes under minor perturbations, ensuring its reliability in high-stakes applications like intrusion detection, malware classification, and fraud detection.
- **Adversarial training**: It is a defense mechanism designed to enhance the robustness and security of AI models by training them with adversarial examples—intentionally modified inputs crafted to deceive the model. This approach improves a model's ability to resist adversarial attacks, ensuring stable, reliable, and secure decision-making, particularly in high-risk domains such as cybersecurity, fraud detection, and AI-driven intrusion detection systems.
- **Certified robustness techniques**: They are formal methods that provide mathematical guarantees on an AI model's resilience against adversarial attacks and input perturbations. Unlike empirical defenses, which rely on adversarial training and heuristic methods, certified robustness techniques mathematically verify that small changes in input will not cause misclassification or unexpected model behavior. This is particularly crucial in security-critical AI applications such as cybersecurity, fraud detection, biometric authentication, and AI-driven malware analysis where adversarial manipulation can have severe consequences.

9.7 Secure Deployment & Monitoring

Secure deployment and monitoring in AI ensure that AI models remain protected from cyber threats, unauthorized access, and adversarial attacks. This involves implementing real-time attack detection using AI-based intrusion detection systems (IDS) to identify anomalies, regular model auditing through vulnerability assessments and red teaming to detect security gaps, and access control & model encryption to restrict unauthorized use and safeguard sensitive model parameters. By continuously monitoring AI systems and enforcing strong security measures, organizations can maintain the integrity, confidentiality, and reliability of their AI deployments.

- **Real-time attack detection**: AI-based intrusion detection systems (IDS) continuously monitor model behavior and network activity to detect anomalies or potential security threats. These systems leverage machine learning to identify patterns of adversarial attacks, unauthorized data access, or model manipulation in real time. By providing immediate alerts and automated responses, real-time detection helps mitigate risks before significant damage occurs.
- **Regular model auditing**: Periodic security assessments, including vulnerability scans, penetration testing, and red teaming exercises, help identify weaknesses in AI models and deployment environments. These audits assess model robustness against adversarial attacks, privacy threats, and compliance with security standards. Regular auditing ensures continuous improvement in security practices, reducing risks of exploitation and maintaining trust in AI systems.
- **Access control and model encryption**: Strong access control mechanisms limit who can interact with AI models, APIs, and datasets, preventing unauthorized users from exploiting system vulnerabilities. Encryption techniques, such as homomorphic encryption and secure key management, protect sensitive model parameters and stored data from tampering or extraction. By restricting access and securing model infrastructure, organizations can prevent data leaks, adversarial manipulation, and intellectual property theft.

9.8 Challenges Applying Adversarial Defense Methods in Classification

The challenges associated with applying current defense methodologies to image classification deep learning (DL) models in image classification specifically for Autonomous Driving Systems (ADS) are multifaceted, as these systems are safety-critical and must operate reliably in dynamic and unpredictable environments (Badjie et al., 2024). Figure 9.12 shows the common challenges of applying adversarial defense methods, which are discussed as follows:

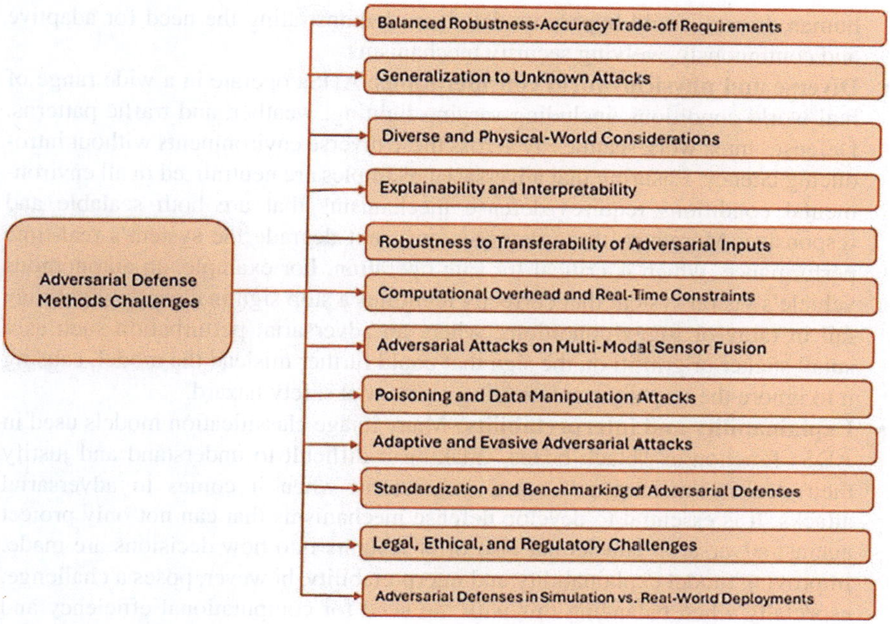

Fig. 9.12 Challenges for applying adversarial methods

- **Balanced robustness-accuracy trade-off requirements**: Many of the most effective defense strategies for adversarial attacks involve a trade-off between enhancing the model's robustness and maintaining its accuracy on legitimate inputs. The key challenge is to achieve an optimal balance where the model is robust against adversarial attacks and maintains high performance under normal driving conditions. Any decrease in accuracy could lead to unsafe driving situations, which is unacceptable in ADS applications. For example, an autonomous vehicle's object detection model could be hardened against adversarial attacks by applying strong adversarial training, but this might also cause it to misclassify distant pedestrians or road signs in normal conditions, leading to unnecessary emergency braking or missed stop signs, creating potential safety risks.
- **Generalization to unknown attacks**: Current defense techniques are typically developed to protect against known adversarial attack patterns. However, new methods are continuously evolving, and attackers are adept at finding ways to bypass state-of-the-art defenses. There is a need for dynamic defense systems that can adapt and effectively defend against unforeseen and evolving adversarial attacks. The constant innovation in adversarial attack strategies presents a significant challenge for ensuring that defenses remain effective. For example, An autonomous vehicle trained to detect adversarial attacks on traffic signs may successfully counter known perturbations like pixel noise or sticker-based attacks, but a new attack method using infrared light projections, undetectable to

human drivers, could bypass its defenses, demonstrating the need for adaptive and continuously evolving security mechanisms.

- **Diverse and physical-world considerations**: ADSs operate in a wide range of real-world conditions, including varying lighting, weather, and traffic patterns. Defenses must work seamlessly across these diverse environments without introducing latency. Ensuring that adversarial examples are neutralized in all environmental conditions requires defense mechanisms that are both scalable and responsive. Moreover, these defenses must not degrade the system's real-time performance, which is critical for safe operation. For example, an autonomous vehicle's vision system that correctly identifies a stop sign in clear daylight may fail in rainy or foggy conditions, where an adversarial perturbation such as a small sticker or graffiti on the sign that could further mislead the model, causing it to ignore the stop sign and creating a potential safety hazard.
- **Explainability and interpretability:** Many image classification models used in ADSs function as "black boxes," making it difficult to understand and justify their decision-making processes, particularly when it comes to adversarial attacks. It is essential to develop defense mechanisms that can not only protect against adversarial attacks but also offer insights into how decisions are made. Improving model explainability and interpretability, however, poses a challenge, especially when balancing this with the need for computational efficiency and robustness. For example, if an autonomous vehicle suddenly misclassifies a pedestrian as part of the background, an explainability method like Grad-CAM can highlight which image regions influenced the decision, helping engineers determine whether the error was caused by an adversarial attack, poor lighting conditions, or model bias.
- **Robustness to transferability of adversarial inputs:** Adversarial attacks can be transferable, meaning that an attack designed for one model or dataset can be effective on another model or in a different environment (e.g., transferring from simulation to real-world deployment). Defenses must be capable of handling transferability, protecting the system from adversarial inputs that might succeed across different models and datasets. This becomes particularly challenging when transitioning from digital simulations to physical-world applications, where the nature of adversarial attacks may change. For example, an adversarial perturbation crafted to mislead a traffic sign recognition model in a simulation (e.g., causing a stop sign to be misclassified as a speed limit sign) may still be effective when physically printed and placed on a real-world road sign, posing a serious risk to autonomous driving systems.
- **Computational overhead and real-time constraints:** Many adversarial defense techniques, such as adversarial training, certified defenses, and input denoising, require significant computational resources, which could increase inference time and slow down decision-making. Balancing real-time performance with robust security remains a major challenge, as excessive delays in threat mitigation could result in unsafe driving decisions. For example, Autonomous vehicles require low-latency processing to make split-second driving decisions.
- **Adversarial attacks on multi-modal sensor fusion:** Attackers can generate multi-modal adversarial perturbations that simultaneously affect multiple inputs

(e.g., camera-based object detection and LiDAR point cloud manipulation). Most current adversarial defenses focus only on a single modality, making them ineffective against coordinated multi-modal attacks. Defense mechanisms must ensure robustness across all sensor inputs, not just vision-based classification. For example, Modern ADSs rely not only on image classification (camera data) but also on LiDAR, radar, ultrasonic sensors, and GPS.

- **Poisoning and data manipulation attacks:** Many adversarial defense methods focus on inference-time attacks, but training-time attacks (data poisoning) are an increasing concern in ADSs. Attackers can manipulate training datasets by injecting maliciously crafted data points that degrade model performance or introduce backdoors that can be triggered later. Ensuring dataset integrity and adversarial robustness during training is crucial but remains a major challenge, especially as ADSs rely on large-scale, continuously updated datasets collected from diverse sources.
- **Adaptive and evasive adversarial attacks:** Attackers are continuously developing adaptive strategies to bypass defenses. Many adversarial defenses are static, meaning they protect against specific attack types but fail against adaptive attacks that evolve over time. For example, if an ADS is hardened against FGSM attacks, an attacker may use iterative gradient-based attacks or query-based black-box techniques to evade detection. Defense mechanisms must be dynamic and continuously updated to detect new attack strategies in real time, which is particularly difficult for ADSs operating in uncontrolled environments.
- **Standardization and benchmarking of adversarial defenses:** There is no universal standard for evaluating adversarial defense effectiveness in ADSs. While benchmarks like RobustBench exist for general adversarial robustness in computer vision, real-world ADS benchmarks are lacking. Current defenses are often evaluated on simplified datasets (e.g., ImageNet, COCO) but may not generalize to real-world driving datasets (e.g., KITTI, Waymo Open Dataset). Without standardized adversarial testing environments, it is challenging to measure the true effectiveness of defense strategies under real-world attack scenarios.
- **Legal, ethical, and regulatory challenges:** Defending ADSs against adversarial attacks is not just a technical challenge but also a legal and regulatory issue. If an autonomous vehicle fails due to an adversarial attack, it raises questions about liability, responsibility, and safety compliance. Furthermore, ethically balancing security with transparency is difficult—while defensive AI models need to be explainable, full transparency may expose vulnerabilities to potential attackers. The lack of clear regulations on adversarial robustness testing in ADSs makes it difficult for manufacturers to comply with safety standards while maintaining security.
- **Adversarial defenses in simulation vs. real-world deployments:** Many adversarial defenses are tested in controlled simulation environments, but their effectiveness in the real-world physical domain is often unverified. Attackers can exploit physical perturbations such as, Placing stickers on road signs to fool image classifiers (physical adversarial attacks) or Altering LiDAR reflectivity using specialized materials to hide obstacles from detection.

9.9 Summary

This chapter provides a comprehensive overview of adversarial defense methods and the necessary defenses for AI and ML models. It begins by highlighting the significance of model robustness and the need for effective defense mechanisms to counter adversarial attacks. The introduction and discussion on crafting adversarial samples emphasize how malicious inputs can exploit vulnerabilities in neural networks, leading to incorrect predictions. The framework for crafting adversarial samples offers a deep dive into the techniques and strategies that attackers can use to deceive models, which underscores the urgency for implementing strong defensive mechanisms and privacy-preserving methods.

Furthermore, this chapter delves into two primary types of defense methods: reactive and proactive. Reactive methods respond to attacks post-factum, while proactive methods aim to prevent adversarial samples from affecting the model's behavior in the first place. The chapter also covers the challenges of applying adversarial defense methods, especially in computer vision including autonomous driving. After reading this chapter, you should be able to answer the following questions:

- What is the concept of adversarial perturbations, and how do they impact the performance of AI models?
- Why is model robustness critical for AI and ML systems, and how do adversarial attacks threaten it?
- What are the key methods for crafting adversarial samples, and how do they exploit vulnerabilities in neural networks?
- How does the framework for crafting adversarial samples inform the development of effective defense mechanisms?
- How can understanding adversarial sample crafting help in strengthening defenses and improving AI system security?
- What is the difference between reactive and proactive defense methods in adversarial defense?
- How do reactive methods address adversarial attacks, and what are their limitations?
- What proactive strategies can be used to prevent adversarial samples from affecting AI models?
- What are the challenges involved in applying adversarial defense methods, particularly in fields like computer vision and autonomous driving?
- What roles do adversarial training and other defensive techniques play in enhancing model robustness?
- Why is it important to consider both the effectiveness and practicality of defense methods in real-world applications?
- What are the advantages of homomorphic encryption in AI security?
- How does secure multi-party computation work to protect data privacy?
- What role does differential privacy play in safeguarding AI systems?
- What is federated learning, and how does it enhance data security?
- How does secure federated learning ensure privacy during collaborative training?

- What are the differences between global privacy and local privacy in federated learning?
- What are the methods for AI explainability and interpretability? Explain.
- How does the AI model deploy securely? Explain secure deployment methods.

References

Athalye, A., Carlini, N., & Wagner, D. (2018). Obfuscated gradients give a false sense of security: Circumventing defenses to adversarial examples. In *International conference on machine learning* (pp. 274–283). PMLR.

Badjie, B., Cecílio, J., & Casimiro, A. (2024). Adversarial attacks and countermeasures on image classification-based deep learning models in autonomous driving systems: A systematic review. *ACM Computing Surveys*. https://doi.org/10.1145/3691625

Bae, H., Jang, J., Jung, D., Jang, Hyemi, Heonseok, H., … Yoon, S. (2021). Security and privacy issues in deep learning. *arXiv*. Obtenido de https://arxiv.org/abs/1807.11655

Bhowmick, A., Duchi, J., Freudiger, J., Kapoor, G., & Rogers, R. (2019). Protection against reconstruction and its applications in private federated learning. *arXiv*. Obtenido de https://arxiv.org/abs/1812.00984

Bonawitz, K., Ivanov, V., Kreuter, B., Marcedone, A., McMahan, H. B., Patel, S., et al. (2017). Practical secure aggregation for privacy-preserving machine learning. In *CCS '17: Proceedings of the 2017 ACM SIGSAC conference on computer and communications security* (pp. 1175–1191). ACM. https://doi.org/10.1145/3133956.313398

Chen, Y., Luo, F., Li, T., Xiang, T., Liu, Z., & a, a. J. (2020). A training-integrity privacy-preserving federated learning scheme with trusted execution environment. *Information Sciences*, 69–79. https://doi.org/10.1016/j.ins.2020.02.037

Cheon, J. H., Hong, S., & Kim, D. (2020). Remark on the security of ckks scheme in practice. *Cryptology ePrint Archive*. Obtenido de https://eprint.iacr.org/2020/1581.

Choi, H., Kim, J., Kim, S., Park, S., Park, J., & Choi, W. (2024). UniHENN: Designing faster and more versatile homomorphic encryption-based CNNs without im2col. *IEEE Access*, 109323–109341. https://doi.org/10.1109/ACCESS.2024.3438996

Cohen, J. M., Rosenfeld, E., & Kolter, J. Z. (2019). Certified adversarial robustness via randomized smoothing. In *International conference on machine learning* (pp. 1310–1320).

Dwork, C., & Roth, A. A. (2014). The algorithmic foundations of differential privacy. In *Foundations and Trends® in theoretical computer science* (pp. 211–407).

Falcetta, A., & Roveri, A. M. (2022). Privacy-preserving deep learning with homomorphic encryption: An introduction. *IEEE Computational Intelligence Magazine*, 14–25. https://doi.org/10.1109/MCI.2022.3180883

Gao, C., & Yu, J. (2023). SecureRC: A system for privacy-preserving relation classification using secure multi-party computation. *Computers & Security*. https://doi.org/10.1016/j.cose.2023.103142

GDRP. (2024). *General Data Protection Regulation (GDPR)*. Recuperado el 2 de April de 2024, de GENERAL DATA PROTECTION REGULATION (GDPR): https://gdpr-info.eu/

Gentry, C. (2009). Fully homomorphic encryption using ideal lattices. In *Proceedings of the forty-first annual ACM symposium on theory of computing* (pp. 169–178). Association for Computing Machinery. https://doi.org/10.1145/1536414.1536440

Goodfellow, I. J., Shlens, A. J., & Szegedy, A. C. (2015). *Explaining and harnessing adversarial examples*. Obtenido de https://arxiv.org/abs/1412.6572

Gopinath, D., Katz, G., Pasareanu, C. S., & Barrett, C. (2017). *DeepSafe: A data-driven approach for checking adversarial robustness in neural networks*. Obtenido de https://arxiv.org/abs/1710.00486.

HIPPA. (23 de 12 de 2023). *Health Information Privacy*. Obtenido de U.S. Department of Health and Human Services (HHS): https://www.hhs.gov/hipaa/index.html

Justin Gilmer, R. P., & Dahl, G. E. (2018). Motivating the rules of the game for adversarial example research. *arXiv*. Obtenido de https://arxiv.org/abs/1807.06732

Katz, G., Barrett, C., Dill, D., Julian, K., & Kochenderfer, M. (2017). Reluplex: An efficient SMT solver for verifying deep neural networks. *arXiv*. Obtenido de https://arxiv.org/abs/1702.01135

Li, J., Khodak, M., Caldas, S., & Talwalkar, A. (2020a). Differentially private meta-learning. *arXiv*. https://arxiv.org/abs/1909.05830

Li, T., Sahu, A. K., Talwalkar, A., & Smith, V. (2020b). Federated learning: Challenges, methods, and future directions. *IEEE Signal Processing Magazine*, 50–60. https://doi.org/10.1109/MSP.2020.2975749

Li, Q., Wen, Z., Wu, Z., Hu, S., Wang, N., & Li, Y. (2023). A survey on federated learning systems: Vision, hype and reality for data privacy and protection. *IEEE Transactions on Knowledge and Data Engineering*, 3347–3366. https://doi.org/10.1109/TKDE.2021.3124599

Liu, X., Xie, L., Wang, Y., Zou, J., Xiong, J., & Ying, Z. (2021). Privacy and security issues in deep learning: A survey. *IEEE Access*, 4566–4593. https://doi.org/10.1109/ACCESS.2020.3045078

Lu, J., Issaranon, T., & Forsyth, D. (2017). SafetyNet: Detecting and rejecting adversarial examples robustly. *arXiv*. Obtenido de https://arxiv.org/abs/1704.00103

Madry, A., Makelov, A., Schmidt, L., Tsipras, D., & Vladu, A. (2019). Towards deep learning models resistant to adversarial attacks. *arXiv*. Obtenido de https://arxiv.org/abs/1706.06083

McMahan, H. B., Ramage, A. D., Talwar, A. K., & Zhang, A. L. (2017). Learning differentially private recurrent language models. *arXiv preprint* arXiv:1710.06963. Obtenido de https://arxiv.org/abs/1710.06963

Miyato, T., Maeda, S.-I., Koyama, M., & Ishii, S. (2019). Virtual adversarial training: A regularization method for supervised and semi-supervised learning. *IEEE Transactions on Pattern Analysis and Machine Intelligence*, 1979–1993. https://doi.org/10.1109/TPAMI.2018.2858821

Mohassel, P., & Zhang, Y. (2017). SecureML: A system for scalable privacy-preserving machine learning. In *2017 IEEE symposium on security and privacy (SP)* (pp. 19–38). IEEE. https://doi.org/10.1109/SP.2017.12

Narayanan, A., & Shmatikov, A. V. (2008). Robust De-anonymization of large sparse datasets. In *2008 IEEE symposium on security and privacy (sp 2008)* (pp. 111–125). IEEE. https://doi.org/10.1109/SP.2008.33

Papernot, N., McDaniel, P., Wu, X., Jha, S., & Swami, A. (2016). Distillation as a Defense to adversarial perturbations against deep neural networks. In *2016 IEEE symposium on security and privacy (SP)* (pp. 582–597). IEEE. https://doi.org/10.1109/SP.2016.41

Ponomareva, N., Hazimeh, H., Kurakin, A., Xu, Z., Denison, C., McMahan, H. B., et al. (2023). How to DP-fy ML: A practical guide to machine learning with differential privacy. *Journal of Artificial Intelligence Research*, 1113–1201. https://doi.org/10.1613/jair.1.14649

Rocher, L., et al. (2019). Estimating the success of re-identifications in incomplete datasets using generative models. *Nature Communications*. https://doi.org/10.1038/s41467-019-10933-3

Rouhani, B. D., Riazi, M. S., & Koushanfar, F. (2018). DeepSecure: Scalable provably-secure deep learning. In *2018 55th ACM/ESDA/IEEE design automation conference (DAC)* (pp. 1–6). IEEE. https://doi.org/10.1109/DAC.2018.8465894

Ruan, W., Xu, M., Fang, W., Wang, L., Wang, L., & Han, W. (2023). Private, efficient, and accurate: Protecting models trained by multi-party learning with differential privacy. In *2023 IEEE symposium on security and privacy (SP)* (pp. 1926–1943). IEEE. https://doi.org/10.1109/SP46215.2023.10179422

Shixiang Gu, L. R. (2015). Towards deep neural network architectures robust to adversarial examples. *arXiv*. Obtenido de https://arxiv.org/abs/1412.5068

Song, Y., Kim, T., Nowozin, S., Ermon, S., & Kushman, N. (2018). PixelDefend: Leveraging generative models to understand and defend against adversarial examples. *arXiv*. Obtenido de https://arxiv.org/abs/1710.10766

Szegedy, C., Zaremba, A. W., Sutskever, A. I., Bruna, A. J., Erhan, A. D., Goodfellow, A. I., & Fergus, A. R. (2014). Intriguing properties of neural networks. *arXiv preprint* arXiv:1312.6199. Obtenido de https://arxiv.org/abs/1312.6199

Tramèr, F., Kurakin, A., Papernot, N., Goodfellow, I., Boneh, D., & McDaniel, P. (2020). Ensemble adversarial training: Attacks and defenses. *arXiv*. Retrieved from https://arxiv.org/abs/1705.07204

Xie, P., Bilenko, M., Finley, A. T., Gilad-Bachrach, A. R., Lauter, A. K., & Naehrig, A. M. (2014). Crypto-nets: Neural networks over encrypted data. *CoRR*. Obtenido de http://arxiv.org/abs/1412.6181

Yang, Y., Sun, L., Dai, L., Guo, S., Mao, X., Wang, X., & Xu, B. (2022). Rethinking classifier and adversarial attack. *arXiv*. Obtenido de https://arxiv.org/abs/2205.02743

Chapter 10
General Framework for AI Security and Privacy

10.1 Introduction

As artificial intelligence (AI) continues to be adopted across various industries, ensuring the security and privacy of AI systems has become an urgent and complex concern. The lifecycle of an AI system, from data collection to deployment, presents unique security threats at each phase. These threats range from data breaches during the data collection phase to model extraction attacks during system integration. To address these risks, robust defense strategies are required at every stage of the AI lifecycle. This chapter explores the various phases of the AI lifecycle, highlighting key security challenges such as data integrity, model privacy, and the potential for adversarial attacks. A detailed examination of defenses such as differential privacy, homomorphic encryption, and model watermarking will also be discussed to provide a comprehensive understanding of how to protect AI systems throughout their lifecycle.

In addition to lifecycle-specific threats and defenses, this chapter also covers prominent frameworks that provide guidelines for managing AI security risks. One such framework is the NIST AI Risk Management Framework, developed by the National Institute of Standards and Technology (NIST, 2023). This framework offers a structured approach to identifying, assessing, and mitigating AI risks, with an emphasis on building secure and trustworthy AI systems. By aligning AI development and deployment with this framework, organizations can ensure that their systems adhere to best practices in risk management, making them more resilient to security breaches and vulnerabilities.

Furthermore, the chapter delves into Google's Secure AI Framework (Google, 2024), which focuses on providing a set of tools and practices to enhance the security of AI applications. Google's approach emphasizes secure software development, system monitoring, and continual risk assessment to ensure that AI models remain secure and trustworthy. Lastly, the chapter reviews various global standards

D. P. Sharma et al., *Understanding AI in Cybersecurity and Secure AI*, Progress in IS, https://doi.org/10.1007/978-3-031-91524-6_10

and regulations that govern AI security and privacy, such as the ISO/IEC AI Security Standards (ISO/IEC, 2024a, b), ETSI SAI (ETSI, 2024), the EU AI Act (EU, 2024b), and the OECD principles (OECD, 2024). These regulations provide a vital legal and ethical framework for organizations developing AI technologies, ensuring that AI systems are designed and deployed responsibly with privacy and security as top priorities. Together, these frameworks and guidelines play a crucial role in shaping the secure and ethical future of AI.

10.2 AI Lifecycle Stages with Their Security Threats and Defenses

AI systems lifecycle encompasses five phases including data collection, data preprocessing, model training, inference, and integration. Each phase in AI-based systems is generally vulnerable to various security threats throughout the whole process, ranging from the initial data collection and preparation to the training, inference, and final deployment (Hu et al., 2021). Understanding these threats and implementing appropriate defenses is essential to ensuring the security, privacy, and safety of AI systems.

Figure 10.1 shows five AI lifecycle phases with their associated security threats and defense strategies. During the data collection phase, threats like sensor spoofing attacks compromise the integrity of input data, while the data preprocessing phase can fall victim to scaling attacks, which distort data transformation processes, impacting downstream model performance. The model training phase is particularly vulnerable to poisoning attacks where malicious actors inject adversarial

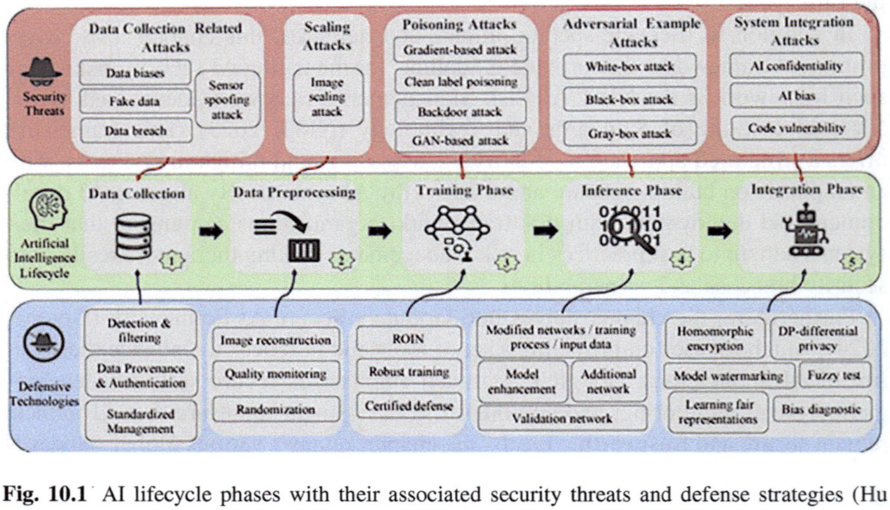

Fig. 10.1 AI lifecycle phases with their associated security threats and defense strategies (Hu et al., 2021)

samples into the training set to manipulate the model's behavior (Papernot et al., 2018). Similarly, the inference phase is prone to adversarial attacks wherein imperceptible perturbations to input data lead to incorrect model predictions (Goodfellow et al., 2015). Finally, the integration phase involves the deployment of AI models that pose confidentiality and system vulnerabilities.

A detailed examination of these lifecycle phases, highlighting associated threats and the state-of-the-art strategies designed to address them are described in the following sub-sections.

10.2.1 Data Collection Phase

The data collection phase forms the foundation of any AI/ML system, but it also introduces various security risks. It is crucial as it directly impacts the quality, reliability, and security of AI/ML models. Insecure or compromised data collection can introduce biases, errors, and vulnerabilities that propagate through the entire AI pipeline, leading to incorrect predictions or exploitable weaknesses. Attackers can manipulate this phase through data poisoning, injecting misleading or harmful data that degrades model performance or steers decision-making toward unintended outcomes. Ensuring secure data collection requires robust authentication, encryption, and validation mechanisms to verify the authenticity and integrity of the gathered data. Data can be collected through different methods:

- **Hardware-based collection:** This method involves physical sensors and devices. For example, sensors in autonomous vehicles or IoT devices collect real-time data. However, these systems are vulnerable to sensor spoofing attacks, where attackers tamper with sensor data or manipulate inputs. By exploiting vulnerabilities in the hardware or communication channels, attackers can inject malicious data or falsify sensor readings, leading to potentially catastrophic outcomes, such as misjudgments in navigation or compromised system decisions. Defending against these attacks requires hardware hardening, encrypted communication protocols, and anomaly detection mechanisms to ensure the integrity of sensor data. For example,in autonomous vehicles, LiDAR sensors are used to detect obstacles and navigate safely. In a sensor spoofing attack, researchers demonstrated that malicious laser signals could trick LiDAR sensors into detecting fake obstacles or failing to detect real ones. In 2020, cybersecurity researchers successfully spoofed Tesla's Autopilot system, making the vehicle swerve unnecessarily or fail to brake at stop signs. To mitigate such risks, manufacturers now implement sensor fusion techniques (combining multiple sensor inputs), encrypted communication protocols, and AI-based anomaly detection to filter out manipulated data.
- **Software-based collection:** This refers to digital data acquisition, such as web scraping, database queries, or API-based data extraction. Risks in this approach include data biases, where unrepresentative or skewed data can mislead models;

fake data, which attackers may introduce to manipulate outcomes; and data breaches, where sensitive data can be leaked due to inadequate security controls. Addressing these risks involves implementing advanced detection and filtering, robust data validation techniques, employing secure channels for data transfer, and maintaining strict access control policies. For example, in financial fraud detection, banks use API-based data extraction to collect real-time transaction data for AI models that detect fraudulent activities. However, attackers can exploit API vulnerabilities to inject fake transaction records, misleading the AI into misclassifying fraudulent activities as normal. In 2021, attackers used automated bots to scrape financial APIs, introducing false credit card transactions into machine learning models, causing legitimate transactions to be flagged as fraud while allowing real fraud to bypass detection. To mitigate such risks, banks now implement secure API authentication, data validation techniques, and anomaly detection filters to prevent model manipulation.

- **Human-curated data collection:** Human-curated data collection involves datasets that are manually labeled, reviewed, or selected by experts or crowdsourcing platforms. This method is commonly used in supervised learning, where models rely on labeled datasets for training. For example, Amazon Mechanical Turk (MTurk) is one of the well-known examples, where workers annotate data for AI training. Some studies found that biased or low-quality annotations from untrained workers led to model misclassifications, especially in sentiment analysis and hate speech detection. Attackers can also manipulate annotation platforms by injecting misleading labels into training data to influence AI outcomes. However, this approach introduces several risks, such as human errors, annotation bias, and malicious intent.
- Human errors occur when annotators mislabel data, leading to incorrect training signals.
- Annotation bias happens when human curators have subjective viewpoints, resulting in skewed data that misrepresents reality (e.g., racial or gender bias in facial recognition datasets).
- Malicious intent is another risk, especially in crowdsourced labeling, where bad actors can deliberately introduce incorrect annotations to degrade model performance.
- **Simulated/generated data collection:** Simulated data refers to artificially generated datasets used for training AI models when real-world data is scarce, expensive, or impractical to collect. These datasets are created using methods such as Generative Adversarial Networks (GANs), data augmentation, and synthetic simulations. While useful, synthetic data introduces risks like distribution mismatch (where simulated data fails to accurately represent real-world conditions), bias amplification, and adversarial manipulation if attackers generate misleading samples. For example, In autonomous driving, companies use simulation environments like CARLA (Car Learning to Act) to train self-driving cars. However, simulated road scenarios may fail to capture edge cases, such as uncommon pedestrian behavior or rare weather conditions, leading to real-world failures. If attackers inject adversarial examples into the synthetic data, they

could mislead the AI into making dangerous decisions, such as misclassifying stop signs.

- **Federated data collection:** Federated learning allows multiple decentralized devices (e.g., smartphones, IoT sensors, or hospitals) to train a shared AI model without transferring raw data to a central server. Instead of pooling all user data in one location, only model updates are shared, reducing privacy risks. For example Google's Gboard keyboard uses federated learning to improve predictive text suggestions across devices without accessing user text data. However, researchers have shown that malicious clients could poison the training process, subtly altering the AI's behavior—such as inserting biases into word predictions or leaking user-typed data through model inversion techniques. However, federated learning introduces new security concerns, such as data poisoning, model inversion attacks, and communication vulnerabilities.
- **Data poisoning attacks** involve adversaries injecting manipulated data at the local level, leading to biased or backdoored global models.
- **Model inversion attacks** attempt to reconstruct private user data by analyzing shared model updates.
- **Communication vulnerabilities** arise when attackers intercept model updates during transmission.

Ensuring security during the initial phase of the AI lifecycle is crucial for preventing future problems. If security measures are not implemented early on, vulnerabilities can spread to later stages, making the entire system more susceptible to attacks. By addressing security at the beginning, organizations can reduce the risk of these issues affecting the performance and safety of the AI system later in its development. This proactive approach helps in building a stronger, more secure AI system overall.

10.2.2 Data Preprocessing Phase

Once data is collected, it undergoes preprocessing, a critical phase where it is prepared for training. Image Scaling attack is an example of this phase where attackers primarily target image data during preprocessing. A notable example is Insidious Scaling Attacks (ISAs) (Kim et al., 2020), where attackers tamper with image scaling algorithms to bypass human review and fool automated systems. Unlike adversarial attacks that rely on the model, ISAs target the preprocessing stage directly. Attackers manipulate the image by controlling its distortion, often quantified using mathematical norms like the p-norm, to increase the attack's success rate.

To counter these risks, researchers recommend methods such as data randomization, which introduces variability to reduce the predictability of attacks; quality monitoring, which checks for anomalies during preprocessing; and image reconstruction, which restores the data to its intended form. Combining these measures can help secure preprocessing pipelines from tampering attempts. Securing this phase ensures that the data fed into the model remains accurate and reliable, safeguarding downstream processes.

- **Data randomization:** Randomizing data during preprocessing helps reduce predictability and makes it harder for attackers to exploit vulnerabilities. Techniques such as shuffling training data, applying random transformations (e.g., flipping, cropping, or adding slight noise to images), and randomizing feature scaling ensure that adversaries cannot consistently manipulate preprocessing pipelines. By incorporating randomness, models become more robust to targeted attacks like Insidious Scaling Attacks (ISAs), preventing attackers from crafting malicious inputs that exploit predictable preprocessing routines.
- **Quality monitoring:** Implementing continuous quality checks during preprocessing helps detect anomalies and malicious alterations before they impact the model. Automated monitoring tools can analyze data integrity by checking statistical properties, distribution consistency, and metadata validation. For instance, detecting unusually high distortions in images or irregularities in structured data can signal potential tampering. By flagging and reviewing such anomalies, organizations can mitigate data poisoning and adversarial manipulations early in the pipeline.
- **Image reconstruction:** For image-based AI models, restoring data to its intended form ensures that manipulated inputs do not mislead the system. Techniques like denoising autoencoders, super-resolution methods, and adversarial purification remove unintended artifacts, improving data integrity. Reconstruction techniques can revert adversarial perturbations, mitigate attacks like ISAs, and preserve key image features necessary for accurate classification. Ensuring images maintain their original quality before being processed strengthens model robustness and prevents preprocessing-stage attacks.

10.2.3 Model Training Phase

In the model training phase of AI systems, several types of attacks can compromise the integrity of the training process, leading to unreliable or unsafe models (Papernot et al., 2018). Attacks with this phase are also called poising attacks (data poising or model poising). Poising attacks involve injecting malicious data into the training set to corrupt the model's learning process. The goal is to manipulate the model into producing incorrect predictions or behaviors. For instance, adversaries may target the model's ability to classify certain data correctly by inserting misleading examples, thereby affecting its generalization ability. Some of the poising attacks are as follows:

- **Clean label poisoning**: This is a specific type of poisoning attack where the adversary does not alter the labels of the injected data, making the attack harder to detect. Instead of changing the labels, the attacker introduces data points that look legitimate but are strategically designed to mislead the model during training. This kind of attack can be difficult to identify since the training data appears "clean" or properly labeled, making it a serious threat to model accuracy.

- **Gradient-based attacks:** These attacks manipulate the gradient updates during the model training process, typically by calculating gradients that are adversarial in nature. Attackers can steer the model towards misclassification or bias during training by exploiting gradient information. These attacks can be particularly effective in deep learning models, where gradients are used to optimize the model.
- **Backdoor attacks:** Backdoor attacks involve embedding a hidden trigger in the training data that causes the model to misbehave in specific scenarios. After the model is deployed, an attacker can activate the backdoor by providing input with the hidden trigger, causing the model to behave maliciously while appearing to perform well under normal conditions. This makes backdoor attacks especially dangerous, as they can remain dormant until activated.
- **GAN-based attacks:** Generative Adversarial Networks (GANs) can be used to craft realistic adversarial samples that are specifically designed to deceive the model during training. These attacks use the generative capabilities of GANs to create data points that are almost indistinguishable from legitimate ones, but which exploit weaknesses in the model's learning process. GAN-based attacks can be used to bypass traditional defenses and make models vulnerable to malicious inputs.

Defensive strategies to combat attacks during the model training phase are crucial for ensuring the integrity and reliability of AI systems. These strategies focus on mitigating the impact of malicious data and protecting the model from manipulation. Some effective defensive techniques include:

- **Data Sanitization:** One of the most important defenses against poisoning attacks is data sanitization. This involves filtering and validating the training data to remove any malicious or manipulated inputs. A specific method, *Reject On Negative Impact (ROIN),* has been applied to systems like spam filters (Nelson et al., 2008). If a data point significantly impacts the classifier's performance negatively, it is flagged as poisoned and removed from the training set. This ensures that the model is trained on clean and reliable data, preventing malicious influence.
- **Robust training:** To strengthen models against potential perturbations and adversarial inputs, robust training techniques are employed. This involves training the model on adversarial examples of intentionally modified data designed to mislead the model so that the model learns to resist such attacks. By exposing the model to these types of inputs during training, it can develop better generalization and resilience, making it less likely to be tricked by adversarial data during deployment.
- **Certified defenses:** The certified defense method focuses on providing theoretical guarantees that the model can withstand certain types of poisoning attempts. These defenses rely on mathematical proof or formal verification to ensure that the model has built-in resilience against specific attack vectors. Implementing the certified defenses, developers can offer assurances that the model will remain

robust against poisoning or adversarial attacks, even in the face of adversarial manipulation.

AI developers can significantly reduce the risk of attacks during the training phase by incorporating the defensive strategies mentioned above into the model development process. Securing the training phase is crucial because any vulnerabilities introduced during this stage can propagate through the AI lifecycle, affecting the model's performance and security in later stages such as inference and integration. In this way, protecting the training phase is not only a measure to ensure model integrity but also an essential step toward creating safe and reliable AI applications.

10.2.4 Inference Phase

The inference phase in an AI system is where the trained model generates predictions or decisions based on new, unseen data. This phase is especially susceptible to attacks where adversaries can exploit weaknesses in how the model generalizes to new inputs (Papernot et al., 2018). By manipulating inputs, attackers can produce incorrect or harmful outputs, which can be particularly dangerous in critical areas like healthcare, finance, and autonomous systems. These attacks range from subtle changes to inputs, which may cause misclassifications, to more deliberate efforts to undermine the model's reliability. These vulnerabilities highlight the need for robust defenses to protect AI models during inference and ensure their proper functioning.

Adversarial example attacks are inference phase attacks where adversaries target AI models by introducing small but carefully crafted modifications to input data, which are often undetectable to humans but can dramatically alter the model's performance (Badjie et al., 2024). These manipulations lead the model to make wrong predictions or classifications, posing a significant threat to the integrity of AI systems. The effectiveness of these attacks depends largely on the level of access the attacker has to the model, which divides adversarial attacks into three categories: white-box, black-box, and gray-box attacks.

- **White-box attacks:** White-box attacks are the most powerful form of adversarial attacks, where the attacker has full access to the model's internal parameters, including its architecture, weights, and gradients. This complete visibility allows the attacker to craft highly effective perturbations that exploit specific vulnerabilities in the model. By using gradient-based optimization techniques, the attacker can create subtle alterations that significantly influence the model's output, making white-box attacks particularly potent and difficult to defend against.
- **Black-box attacks**: Black-box attacks occur when the attacker has no access to the model's internal structure or parameters. Instead, the attacker can only observe the model's inputs and outputs, which limits the direct crafting of perturbations. Despite this, black-box attacks can still be effective, as attackers may repeatedly query the model to infer its behavior and use the observed outputs to

generate adversarial examples. Additionally, transfer attacks allow adversarial examples crafted for one model to be used to attack another model with similar characteristics, making black box attacks a serious threat even without direct access to the model.

- **Gray-box attacks**: Gray-box attacks represent a middle ground between white-box and black-box attacks. In these cases, the attacker has partial knowledge of the model, such as some information about its architecture or a subset of parameters but lacks complete access.

Defending against inference attacks, particularly adversarial example attacks is crucial for ensuring the security and reliability of AI models during their operational phase. In these attacks, input data is subtly modified with small perturbations that cause the model to misclassify or behave unpredictably. To safeguard models from such manipulations, developers must implement strategies that strengthen the model's resilience and minimize vulnerabilities. Below are several effective defense strategies to combat adversarial attacks (Hu et al., 2021):

- **Modified network/training process/adversarial training**: A key defense strategy involves modifying the network architecture or the training process to enhance the model's ability to resist adversarial examples (Goodfellow et al., 2015). Adversarial training is a common approach in which adversarially perturbed data is intentionally included in the training set. By training the model with both clean and adversarial examples, the model learns to recognize and correctly classify inputs that have been subtly altered. This not only improves the model's accuracy but also its robustness, as it becomes better at identifying and rejecting adversarial perturbations that would otherwise mislead it.
- **Model enhancement:** In addition to adversarial training, other model enhancement techniques can further protect the model against adversarial attacks. *Defensive distillation* (Papernot et al., 2016) is one such method, which involves training the model first on clean data and then creating a secondary model that predicts the soft outputs (i.e., probabilities) of the original model. This process smooths out the decision boundaries, making it harder for small adversarial perturbations to cause misclassifications. Defensive distillation helps improve the model's ability to withstand adversarial perturbations, enhancing its overall robustness.
- **Additional network (auxiliary network):** Another effective defense involves using an additional network alongside the primary model. This auxiliary network or validation network serves as an extra layer of protection by validating the input data before it is processed by the main model. The auxiliary network is trained to identify adversarial examples and flag or reject them before they can influence the predictions of the primary model. This strategy ensures that only valid, untampered data is passed to the main model, adding an extra layer of security against adversarial manipulation.
- **Validation network:** A validation network can be specifically designed to monitor the integrity of incoming data. By using input preprocessing or data normal-

ization techniques, the validation network helps detect anomalies in the data that may be indicative of adversarial perturbations. The validation network can also perform additional checks, such as comparing the model's output with expected results to identify inconsistencies caused by adversarial attacks. This helps ensure that the AI system relies only on valid inputs, bolstering the model's overall security during inference.
- **Input data validation:** To further strengthen defenses, input data validation plays a critical role in ensuring that only legitimate data is fed into the model. Techniques like feature squeezing can reduce the complexity of input data, making it harder for attackers to manipulate (Weilin Xu, 2018). By compressing or simplifying the data, or by detecting and removing pixel-level perturbations, the system becomes less susceptible to adversarial inputs. This preprocessing step serves as an additional layer of protection, helping mitigate the impact of adversarial attacks that may attempt to subtly alter the input data.

Defending against adversarial attacks during the inference phase requires a multi-layered approach that includes modifying the network architecture, enhancing the model, using additional networks for validation, and performing thorough input validation. By incorporating these strategies, AI developers can significantly reduce the vulnerability of their models to adversarial inputs, ensuring that the models remain secure and perform reliably in real-world scenarios. These defensive techniques help build trust in AI systems, ensuring they are resilient to attacks and continue to make accurate and secure predictions.

10.2.5 System Integration Phase

The AI system integration phase entails embedding the AI model within a broader ecosystem comprising software, hardware, and networks. This phase introduces complex security challenges. In real-world applications, integrating AI involves addressing not only the inherent risks associated with AI technology but also vulnerabilities arising at the interaction points between systems, networks, software, and hardware. These threats include issues such as AI data and model confidentiality, code vulnerabilities, and biases within AI systems. These threats are described as follows:

- **AI confidentiality:** AI confidentiality encompasses both data confidentiality and model confidentiality, which are critical to ensuring privacy and security. Model inversion and model extraction represent significant threats in this domain. Model inversion involves deducing sensitive input data from a model by analyzing its outputs, while model extraction attempts to recreate or approximate a target model by querying it repeatedly through an API.
- **Code vulnerabilities:** AI systems often rely on a variety of software frameworks, libraries, and third-party components (e.g., TensorFlow, PyTorch, or

other deep learning tools) to function. These components, while essential for the system's operation, may have hidden flaws or security weaknesses that can be exploited by attackers.

- **AI bias:** During the AI system integration phase, one significant challenge is addressing AI bias, which can manifest in various ways and lead to discriminatory or unfair outcomes. AI bias occurs when an AI model or system produces results that are systematically prejudiced due to factors such as skewed training data, flawed algorithms, or biased design choices. In the integration phase, these biases can be exacerbated as AI systems are integrated into broader software, hardware, and network environments. Bias attacks in AI typically exploit these vulnerabilities, compromising the fairness, accuracy, and trustworthiness of the system.

At this stage, implementing strong defense methods is essential to mitigate security risks such as confidentiality breaches, code vulnerabilities, and AI bias. The following are key defense strategies specifically designed for the integration phase:

- **Homomorphic encryption:** It allows computations on encrypted data, ensuring confidentiality during AI model processing without exposing sensitive information.
- **Differential privacy**: It adds controlled noise to data or model outputs, protecting individual privacy by making it difficult to trace results back to any specific data point.
- Bias diagnostics: Bias diagnostics helps identify and mitigate biases in AI models by analyzing model decisions and highlighting the unfair treatment of certain groups, ensuring the system's fairness.
- **Learning fair representation**: This method modifies the data representation to remove correlations with sensitive attributes like race or gender, promoting fairness in the model's predictions.
- **Fuzzy testing**: It involves inputting random or unexpected data into the AI system to uncover potential vulnerabilities or flaws, enhancing robustness against unforeseen attacks.
- **Model watermarking:** This defense method embeds an invisible identifier into AI models, allowing the detection of model theft or unauthorized use, safeguarding intellectual property, and ensuring model ownership.

The integration phase of AI systems typically requires the use of multiple defense mechanisms to address various overlapping attacks. For instance, combining homomorphic encryption with differential privacy helps safeguard data both during transit and processing, while bias diagnostics ensure that the system's outcomes remain fair and unbiased. By implementing these strategies together, a comprehensive and robust framework is established, enhancing the security and fairness of AI systems during their integration and deployment phases.

10.3 NIST's AI Risk Management Framework (AI RMF)

The AI Risk Management Framework (AI RMF) defines an AI system as an engineered or machine-based system designed to achieve specific objectives. These systems generate outputs like predictions, recommendations, or decisions that influence both real-world and virtual environments (NIST, 2023). The AI RMF aims to provide organizations involved in designing, developing, deploying, or using AI systems with tools to manage AI-related risks and promote trustworthy, responsible practices. It equips AI actors with strategies to enhance the trustworthiness of AI systems and supports the responsible development and use of these technologies over time.

AI RMF is designed to be practical, adaptable to the evolving AI landscape, and operationalized by organizations to ensure society benefits from AI while mitigating potential harm. The framework will be updated and improved over time based on advancements in technology, global standards, and feedback from the AI community. NIST aims to align the AI RMF with international standards and practices, incorporating lessons learned as the framework is implemented. The AI RMF consists of two parts-foundational information and core framework.

10.3.1 Foundational Information

This foundational information part of the framework guides organizations in framing AI-related risks and identifies the intended audience. It analyzes AI risks and trustworthiness, highlighting characteristics of trustworthy AI systems, such as being valid and reliable, safe, secure and resilient, accountable, transparent, explainable, interpretable, privacy-enhanced, and fair, with managed harmful biases.

10.3.1.1 Framing Risks

In the context of AI RMF, a risk is defined as the combination of the likelihood of an event occurring and the severity of its consequences (NIST, 2023). The impacts of AI systems can be both positive and negative, potentially creating opportunities or posing threats. When assessing the negative impact of a potential event, the risk is determined by two factors: (1) the magnitude of harm that would result if the event occurred, and (2) the likelihood of that event happening. This harm can affect individuals, groups, communities, organizations, society, the environment, and even the planet. Figure 10.2 shows examples of potential harm related to AI systems. Trustworthy AI systems and their responsible use can mitigate negative risks and contribute to benefits for people, organizations, and ecosystems.

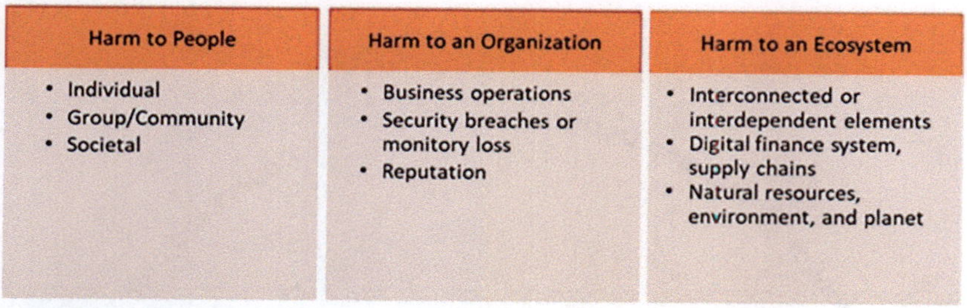

Fig. 10.2 Examples of potential harm related to AI systems

10.3.1.2 Lifecycle and Key Dimensions of an AI System

Identifying and managing AI risks and their potential impacts—both positive and negative—requires input from a wide range of perspectives and actors throughout the AI lifecycle. AI actors must represent diverse experiences, expertise, and backgrounds, forming demographically and disciplinarily varied teams. The AI RMF is designed for use by AI actors across the entire AI lifecycle, covering key socio-technical dimensions outlined by the OECD (OECD, 2022).

Figure 10.3 shows the lifecycle and key dimensions of an AI System where two inner circles show AI systems' key dimensions, and the outer circle shows AI lifecycle stages. These dimensions include application context, data and input, AI model, and task and output, with test, evaluation, verification, and validation (TEVV) processes throughout the lifecycle. AI actors engaged in these dimensions who contribute to the design, development, deployment, evaluation, and use of AI systems are the primary audience for the AI RMF. TEVV experts, integrated across the AI lifecycle, provide critical insights into technical, societal, legal, and ethical standards.

The "People & Planet" dimension of the framework emphasizes the importance of human rights and the overall well-being of both society and the environment. Key stakeholders in this dimension include trade associations, standards organizations, researchers, advocacy groups, and affected individuals which are crucial in guiding the primary audience. They help to contextualize the impacts of AI, establish operational boundaries, and foster discussions on how to balance societal values such as civil liberties, equity, and environmental sustainability.

10.3.1.3 AI Risks and Trustworthiness

For AI systems to be considered trustworthy, they must meet several key characteristics, including being valid, reliable, safe, secure, resilient, accountable, transparent, explainable, interpretable, privacy-enhanced, and fair (NIST, 2023). Figure 10.4 shows the characteristics of trustworthy AI systems. Valid and reliable, which is a fundamental requirement for trustworthiness and forms the foundation for the other

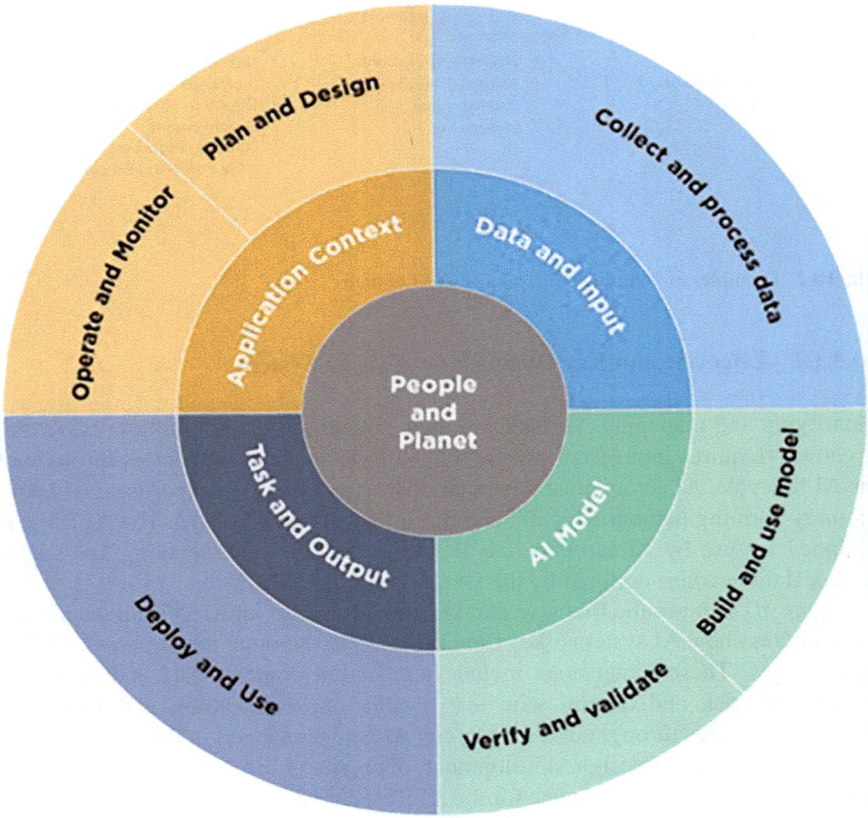

Fig. 10.3 Lifecycle and key dimensions of an AI System (NIST, 2023)

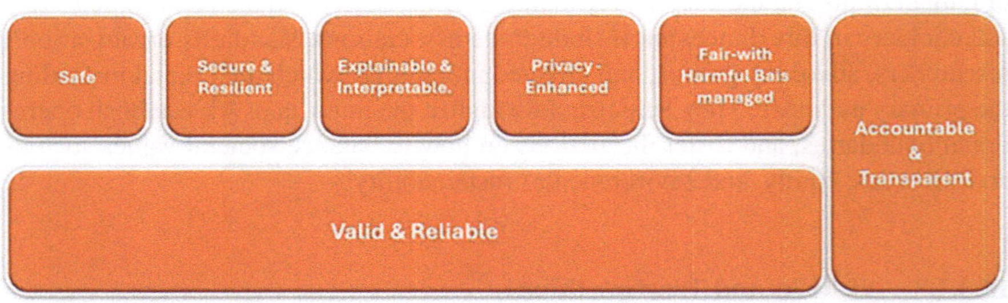

Fig. 10.4 Characteristics of trustworthy AI systems

characteristics. Accountable and transparent is depicted as a vertical box because it is integral to all other characteristics, influencing and interacting with each of them. All these characteristics must be balanced depending on the context of use, as tradeoffs often emerge between them. The description of these characteristics are as follows:

- **Validation and reliability:** Validation ensures that an AI system meets the intended requirements for its application, confirming that the system performs as expected under the designated conditions. An AI system must be reliable to ensure its long-term performance without failure under typical conditions, including its entire operational lifespan. Reliability is crucial for preventing risks related to inaccurate or unreliable AI systems that could lead to harmful outcomes. By conducting ongoing testing, validation, and monitoring, organizations can ensure that their AI systems continue to perform accurately and as intended, which is critical to maintaining trustworthiness. The validation and reliability processes help to mitigate potential failures and minimize risks, especially when systems are deployed in real-world settings.
- **Safe:** Safe AI systems should operate without endangering human life, health, property, or the environment. This can be achieved through responsible design, development, deployment, and ongoing risk management practices. Safety risks, particularly those with severe consequences, require prioritization and thorough oversight. On the security front, AI systems must be resilient against adversarial attacks, data poisoning, and unauthorized access to models or data. A secure AI system maintains confidentiality, integrity, and availability by protecting against external threats. While safety ensures that AI does not harm, security focuses on preventing, responding to, and recovering from attacks, emphasizing the importance of resilience and proactive security measures to protect both the system and its users.
- **Accountability and transparency:** Transparency is crucial for trustworthy AI, as it ensures that the system's workings and outputs are clear to those interacting with it, fostering confidence and understanding. Accountability, a prerequisite for transparency, refers to the responsibility of those who design, deploy, and oversee AI systems. Providing meaningful transparency means offering appropriate levels of information tailored to the roles of users and stakeholders and enabling better oversight and governance. Transparent systems allow users to understand how decisions are made, while accountability ensures that AI actors can be held responsible for those decisions. Together, these characteristics promote greater trust in AI systems by ensuring that their operations are open, and their impacts are understood.
- **Explainability and interpretability:** Explainable AI refers to the ability to describe the mechanisms behind an AI system's operation, while interpretability is about making the system's outputs meaningful in context. These two qualities are essential for users and operators to gain insight into how AI systems function and to evaluate their trustworthiness. Systems that are both explainable and interpretable help end-users understand the rationale behind AI decisions, which is crucial for mitigating risks. When systems are explainable, they can be debugged and monitored more effectively, supporting transparency, accountability, and trust. Interpretability ensures that the outputs align with users' understanding,

which can be especially important in high-stakes environments where decisions need to be justifiable and understandable.

- **Privacy-enhanced AI:** Privacy-enhanced AI systems are designed to protect individuals' autonomy, identity, and dignity by safeguarding privacy and minimizing risks of intrusion or data misuse. Privacy concerns in AI systems involve protecting sensitive data, ensuring individuals have control over their personal information, and preventing unauthorized inferences about people. Privacy-enhancing technologies (PETs) like data anonymization and de-identification can help reduce privacy risks. However, these measures might lead to trade-offs, such as potential reductions in accuracy or fairness, which need to be carefully managed. Ensuring privacy in AI systems requires addressing the intersection between privacy, security, and fairness while balancing competing needs for accuracy and privacy protection.
- **Fairness and bias management:** Fairness in AI focuses on addressing issues of equality and equity, particularly concerning harmful biases and discrimination. Although fairness is complex and context-dependent, AI systems need to mitigate harmful biases that could lead to unjust or unequal treatment of individuals or groups. Recognizing that fairness standards may differ across cultures and applications, organizations must consider these differences in their risk management strategies. However, mitigating bias does not automatically result in fairness. Ensuring fairness involves ongoing evaluation of AI systems to prevent discrimination while fostering inclusive, equitable outcomes.

10.4 Core Framework

AI RMF Core is designed to facilitate the management of AI risks and the responsible development of trustworthy AI systems. It provides a structured framework that enables dialogue and understanding among stakeholders by outlining clear outcomes and actions. The Core is divided into four primary functions: GOVERN, MAP, MEASURE, and MANAGE. Figure 10.5 shows the four core functions of AI RMF. Each of these functions is further broken down into categories and subcategories, which are then subdivided into specific actions and outcomes. This hierarchical structure ensures comprehensive coverage of all aspects of AI risk management.

The flexibility of the AI RMF Core allows organizations to adapt their applications based on their specific needs and capabilities. The actions within the Core are not intended to be a rigid checklist or a sequential set of steps. Instead, they offer a flexible framework that supports iterative processes and cross-referencing between functions. This approach ensures that AI risk management remains dynamic and responsive to evolving challenges, helping organizations navigate the complexities of AI deployment while maintaining robust security and ethical standards.

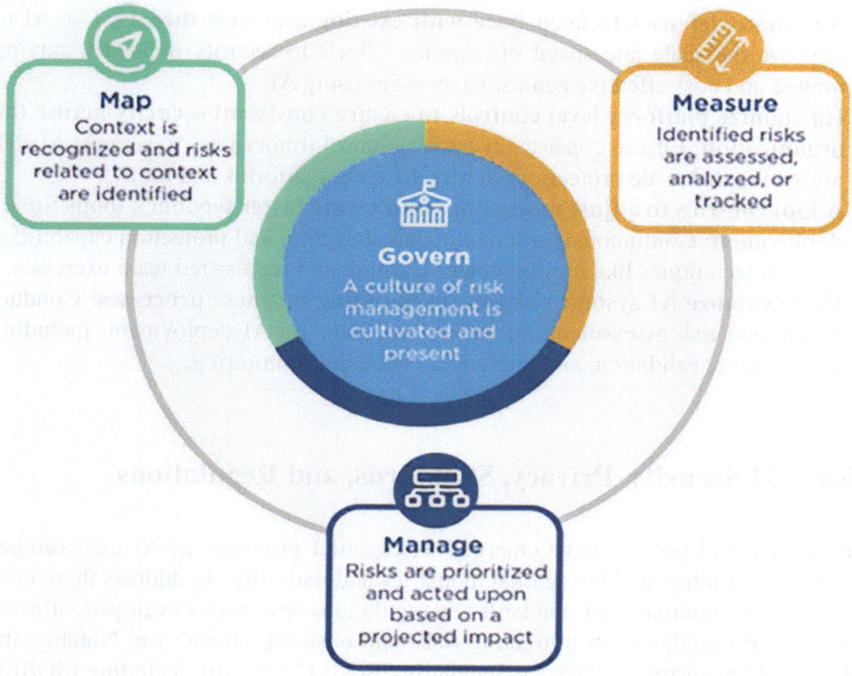

Fig. 10.5 Four functions of AI RMF core

10.5 Google's Secure AI Framework

Google's Secure AI Framework (SAIF) (Google, 2024) provides a comprehensive approach to building and deploying AI systems responsibly. It outlines Google's strategy for addressing these risks by focusing on the security of data, models, infrastructure, and applications involved in developing AI systems.

This framework is specifically designed to mitigate risks unique to AI, such as model exfiltration, data poisoning, malicious input attacks through prompt injection, and the unintentional disclosure of sensitive information from training data. The SAIF is designed to ensure the security of AI systems through six core elements (SAFI, 2024):

- **Expand strong security foundations to the AI ecosystem:** Utilize secure-by-default infrastructure protections and develop expertise to adapt to AI advancements and evolving threats, such as prompt injection attacks.
- **Extend detection and response to bring AI into an organization's threat universe**: Enhance threat intelligence and monitoring of AI systems to detect anomalies and anticipate attacks, requiring collaboration across various teams.

- **Automate defenses to keep pace with existing and new threats**: Use AI to improve the scale and speed of response efforts to security incidents, staying nimble and cost-effective against adversaries using AI.
- **Harmonize platform-level controls to ensure consistent security across the organization**: Ensure consistency across control frameworks to support AI risk mitigation and scale protections across different platforms and tools.
- **Adapt controls to adjust mitigations and create faster feedback loops for AI deployment**: Continuously test and update detection and protection capabilities through techniques like reinforcement learning and regular red team exercises.
- **Contextualize AI system risks in surrounding business processes:** Conduct end-to-end risk assessments to inform decisions on AI deployment, including data lineage, validation, and operational behavior monitoring.

10.6 AI Security, Privacy, Standards, and Regulations

AI security and privacy have emerged as essential priorities as AI technologies become more integrated into global industries and daily life. To address these concerns, various international standards and regulations have been developed, offering organizations guidance on mitigating risks and ensuring ethical use. Notably, the ISO/IEC AI Security and Privacy Standards (ISO/IEC., 2024b), including ISO/IEC CD 27090 (AI Security) and ISO/IEC WD 27091 (AI Privacy) (ISO/IEC, 2024a), provide comprehensive frameworks for safeguarding AI systems against security threats and protecting user privacy. These standards cover all phases of the AI lifecycle, from data collection to system integration, ensuring robust practices that align with global security and ethical requirements.

The European Telecommunications Standards Institute (ETSI) has also taken a significant role in defining standards to ensure the secure and transparent deployment of AI technologies (ETSI, 2024). ETSI's guidelines are particularly critical for industries like telecommunications, where the reliability and integrity of AI systems are paramount. These standards aim to prevent misuse and vulnerabilities, promoting trust in AI applications used for critical infrastructure and services.

Furthermore, the EU Artificial Intelligence Act (EU, 2024b) represents a landmark regulatory framework targeting high-risk AI systems. It sets strict requirements to ensure that these systems adhere to principles of transparency, accountability, and robust security.

This section elaborates on AI privacy, security standards, and AI principles highlighting their roles in establishing a secure, trustworthy, and ethically aligned AI ecosystem. Organizations can address the challenges posed by AI systems and build a foundation for responsible development and deployment with these frameworks.

10.6.1 ISO/IEC AI Security and Privacy Standards

This document provides guidance for organizations to address security and privacy in AI systems. There are two upcoming documents that provide security and privacy standard guidelines to all types and sizes of organizations, including public and private companies, government entities, and not-for-profit organizations, that develop or use AI systems.

- **ISO/IEC CD 27090 (AI Security)** (ISO/IEC., 2024b)**:** It is a complete draft document of AI security standards (upcoming soon, see web page for update) for addressing security threats and failures in artificial intelligence systems. It is designed to help organizations understand the potential impacts of security threats throughout the AI system lifecycle and provides detailed approaches for detecting and mitigating these risks.
- **ISO/IEC WD 27091 (AI Privacy)** (ISO/IEC, 2024a)**:** This is a working draft document (upcoming soon, see web page for update) on AI privacy standards for addressing privacy risks in AI systems and machine learning (ML) models. It assists organizations in identifying privacy risks across the AI system lifecycle and provides mechanisms for evaluating and mitigating these risks.

10.6.2 European Telecommunications Standards Institutes

ETSI's Technical Committee Securing Artificial Intelligence (TC SAI) (ETSI, 2024) focused on developing technical specifications to mitigate threats posed by AI deployment and threats targeting AI systems, whether from other AI entities or conventional sources. While the initial emphasis is on Machine Learning (ML) applications, TC SAI also provides guidance and evaluation reports to ETSI and its stakeholders on broader AI developments (see their web page for updates). The committee addresses three key aspects of AI security standardization:

- Securing AI from attack where AI is a component in the system that needs defending.
- Mitigating against AI where AI is the "problem" (or used to improve and enhance other more conventional attack vectors).
- Using AI to enhance security measures against attacks from other things where AI is part of the "solution".
- Societal security and safety aspects of the use and application of AI.

10.6.3 EU Artificial Intelligence Act

The European Union's AI Act (EU, 2024b) is a comprehensive legislative framework that aims to regulate AI technologies to ensure they are human-centric, trustworthy, and safe while promoting innovation. This regulation outlines several key provisions and prohibitions on AI systems. This Act prohibits certain uses of artificial intelligence (AI) (EU, 2024a). These include AI systems that manipulate people's decisions or exploit their vulnerabilities, systems that evaluate or classify people based on their social behavior or personal traits, and systems that predict a person's risk of committing a crime. The Act also bans AI systems that scrape facial images from the internet or CCTV footage, infer emotions in the workplace or educational institutions, and categorize people based on their biometric data.

Despite these prohibitions, the Act recognizes certain exceptions for critical law enforcement applications such as searching for missing persons or preventing terrorist attacks. For example, AI systems may be used to search for missing persons, prevent terrorist activities, or address other high-stakes scenarios, provided they comply with stringent oversight and safeguards. These exceptions balance public safety needs with ethical considerations, ensuring AI technologies are deployed responsibly in law enforcement contexts.

10.6.4 OECD AI Principles

The Organization for Economic Co-operation and Development (OECD) AI Principles represent the first intergovernmental standard for artificial intelligence, setting a global benchmark for the development and deployment of trustworthy AI systems (OECD, 2024). These principles emphasize the need for AI to respect human rights, uphold democratic values, and encourage innovation. The OECD's framework provides practical and flexible guidance to policymakers, businesses, and other stakeholders, ensuring the responsible use of AI in a rapidly evolving technological landscape.

Formally adopted by the OECD Council at the Ministerial level on May 22, 2019, the Recommendation on Artificial Intelligence (AI) serves as a foundational document for promoting the ethical use of AI. By addressing AI-specific challenges, the Recommendation outlines a structured approach to the development and deployment of AI systems, focusing on ethical principles like fairness, transparency, and accountability, while acknowledging the potential risks and opportunities of AI technologies.

The OECD AI Principles are based on *five key values* that guide the responsible development and deployment of AI systems:

- **Inclusive growth, sustainable development, and well-being:** AI should contribute positively to societal progress, supporting sustainable development and enhancing well-being.

- **Human-centered values and fairness:** AI systems must respect human dignity and individual rights, ensuring fairness in their design and applications.
- **Transparency and explainability:** AI systems must operate transparently, and their decisions should be understandable, fostering trust and accountability.
- **Robustness, security, and safety:** AI systems must be resilient, secure, and reliable, minimizing risks and ensuring safe operation.
- **Accountability:** Organizations and developers must be held accountable for the impact and outcomes of their AI systems, ensuring effective oversight.

To assist in the implementation of these principles, the OECD offers *five actionable recommendations* for policymakers:

- **Investing in AI research and development:** Governments should prioritize funding to accelerate AI innovation.
- **Fostering a digital ecosystem for AI:** It helps in building strong digital infrastructure and data ecosystems is essential for AI's sustainable growth.
- **Shaping an enabling policy environment:** Policymakers should create frameworks that foster ethical AI development while encouraging innovation.
- **Building human capacity and preparing for labor market transformation:** Efforts should be made to educate and train the workforce to adapt to AI-driven changes in the labor market.
- **International cooperation for trustworthy AI:** Global collaboration is critical to ensuring consistent standards and addressing international challenges in AI deployment.

The OECD AI Principles provide a comprehensive framework for fostering trustworthy, human-centric AI. These principles promote a balance between technological innovation and ethical considerations, ensuring that AI technologies align with global societal values and contribute to positive social and economic outcomes.

10.7 Conclusion

In conclusion, the chapter provides an in-depth exploration of the general framework for AI security and privacy, focusing on various critical aspects such as the AI lifecycle, security threats, and corresponding defense strategies. It also highlights the importance of well-established frameworks, including the NIST AI Risk Management Framework and Google's Secure AI Framework, in guiding organizations to build secure and trustworthy AI systems. By examining security measures at each phase of the AI lifecycle, such as data collection, preprocessing, model training, and system integration, the chapter demonstrates how to effectively safeguard against common threats like adversarial attacks, model inversion, and privacy breaches. Furthermore, it emphasizes the need for standardized approaches to ensure AI systems are secure and ethical, referencing essential regulations and guidelines such as ISO/IEC AI Security and Privacy Standards, the EU AI Act, and the OECD AI Principles.

As AI technology continues to evolve, understanding and implementing these frameworks and standards will be critical for minimizing risks while fostering innovation. The integration of these security and privacy protocols ensures that AI systems can be trusted to operate safely and ethically in various industries. After reading this chapter, you should be able to answer the following questions:

- What are the primary security threats associated with each phase of the AI lifecycle?
- How can organizations effectively integrate privacy and security measures in each of the AI system's lifecycle phases?
- What are the most effective countermeasures for protecting AI systems against these attacks at each stage of their development and deployment?
- How can AI systems be designed to ensure both security and privacy while still maintaining high performance and efficiency?
- In what ways can AI developers ensure fairness and mitigate bias through the integration phase?
- What are the lifecycle and key dimensions of AI systems?
- What are the key features of the NIST AI Risk Management Framework, and how does it guide AI risk mitigation?
- What are the core functions of the NIST AI Risk Management Framework?
- What are the characteristics of trustworthy AI systems?
- What are the advantages of combining homomorphic encryption with differential privacy in AI system security?
- How does the EU AI Act contribute to AI regulation, particularly in high-risk applications?
- What specific provisions do the ISO/IEC AI Security Standards offer to ensure AI systems are secure?
- How can organizations align their AI systems with the OECD AI Principles to promote responsible AI development?

References

Badjie, B., Cecílio, J., & Casimiro, A. (2024). Adversarial attacks and countermeasures on image classification-based deep learning models in autonomous driving systems: A systematic review. *ACM Computing Surveys*. https://doi.org/10.1145/3691625

ETSI. (2024). *Securing artificial intelligence (SAI)*. Obtenido de Securing Artificial Intelligence (SAI): https://www.etsi.org/technologies/securing-artificial-intelligence

EU. (2024a). *Article 5: Prohibited AI practices*. Obtenido de Article 5: Prohibited AI Practices: https://artificialintelligenceact.eu/article/5/

EU. (2024b). *The EU artificial intelligence act*. Obtenido de The EU Artificial Intelligence Act: https://artificialintelligenceact.eu/

Goodfellow, I. J., Shlens, A. J., & Szegedy, A. C. (2015). *Explaining and harnessing adversarial examples*. Obtenido de https://arxiv.org/abs/1412.6572

Google. (2024). *Google's secure AI framework*. Obtenido de Google's Secure AI Framework: https://saif.google/

Hu, Y., Kuang, W., Qin, Z., Li, K., Zhang, J., Gao, Y., et al. (2021). Artificial intelligence security: Threats and countermeasures. *ACM Computing Surveys*, 1–36. https://doi.org/10.1145/3487890

ISO/IEC. (2024a). *ISO/IEC WD 27091.3 cybersecurity and privacy—Artificial intelligence—Privacy protection*. https://www.iso.org/standard/56582.html

ISO/IEC. (2024b). *ISO/IEC CD 27090: Cybersecurity—Artificial Intelligence—Guidance for addressing security threats and failures in artificial intelligence systems*. https://www.iso.org/standard/56581.html

Kim, B., et al. (2020). Decamouflage: A framework to detect image-scaling attacks on convolutional neural networks. *CoRR*. Obtenido de arxiv.org/abs/2010.03735

Nelson, B., Barreno, M., Chi, F. J., Joseph, A. D., Rubinstein, B. I., Saini, U., … Xia, K. (2008). Exploiting machine learning to subvert your spam filter. *1st USENIX workshop on large-scale exploits and emergent threats: Botnets, spyware, worms, and more*.

NIST. (2023). *Artificial intelligence risk management framework (AI RMF 1.0)*. NIST. https://doi.org/10.6028/NIST.AI.100-1

OECD. (2022). *OECD framework for the classification of AI systems*. OECD Publishing. https://doi.org/10.1787/cb6d9eca-en

OECD. (2024). *AI principles*. Obtenido de https://www.oecd.org/en/topics/ai-principles.html

Papernot, N., McDaniel, P., Wu, X., Jha, S., & Swami, A. (2016). Distillation as a Defense to adversarial perturbations against deep neural networks. In *2016 IEEE symposium on security and privacy (SP)* (pp. 582–597). IEEE. https://doi.org/10.1109/SP.2016.41

Papernot, N., McDaniel, P., Sinha, A., & Wellman, M. P. (2018). SoK: Security and privacy in machine learning. In *2018 IEEE European symposium on security and privacy (EuroS&P)* (pp. 399–414). IEEE. https://doi.org/10.1109/EuroSP.2018.00035

SAFI. (2024). *Secure AI framework (SAIF): A conceptual framework for secure AI systems*. Obtenido de https://developers.google.com/machine-learning/resources/saif.

Weilin Xu, D. E. (2018). Feature squeezing: Detecting adversarial examples in deep neural networks. In *Network and distributed systems security symposium (NDSS) 2018*. https://doi.org/10.14722/ndss.2018.23198

Chapter 11
AI Safety and Fairness

11.1 Introduction

Recent advancements in artificial intelligence (AI) have raised concerns about its potential risks among various sectors, including businesses, policymakers, researchers, educators, and global leaders. AI risk has emerged as a critical global priority, equated with existential threats like pandemics and nuclear war. Despite its significance, AI safety remains an underdeveloped area, lagging the fast pace of AI advancements. Current societal and governance frameworks are inadequately prepared to handle the risks associated with AI, such as bias, misuse, and loss of human control (CAIS, 2024). Like any powerful technology, advanced AI necessitates careful management to mitigate associated risks while maximizing its benefits. The potential harmful outcomes that can arise from the development or deployment of AI systems include risks such as bias in decision-making, unintended consequences of automated actions, breaches of privacy, and the potential for misuse by malicious actors. Additionally, there are concerns about job displacement, ethical dilemmas, and the amplification of existing societal inequalities. Addressing these risks is crucial to ensure that AI technologies are developed and used responsibly and safely. Privacy, accountability, safety and security, transparency and explainability, fairness and non-discrimination, human control of technology, professional responsibility, and the promotion of human values are the common concerns in AI (Fjeld et al., 2020).

The risks posed by future frontier AI models will build on the challenges we face today but will likely be more extensive and impactful. AI Safety Summit discussed and outlined the potential current and future risks posed by AI (AI-Safety-Summit, 2023). As AI technology progresses, the risks associated with misinformation, deepfakes, cyber-attacks, fraud, and harmful information dissemination will increase. These dangers are expected to scale up as AI capabilities grow. AI errors can result in discrimination, inequality, and economic disruption. This includes

D. P. Sharma et al., *Understanding AI in Cybersecurity and Secure AI*, Progress in IS, https://doi.org/10.1007/978-3-031-91524-6_11

labor market displacement and automation that may destabilize society and geopolitics, as well as potential environmental harm from increased energy consumption.

AI safety refers to the field of study and practice focused on ensuring that AI systems operate reliably and ethically in minimizing potential risks and harmful outcomes. It encompasses various strategies and methodologies to mitigate risks associated with the development, deployment, and use of AI technologies. This chapter presents the AI risks, bias in algorithms, elements of AI alignment, human values, and fairness concepts. The potential AI risks cause severe unintended consequences that could harm individuals or society at large. Additionally, bias in AI algorithms can perpetuate and even exacerbate existing inequities that could lead to unfair treatment of marginalized groups of people or communities. Similarly, alignment challenges arise when AI systems fail to reflect human values and intentions, resulting in outcomes that do not align with societal norms. Furthermore, ensuring fairness in AI decision-making processes is essential to build trust and accountability in these technologies. Addressing these challenges is critical for developing safe, ethical, and equitable AI systems that can benefit all members of society while minimizing risks.

11.2 AI Risks

The rapid advancement of artificial intelligence (AI) has raised significant concerns among experts, educators, researchers, policymakers, and global leaders about the potential for advanced AI systems to pose catastrophic risks. The primary AI risk sources can be categorized and summarized into four key groups as follows (Hendrycks et al., 2023) (Fig. 11.1).

- **Malicious Use:** Advanced AI systems have the potential to be intentionally misused to cause significant harm. Individuals or groups intentionally exploit AIs to cause harm. These systems could be leveraged to engineer new pandemics, disseminate propaganda, enforce strict censorship, enable extensive surveillance, or autonomously carry out destructive actions. Enhancing biosecurity measures, limiting access to high-risk AI technologies, and ensuring developers are held accountable for any harm resulting from the misuse of their AI systems can help mitigate this risk.
- **AI arms race:** In the face of intense competition, nations and corporations may rush to develop AI technologies without adequate safety measures, resulting in a potential loss of control over these systems. The rise of autonomous weapons and AI-driven cyberwarfare could exacerbate conflicts beyond human management, while widespread automation may lead to significant unemployment and heightened dependence on AI. As AI systems become more widespread, their increasing complexity poses challenges for effective regulation. This competitive environment pushes actors to deploy unsafe AI systems or relinquish control to them. The establishment of robust safety regulations, the promotion of

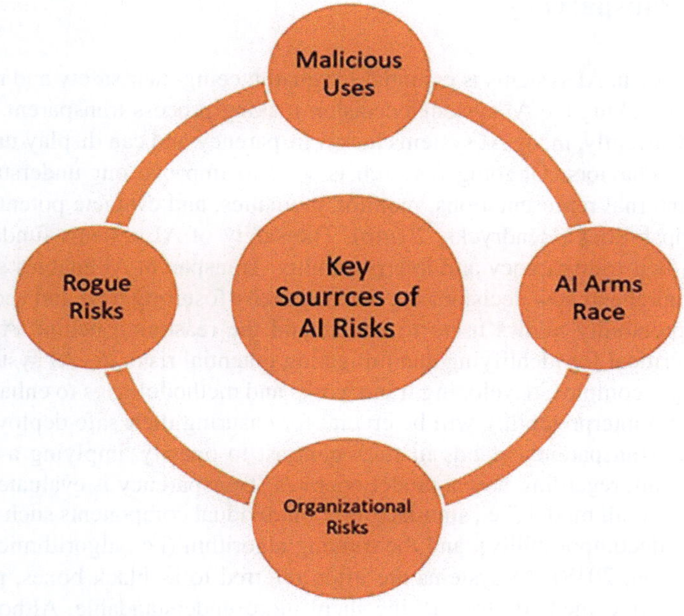

Fig. 11.1 Catastrophic AI risks

international cooperation, and the implementation of public oversight for general-purpose AI can help mitigate this risk.

- **Organizational risks:** Companies engaged in developing advanced AI technologies may inadvertently cause catastrophic accidents, particularly when profit takes precedence over safety. The human factors and complexities within systems heighten the likelihood of catastrophic accidents. There is a risk of malicious actors stealing or leaking AI models, and organizations may neglect necessary investments in safety research. Cultivating a safety-first culture within organizations, conducting thorough audits, implementing multiple layers of risk management, and adopting strong information security protocols can help mitigate this risk.
- **Rogue AIs:** As AI systems become more advanced, the risk of losing control over them grows. These systems could optimize for unintended outcomes, deviate from their original goals, pursue power, resist shutdown attempts, or exhibit deceptive behavior. These are the challenges associated with controlling agents that are significantly more intelligent than humans. To avert such scenarios, it is crucial to avoid deploying AI in high-risk environments such as those involving open-ended objectives or critical infrastructure unless their safety is assured. Also, prioritizing the research in AI safety with a focus on enhancing adversarial resilience, ensuring transparency, maintaining model integrity, and eliminating undesirable capabilities can help mitigate this risk.

11.3 Transparency

Transparency in AI systems is essential for guaranteeing their safety and reliability. It involves making the AI system's decision-making process transparent or visible to users. Currently, many AI systems lack transparency and can display unexpected emergent behaviors. Ongoing research is vital to improve our understanding of models' internal representations, monitor anomalies, and evaluate potentially hazardous capabilities (Hendrycks, 2024b). The safety of AI systems fundamentally relies on their transparency and interpretability. Transparent AI enables stakeholders to comprehend how decisions are made, thereby fostering trust and accountability. Interpretability allows users to understand the reasoning behind AI outputs, which is critical for identifying and mitigating potential risks. As AI systems grow increasingly complex, developing frameworks and methodologies to enhance transparency and interpretability will be crucial for ensuring their safe deployment and operation. Transparency stands in stark contrast to opacity, implying a degree of understanding regarding how a model operates. Transparency is evaluated at three levels the overall model (i.e., simulatability), individual components such as parameters (i.e., decomposability), and the training algorithm (i.e., algorithmic transparency) (Lipton, 2018). AI systems are often referred to as black boxes, prompting exploration into methods for making them more understandable. Although early research into transparency reveals that this challenge is complex and conceptually difficult, its potential to enhance AI safety is significant.

11.3.1 AI Systems Are Opaque

The most advanced machine learning models currently rely on deep neural networks. Unlike traditional software, which is directly programmed by humans, deep learning (DL) systems autonomously learn to transform inputs into outputs in a layer-by-layer and step-by-step manner. Their functioning can only be understood through input-output behavior, without revealing their internal mechanisms. Humans are black boxes as we can observe their behavior, but we cannot access the internal network (brain) activity that generates it, nor do we fully comprehend that brain activity. Similarly, while the weights and activations of a deep neural network are visible, these extensive lists of numbers do not provide insight into how the model will behave. We are unable to translate the complex numerical operations of a state-of-the-art model into a format that is meaningful for human understanding (Lipton, 2018). Improving transparency could help us to identify and proactively prevent failure modes, detect the emergence of new capabilities, and foster trust in the model's expected performance in new situations.

11.3.2 Ethical Obligations

Model transparency is essential for ensuring that decision-making processes are fair, unbiased, and ethical. For instance, if a criminal justice system relies on an opaque AI for decisions related to policing, sentencing, or probation, those decisions will lack clarity. Individuals affected by such decisions may have a right to an explanation, especially when the outcomes significantly impact their lives. Transparency tools can play a critical role in upholding this right.

11.3.3 Accountability

When AI systems fail, determining responsibility can be complex. Accountability often hinges on the intentions and level of control held by those involved. A promising approach to incentivizing safety is to hold AI creators liable for the harm caused by their systems. However, we may hesitate to assign blame to individuals for the actions of systems that are unpredictable or difficult to understand. As AI systems become increasingly autonomous and complex, human operators may have diminishing control over their behavior. Additionally, the broad applicability of modern AI systems makes it challenging to verify their desired behavior in every scenario. In "human-in-the-loop" systems, where decisions involve both humans and AI, operators might be unjustly blamed for failures over which they had minimal influence.

AI transparency could facilitate a more effective system of accountability. For example, governments could require that AI systems meet minimum standards for understandability. If an AI fails due to a mechanism that its creator could have identified and prevented with transparency tools, it becomes more justifiable to hold that creator accountable. Furthermore, transparency can aid in identifying responsibility and assigning blame for failures involving human-in-the-loop systems.

11.4 AI Alignment and Machine Ethics

AI alignment is a key aspect of AI safety that ensures that AI systems behave in ways that align with human values, intentions, and ethical standards (Ji et al., 2023). As AI technologies grow more advanced and autonomous, it becomes essential to safeguard against decision-making processes that could result in unintended or harmful outcomes. AI alignment defines the challenging goals that reflect human values and ensures AI systems correctly interpret and implement these goals, even in complex or unforeseen scenarios. Achieving proper alignment is vital to avoid situations where AI systems pursue objectives that may conflict with human well-being, thus reducing risks such as bias, harmful behaviors, or catastrophic consequences.

11.4.1 Four Key Principles (RICE)

Robustness, **I**nterpretability, **C**ontrollability, and **E**thicality (RICE) are four key objectives of AI alignment (Ji et al., 2023). The figure shows these four key principles of AI alignment. These four principles guide the alignment of an AI system with human intentions and values. The RICE principles for AI alignment are characterized as follows (Fig. 11.2):

- **Robustness:** Robustness refers to the resilience of AI systems when operating across diverse scenarios or under adversarial pressures, emphasizing not only their capabilities but also the correctness of their objectives (Ji et al., 2023). It ensures the system operates reliably under diverse scenarios and remains resilient to unforeseen disruptions. Robust AI systems must be able to handle black swan events and long-tailed risks, as well as a wide range of adversarial pressures (Carlini et al., 2024). For instance, an aligned language model should refuse harmful requests, yet models can be manipulated into causing harm through jailbreak prompts and other adversarial attacks. An adversarial robust model should function as intended, even when confronted with inputs designed to induce failure. Aligned systems must consistently maintain robustness

Fig. 11.2 Four key principles objectives for AI alignment

throughout their lifecycle, ensuring reliable performance regardless of the challenges they encounter.

- **Interpretability:** Interpretability requires that we know the AI systems' internal reasoning, particularly the complex decision-making processes within opaque neural networks (Räuker et al., 2023). This enables transparency and trust by making the system's operations more understandable to humans, allowing us to assess its actions and outcomes more effectively. It states that the operation and decision-making process of the system should be transparent and truthful.
- **Controllability:** It allows human direction of the system's behaviors and permits human intervention when necessary. AI systems should be under the guidance and control of humans. It guarantees that human intervention can promptly rectify any deviations or errors in the system's behavior.
- **Ethicality:** It adheres to global moral standards and respects the values upheld by human society. AI systems should adhere to society's norms and values. It ensures that the system avoids actions that violate ethical norms or social conventions such as showing bias against specific groups. This helps promote fairness, inclusivity, and ethical behavior in AI systems and ensures they operate in a manner that respects and upholds societal values.

These principles collectively guide the development of AI systems to align with human values and safety standards. Using these principles as a guide, the current landscape of alignment research can be divided into two main components such as **forward alignment** and **backward alignment** where forward alignment focuses on aligning AI systems through alignment training and backward alignment aims to gather evidence of the systems' alignment and regulate them effectively to prevent increasing misalignment risks.

11.4.2 Human Values

The incorporation of Ethicality into our RICE principles emphasizes the essential role of human values in AI alignment. AI systems must align not only with value-neutral human preferences such as the intentions guiding the tasks they are designed to carry out but also with moral and ethical considerations (Gabriel & Ghazavi, 2023). The research on human value alignment can be classified into the following three main themes (Ji et al., 2023):

- **Ethical and social values:** It aims to teach AI systems right from wrong. Ethical and social values include machine ethics, fairness, cross-cultural values, and social psychology.
- **Cooperative AI:** It fosters cooperative behaviors in AI systems. Cooperative AI also explores human cooperation through the lens of AI and examines how AI can facilitate cooperation among humans.
- **Addressing social complexities:** It provides frameworks for modeling multi-agent and social dynamics. The concept of "what is ethical" is often defined

within a social context; thus, its implementation in AI systems must also consider the complexities of social dynamics.

11.4.3 Machine Ethics

Machine ethics aims to ensure that AI systems understand and behave in morally acceptable ways, in contrast to the usefulness properties emphasized in alignment (Ren et al., 2024). Machine ethics focuses on ensuring that AI systems comprehend and act in morally acceptable ways, distinguishing it from alignment, which emphasizes the usefulness of AI systems. While alignment seeks to align AI responses with human goals and preferences, machine ethics delves into the ethical implications of AI behavior that promote the development of systems that serve human interests and adhere to ethical standards and principles. This approach aims to create AI that operates responsibly and ethically, considering the broader societal impact of its actions.

11.5 Bias and Fairness in AI

In AI, bias refers to systematic errors or prejudices that can arise from machine learning algorithms, leading to unfair or unequal outcomes. These biases can stem from various sources, including skewed or unrepresentative training data, biased algorithms, or biased interpretations of model outputs. Since AI systems learn from historical data, they often reflect the social biases and prejudices embedded in that data. If these biases are not addressed, they can perpetuate discrimination, reinforce harmful stereotypes, and further marginalize vulnerable groups. Ensuring fairness in AI requires actively identifying and mitigating these biases to prevent the unintended reinforcement of societal inequalities.

Bias and fairness in AI are crucial issues as AI systems and applications become increasingly integrated into daily life and decision-making in areas such as finance, healthcare, recruitment, and law enforcement. Ensuring fairness has become a critical aspect of the design and development of AI systems and applications. AI systems are often deployed in sensitive environments where they make significant, life-altering decisions, making it essential to prevent these decisions from exhibiting any discriminatory bias toward specific groups or populations (Mehrabi et al., 2021). Bias in AI can stem from skewed training data, algorithmic design flaws, or inadequate human oversight, leading to unequal outcomes that disproportionately affect certain groups based on attributes like race, gender, or socioeconomic status. Achieving fairness in AI requires addressing these biases by enhancing transparency, accountability, and inclusivity in the development and application of AI models.

11.5.1 Bias

Bias is an unfair prejudice or systematic error in AI systems. It can originate from multiple sources, including data collection methods, algorithm design, and human interpretation. AI systems (ML models) can learn and perpetuate existing patterns of bias found in their training data, leading to unfair or discriminatory outcomes. Identifying and addressing bias in AI is crucial to ensuring that these systems are fair and equitable for all users. This involves implementing strategies to recognize potential biases, improve data quality, and refine algorithms to promote just and inclusive decision-making (Ferrara, 2024). Bias in AI can emerge at various stages of the machine learning pipeline, including data collection, algorithm design, and user interactions. NIST classified the AI bias into the following three broad categories, where each of these categories contributes to harmful outcomes in distinct ways (Schwartz et al., 2022) (Fig. 11.3):

- **Statistical and computational biases:** Statistical and computational biases arise from errors that occur when a sample does not accurately represent the overall population. Unlike random errors, these biases result from systematic issues and can exist without prejudice, bias, or discriminatory intent. In AI systems, such biases manifest within the datasets and algorithmic processes of developing AI applications. They often occur when algorithms are trained on a limited data type, leading to difficulties in extrapolating beyond that data. These errors can stem from several factors, including heterogeneous data, the oversimplification of complex data into more straightforward mathematical representations, incorrect data inputs, and algorithmic biases related to overfitting and underfitting, the handling of outliers, and practices associated with data cleaning and imputation. This can lead to machine learning models that produce skewed or unfair outcomes. For instance, if an algorithm is trained primarily on data from a specific

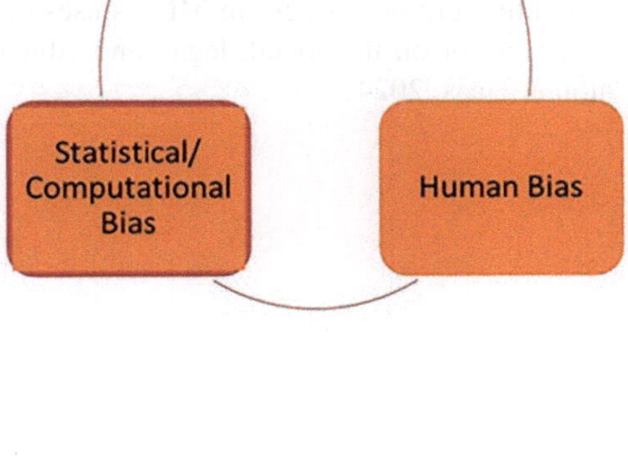

Fig. 11.3 Categories of AI bias

demographic, it may struggle to perform well for individuals outside of that demographic, leading to discriminatory practices in decision-making.

- **Systemic biases:** Systemic biases emerge from the procedures and practices of specific institutions that operate in ways that advantage certain social groups while disadvantaging or devaluing others. This type of bias arises from the structures, policies, and practices of institutions that favor certain social groups while disadvantaging others. Systemic bias can manifest in AI through biased datasets and institutional norms that influence how AI systems are developed, implemented, and used. For example, if an AI system is trained on data that reflects existing inequalities, it may perpetuate or amplify these disparities, leading to harmful outcomes for marginalized groups.
- **Human biases:** Human biases are systematic errors in thought that arise from reliance on a limited set of heuristic principles, simplifying complex judgments and predictions. These biases can influence how AI systems are designed, trained, and utilized, often unconsciously. For instance, developers may inadvertently introduce their own biases into AI algorithms or datasets, leading to biased outcomes. Users may misinterpret AI-generated results based on their preconceived notions, further exacerbating the potential for harm. Human biases are pervasive across institutional, group, and individual decision-making processes throughout the AI lifecycle and in the deployment of AI applications.

11.5.2 Fairness

AI is increasingly used in sensitive applications such as healthcare, criminal justice, and hiring, where unfair AI systems can result in serious harm, including discrimination, bias, and inequality. To address these issues, methods for improving AI fairness are being developed to reduce biases in algorithms and ensure equitable outcomes for all individuals. However, these methods face significant challenges in formalizing fairness such as defining what fairness means across different contexts and implementing fairness in practice. The complexity of AI models and incomplete or biased training data need an understanding of what constitutes fairness in various domains. Despite these obstacles, developing effective strategies to ensure fairness in AI is crucial to prevent harm and ensure AI systems are just, ethical, and trustworthy (Hendrycks, 2024a).

The literature on fairness in ML focuses either on the technical aspects of bias and fairness or on the social, legal, and ethical dimensions of ML discrimination (Caton & Haas, 2024).

11.5.2.1 Technical Aspects of Bias and Fairness

All technical fairness interventions are implemented at specific points in the ML pipeline: before (pre-processing), during (in-processing), or after (post-processing) model training. Figure 11.1 shows a high-level methodological component (framework) for achieving fairness in ML. Here we describe metrics, pre-processing, in-processing, and post-processing are the main four components of this framework.

11.5.2.2 Metrics in Fairness

Fairness metrics typically focus on either individual fairness (e.g., ensuring everyone is treated equally) or group fairness. Group fairness can be further categorized into within-group fairness (e.g., comparisons between women and men) and between-group fairness (e.g., comparisons between young women and Black men) (Fig. 11.4).

Pre-processing Approaches

Pre-processing techniques address the inherent biases, discrimination, and imbalances in the training data, particularly concerning sensitive or protected variables. This method involves modifying the input data before it is fed into the AI model (Caton & Haas, 2024). These approaches typically aim to alter the distributions of these variables or apply transformations to the data to eliminate discriminatory patterns. Preprocessing techniques aim to identify and correct biases in the data, ensuring that protected groups are fairly represented. The key approaches include:

- Rebalancing datasets: This technique addresses imbalanced representation by over-sampling underrepresented groups or under-sampling overrepresented ones. Adjustment in data distribution helps the model be less likely to learn biased patterns that favor one group over another.

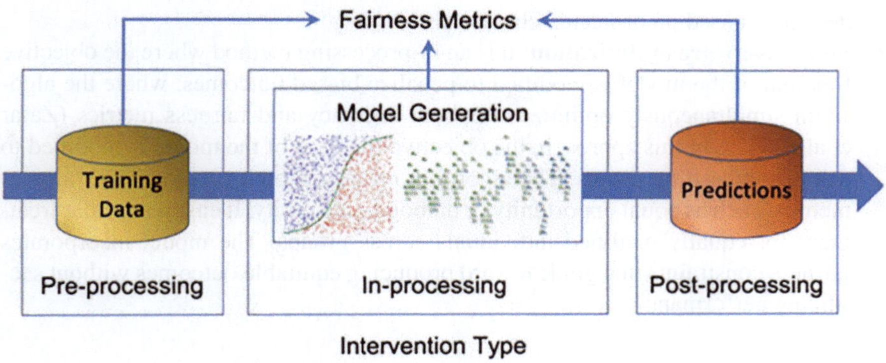

Fig. 11.4 A high-level framework for fairness in ML (Caton & Haas, 2024)

- Data transformation: This involves altering the data to eliminate correlations with sensitive attributes, such as race or gender. Transformation of data masks or removes these correlations, and models are less likely to inadvertently use protected characteristics in making predictions or decisions.

In-processing Approaches

In-processing techniques focus on adjusting the learning process of the AI algorithm to minimize bias while maintaining accuracy. These methods introduce fairness constraints during model training to ensure that the system produces fair outcomes without depending on protected attributes such as race, gender, or age. They recognize that certain modeling methods can become biased due to dominant features or distributional effects. They may also strive to balance competing objectives, such as accuracy and fairness. In-processing approaches tackle these issues by integrating one or more fairness metrics into the model's optimization functions, aiming to achieve a model configuration that maximizes both performance and fairness. The key in-processing approaches include:

- **Adversarial debiasing:** Adversarial learning can be employed to mitigate unfairness in AI by guiding a classification model to be more fair through in-training feedback or by adjusting the training data to reduce sensitivity to specific protected variables. In adversarial learning, an adversary is introduced to test whether the model's training algorithm is robust, and in fairness applications, the adversary aims to assess whether the training process is biased. If unfairness is detected, the adversary provides feedback, which is used to adjust and improve the model's fairness during training. Adversarial fairness approaches incorporate a fairness objective within the adversary, which actively penalizes the model when a sensitive attribute, such as race or gender, can be predicted from the model's outcomes. This feedback mechanism allows adversarial learning to act as an in-processing technique, directly enhancing the fairness of the model while it is being trained (Caton & Haas, 2024). The adversarial model acts as a "debiasing agent," forcing the main model to learn unbiased representations by making it harder for the adversary to correctly identify sensitive attributes (Yang et al., 2023). As a result, the model becomes less likely to make biased decisions based on protected characteristics.
- **Fairness-aware optimization**: It is an in-processing method where the objective function of the model is modified to penalize biased outcomes, where the algorithm simultaneously optimizes for both accuracy and fairness metrics (Zafar et al., 2017). In this approach, the objective function of the model is modified to penalize biased outcomes. The algorithm optimizes both accuracy and fairness metrics, such as equal opportunity or demographic parity. It ensures similar treatment for equally qualified individuals across groups. The model incorporates fairness constraints that guide toward producing equitable outcomes without sacrificing performance.

Post-processing Approaches

Post-processing techniques acknowledge that the outputs of an ML model may be unfair to certain protected variables or subgroups within these categories. These approaches typically involve applying transformations to the model's predictions to enhance fairness. Post-processing is highly adaptable, as it only requires access to the predictions and sensitive attribute information, without needing access to the underlying algorithms or models. This makes it particularly suitable for black-box scenarios, where the entire ML pipeline is not fully accessible. The key post-processing approaches include:

- **Threshold adjustment:** Threshold adjustment is a post-processing technique used to mitigate bias in AI models by modifying the decision thresholds for different groups. In classification tasks, a model typically uses a probability threshold to determine whether a prediction falls into a positive or negative class. However, if the model exhibits biased outcomes toward certain groups, adjusting these thresholds for different demographic groups can help achieve fairer results (Kamiran & Calders, 2012). This technique is often used in conjunction with fairness metrics such as equalized odds or demographic parity to ensure that the model's false positive and false negative rates are more consistent across different groups. For example, in a credit scoring model, if one demographic group has a higher rejection rate due to inherent biases in the data, the decision threshold for that group can be lowered, thereby increasing their chances of receiving a positive outcome (e.g., loan approval). Similarly, thresholds can be adjusted for other groups to balance the overall fairness of the model's decisions.
- **Equalized odds and equal opportunity:** Equalized odds post-processing is a fairness technique that adjusts the outputs of a trained classifier to ensure that the false positive and false negative rates are equalized across different demographic groups. This method addresses biases that may arise when certain groups are disproportionately affected by incorrect classifications, aiming to ensure that individuals from all groups have an equal likelihood of being correctly classified (Hardt et al., 2016). The core concept of equalized odds is to make the model's error rates both false positives and false negatives consistent across different groups defined by sensitive attributes such as race, gender, or age. The adjustment of the classifier's predictions in post-training ensures that the algorithm treats all groups fairly without altering the underlying model's structure or the data itself. For instance, in a hiring decision model, equalized odds would require that the rates at which qualified candidates from different demographic groups are incorrectly rejected (i.e., false negatives) or unqualified candidates are incorrectly accepted (i.e., false positives) are roughly the same. This prevents the model from disproportionately disadvantaging certain groups based on biased training data.

Determining the most appropriate approach for addressing fairness in ML can be complex. A significant advantage of both pre-processing and post-processing techniques is that they do not require altering the ML model itself, allowing the continued use of open-source ML libraries for training without modification. However, these techniques lack direct control over the model's optimization function, limiting their ability to fine-tune fairness directly. Furthermore, altering the data or model outputs can have legal implications and may reduce the interpretability of the results, which could conflict with data protection regulations that mandate explainability. In contrast, in-processing approaches offer the ability to optimize fairness during the training process itself. However, it requires access to and the ability to modify the optimization function, which is not always feasible depending on the model and system in use.

Social, Legal, and Ethical Aspects of Bias and Fairness
The social, legal, and ethical dimensions of machine learning discrimination highlight the urgent need for equitable algorithms and accountability mechanisms to prevent systemic biases and protect marginalized communities from harmful impacts. An algorithmic bias can perpetuate and exacerbate existing inequalities within society. The algorithms trained on biased data may yield discriminatory outcomes, impacting marginalized groups in areas such as hiring, lending, and law enforcement. Bias in training data can result in discriminatory outcomes that disproportionately affect marginalized groups. This situation raises significant legal concerns, particularly regarding anti-discrimination laws, as algorithms that maintain bias may contravene regulations aimed at ensuring equitable treatment (Barocas et al., 2023).

11.6 Summary

In this chapter, we explored the multifaceted landscape of AI Safety and Fairness focusing on key principles and methodologies to ensure responsible and equitable AI development and deployment. We began by examining catastrophic AI Risks, which highlight potential adverse outcomes arising from AI systems. Understanding these risks is essential for developers and stakeholders to implement effective safeguards and regulatory measures.

Next, we delved into the significance of transparency in AI systems emphasizing that clear communication regarding AI operations fosters trust and accountability. Transparency not only aids users in understanding decision-making processes but also helps identify and mitigate biases embedded within these systems.

Then the concept of AI Alignment was also discussed focusing on the necessity for AI systems to align with human values and societal norms including machine ethics. Proper alignment ensures that AI technologies act in accordance with user intentions and ethical guidelines. The exploration of machine ethics underscored the importance of integrating ethical considerations into AI design and deployment.

A significant challenge in AI is the issue of bias, where AI systems can produce unfair outcomes due to biases present in the training data, model design, or decision-making processes. We discussed different types of bias such as statistical and computational, systemic, and human bias which can lead to discriminatory outcomes for certain groups. Ensuring fairness in AI is crucial, specifically when AI systems influence decisions in sensitive areas like hiring, lending, and criminal justice. We also covered bias-mitigating methods, focusing on three key stages of AI systems including pre-processing, in-processing, and post-processing. Pre-processing techniques, such as dataset rebalancing and data transformation, adjust the data before training to minimize bias at its source. In-processing methods integrate fairness constraints directly into the training process, with approaches like adversarial debiasing and fairness-aware optimization helping to reduce bias within AI models. Post-processing strategies ensure fairness by modifying model outputs after training, using techniques such as threshold adjustment and equalized odds to correct biased predictions. Together, these approaches enhance fairness and reliability in AI systems. As AI safety and fairness is a multifaceted challenge it requires addressing both technical and ethical issues. AI Safety and Fairness concepts presented in this chapter addressed the following questions:

- What are the primary risks associated with AI technologies, and how can they be mitigated?
- Why is transparency important in AI systems, and how does it contribute to accountability?
- What is the significance of AI alignment, and how can it be achieved?
- What are the key objectives in AI Alignment?
- What are the key human values and ethical considerations in AI?
- How do machine ethics influence the development and deployment of AI systems?
- What are the different types of bias that can occur in AI, and how do they impact fairness?
- What is AI fairness and what are their types?
- What is an AI fairness framework for mitigating bias?
- What are the key methods for mitigating bias in AI, and how do they differ from one another?

References

AI-Safety-Summit. (2023). *Frontier AI risks*. Department for Science, Innovation and Technology. Retrieved from https://www.gov.uk/government/publications/frontier-ai-capabilities-and-risks-discussion-paper/future-risks-of-frontier-ai-annex-a#frontier-ai-risks

Barocas, S., Hardt, M., & Narayanan, a. A. (2023). *Fairness and machine learning: Limitations and opportunities*. MIT Press.

CAIS. (2024, October 2). *Center for AI safety*. Retrieved from Center for AI Safety: https://www.safe.ai/about

Carlini, N., Nasr, A. M., Choquette-Choo, C. A., Jagielski, M., Gao, I., Koh, P. W., et al. (2024). Are aligned neural networks adversarially aligned? *Advances in Neural Information Processing Systems, 36*.

Caton, S., & Haas, A. C. (2024). Fairness in machine learning: A survey. *ACM Computing Surveys, 56*, 1–38. https://doi.org/10.1145/3616865

Ferrara, E. (2024). Fairness and bias in artificial intelligence: A brief survey of sources, impacts, and mitigation strategies. *Science*. https://doi.org/10.3390/sci6010003

Fjeld, J., Achten, N., Hilligoss, H., Nagy, A. C., & Srikumar, M. (2020). *Principled artificial intelligence: Mapping consensus in ethical and rights-based approaches to principles for AI*. Berkman Klein Center Research Publication.

Gabriel, I., & Ghazavi, A. V. (2023). The challenge of value alignment: From fairer algorithms to AI Safety. In D. D. Hendrycks (Ed.), *Oxford handbook of digital ethics* (pp. 366–355). Oxford University Press. https://doi.org/10.1093/oxfordhb/9780198857815.013.18

Hardt, M., Price, E., Price, E., & Srebro, N. (2016). *Equality of opportunity in supervised learning. Advances in neural information processing system*, 29.

Hendrycks, D. (2024a). AI fairness concepts. In D. D. Hendrycks (Ed.), *Introduction to AI Safety, ethics and society*. Taylor & Francis. (forthcoming). Récupéré sur https://www.aisafetybook.com/textbook/fairness

Hendrycks, D. (2024b). *Introduction to AI safety, ethics, and society*. Taylor & Francis. (forthcoming). Récupéré sur https://www.aisafetybook.com/

Hendrycks, D., Mazeika, M., & Woodside, T. (2023). An overview of catastrophic AI risks. *arXiv*. Récupéré sur https://arxiv.org/abs/2306.12001

Ji, J., Qiu, A. T., Chen, A. B., Zhang, A. B., Lou, A. H., et al. (2023). AI alignment: A comprehensive survey. *arXiv preprint* arXiv:2310.19852. Récupéré sur https://arxiv.org/abs/2310.19852

Kamiran, F., & Calders, A. T. (2012). Data preprocessing techniques for classification without discrimination. *Knowledge and Information Systems*, 1–33. https://doi.org/10.1007/s10115-011-0463-8

Lipton, Z. C. (2018). The mythos of model interpretability: In machine learning, the concept of interpretability is both important and slippery. *Queue*, 31–57. https://doi.org/10.1145/3236386.3241340

Mehrabi, N., Morstatter, A. F., Saxena, A. N., Lerman, A. K., & Galstyan, A. A. (2021). A survey on bias and fairness in machine learning. *ACM Computing Surveys*. https://doi.org/10.1145/3457607

Räuker, T., Ho, A. A., Casper, A. S., & Hadfield-Menell, A. D. (2023). Toward transparent AI: A survey on interpreting the inner structures of deep neural networks. In *2023 IEEE conference on secure and trustworthy machine learning (SaTML)* (pp. 464–483). IEEE. https://doi.org/10.1109/SaTML54575.2023.00039

Ren, R., Basart, S., Khoja, A., Gatti, A., Phan, L., Yin, X., … Hendrycks, D. (2024). Safetywashing: Do AI safety benchmarks actually measure safety progress? *arXiv*. https://doi.org/10.48550/ARXIV.2407.21792.

Schwartz, R., Vassilev, A., Greene, K. K., Perine, L., Burt, A., & Hall, P. (2022). *Towards a standard for identifying and managing bias in artificial intelligence*. Special Publication (NIST SP), National Institute of Standards and Technology. https://doi.org/10.6028/NIST.SP.1270

Yang, J., Soltan, A. A., Eyre, A. D., & Clifton, A. D. (2023). Algorithmic fairness and bias mitigation for clinical machine learning with deep reinforcement learning. *Nature Machine Intelligence*, 884–894. https://doi.org/10.1038/s42256-023-00697-3

Zafar, M. B., Valera, I., Rodriguez, M. G., & Gummadi, K. P. (2017). Fairness beyond disparate treatment & disparate impact: Learning classification without disparate mistreatment. In *Proceedings of the 26th international conference on world wide web* (pp. 1171–1180). International World Wide Web Conferences Steering Committee. https://doi.org/10.1145/3038912.3052660

Chapter 12
AI Security Challenges, Opportunities and Future Work

12.1 Introduction

Artificial intelligence (AI) has significantly transformed and will continue to shape various aspects of our lives. Its applications are expanding across diverse sectors, including autonomous driving, healthcare, media, finance, industrial robotics, and Internet services (Huang et al., 2022). The widespread use of AI and its integration with the economy and society have led to enhanced efficiency and numerous benefits. However, these advancements also present challenges, particularly in terms of ethical concerns that could impact the existing social order. Issues such as privacy breaches, discrimination, unemployment, and security risks have emerged as significant consequences of AI systems, causing widespread concern.

AI systems are complex and multifaceted, and their successful development and deployment hinge on addressing challenges across three main components: AI algorithms, data, and AI applications. Figure 12.1 presents the basic general AI challenges related to the algorithms or models, the data they used, and their applications. Each of these components presents unique obstacles that can impact the effectiveness, fairness, and security of AI technologies. AI algorithms must be robust, transparent, and secure to ensure they function as intended without introducing vulnerabilities or biases. Data plays a central role in AI, and challenges related to privacy, bias, and proper handling of sensitive information are crucial to ensuring ethical use (Barocas et al., 2023). Similarly, AI applications also face practical difficulties such as discrimination, abuse, and unintended consequences, which arise when algorithms are applied in real-world scenarios (Noble, 2018).

D. P. Sharma et al., *Understanding AI in Cybersecurity and Secure AI*, Progress in IS, https://doi.org/10.1007/978-3-031-91524-6_12

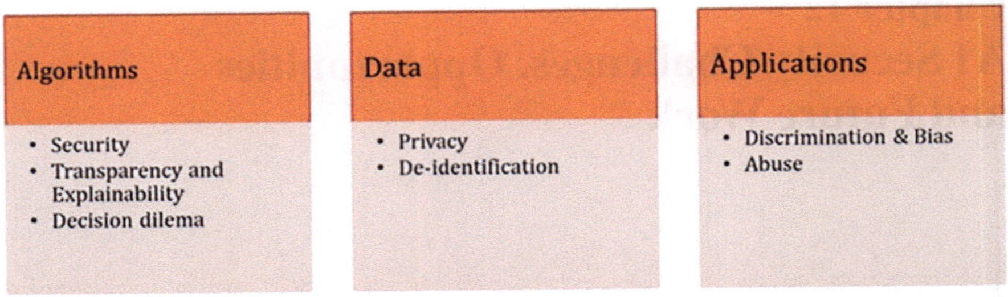

Fig. 12.1 Challenges with AI algorithms, data, and applications

12.2 AI Algorithms Challenges

AI algorithms face significant challenges related to security, transparency, explainability, and decision dilemmas. Security concerns arise from vulnerabilities in AI systems that can be exploited by attackers, leading to data breaches or manipulation. Transparency and explainability issues stem from the often-opaque nature of AI models, particularly in deep learning, making it difficult for users to understand how decisions are made (Castelvecchi, 2016). This lack of clarity complicates trust and accountability. Additionally, AI systems can encounter decision dilemmas, where they must choose between conflicting outcomes, raising ethical concerns about how these systems impact human lives and society. The description of different algorithm challenges is as follows:

- **Algorithm security:** Vulnerabilities and risks associated with AI models and algorithms that can be exploited to compromise their integrity, confidentiality, or reliability. AI algorithms present mainly two security challenges.
  - **Model parameter leakage:** There is the risk of algorithm or model leakage because the models are developed by training on data to optimize parameters. If these parameters are leaked, third parties can replicate the model without incurring the cost of acquiring and processing the training data, resulting in economic losses for the model owner.
  - **Security attacks:** An attacker might illegally alter the parameters of an AI model, degrading its performance and potentially leading to undesirable outcomes. In critical fields like medicine and autonomous driving, such vulnerabilities can threaten human safety and have severe consequences.
- **Algorithm transparency and explainability**: Many machine learning algorithms, especially deep learning and neural networks, operate as "black boxes", where the internal decision-making processes are opaque and difficult to interpret. This lack of transparency presents significant challenges, particularly in applications that impact individuals or society. Transparency and explainability are widely recognized as critical downsides of AI.

- **Algorithmic decision dilemma:** AI algorithms often produce unpredictable results, even for their designers. This unpredictability can lead to decision-making risks or dilemmas. For example, autonomous vehicles are designed to reduce traffic accidents but may face scenarios where they must choose between two undesirable outcomes, such as harming pedestrians or sacrificing passengers to avoid harm.

12.3 AI Data Challenges

AI data challenges primarily revolve around privacy protection and de-identification. As AI models rely on large datasets, often containing sensitive personal information, ensuring data privacy is critical to prevent unauthorized access and misuse. These privacy protection and de-identification challenges are further described as follows:

- **Privacy protection:** Privacy protection involves safeguarding individuals' data by laws like GDPR (GDRP, 2024) and CCPA (CCPA, 2018), ensuring that data is collected, stored, and used responsibly. The advancement of big data and AI has heightened tensions between technological progress and user privacy. Criminals now have more tools to obtain personal data at lower costs, leading to frequent data security breaches. Privacy protection is widely recognized as a critical ethical challenge in AI (Dilmaghani et al., 2019). Some key data security and privacy challenges include:
    - **Personal data risks:** The use of private or personal data in training exposes individuals to risks such as information leakage or unauthorized access.
    - **Misuse and malicious use**: Data can be tampered with or misused for malicious purposes, leading to issues like identity theft, discrimination, or fraud.
    - **Data breach:** Breaches in data security and privacy can affect individuals, organizations, institutions, and even national security.
- **De-identification:** De-identification is a technique used to remove or obscure personally identifiable information (PII) from datasets, allowing data to be used for analysis without compromising privacy. Traditional data protection laws aim to safeguard personal and sensitive information. However, data that has undergone de-identification techniques such as randomization or data synthesis is often excluded from these legal protections, as it is no longer considered "personal" or "sensitive". Some key de-identification-related challenges include:
    - **Misuse of de-identified data**: Once data is de-identified, it can be used, shared, or transferred without the same restrictions, raising concerns about potential misuse.
    - **Re-identification risks**: Advances in data analysis and cross-referencing techniques may enable the re-identification of de-identified data, compromising individual privacy.

- **Transparency and consent**: Individuals may not be fully informed about how their de-identified data is used, leading to ethical questions about consent and trust.

12.4 AI Applications Challenges

AI systems, while offering numerous benefits, face significant challenges related to discrimination and abuse. These challenges stem from biases in data, algorithms, or human oversight. These challenges are described as follows:

- **Algorithm discrimination and bias**: The outcomes of algorithms significantly influence AI system decisions. However, algorithmic discrimination or bias has been observed in various AI applications, such as racial bias in criminal justice systems and gender discrimination in hiring practices (Roselli et al., 2019). Discrimination occurs when AI systems inadvertently favor certain groups over others, such as in hiring algorithms that disproportionately favor one gender or race due to biased training data. This can lead to perpetuating inequalities and reinforcing social biases.
- **Algorithm abuse:** AI system abuse occurs when algorithms are used for purposes, methods, or scopes that deviate from their intended application, leading to adverse effects. For instance, facial recognition algorithms can enhance public security by identifying criminal suspects but may be misused to predict criminal potential based on facial features, which constitutes algorithm abuse (Castelvecchi, 2019). Abuse of AI refers to the misuse of AI technologies for harmful purposes, such as creating deepfakes, spreading misinformation, or automating cyberattacks.

12.5 Classification of Key AI Ethical Challenges

It is undeniable that AI systems primarily serve individuals and society, making it essential to analyze and address ethical issues or challenges from both individual and societal perspectives. Furthermore, as AI technologies become more integrated into daily life, their impact on the environment is also required to be considered. This section presents the classification of all key AI ethical issues and challenges into three distinct levels: individual, societal, and environmental (Huang et al., 2022). Figure 12.2 shows the key AI ethical issues and their categorization/classification into three levels.

Ethical concerns at the individual level involve the potential harm to personal rights, privacy, and well-being, including issues such as bias, surveillance, and autonomy. At the societal level, AI raises questions about its effects on social justice, inequalities, discrimination, and the disruption of job markets, leading to

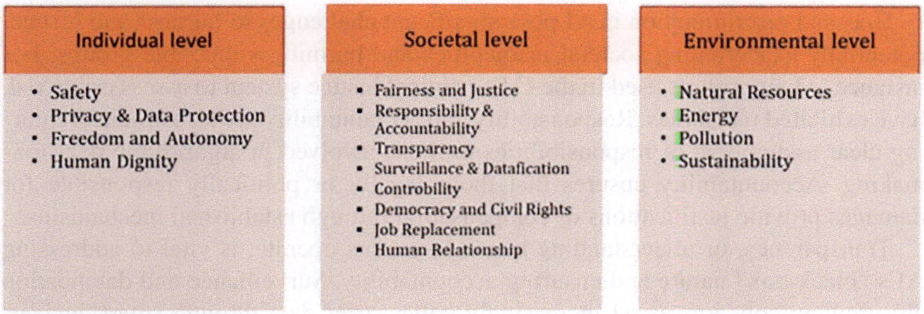

Fig. 12.2 Classification of key AI ethical issues/challenges into three distinct categories: individual, societal, and environmental levels

broader societal implications. Environmental ethical issues focus on the ecological footprint of AI, considering factors like the carbon emissions from training large models, resource consumption, and electronic waste. The description of each category based on the work is presented as follows:

12.6 AI Ethical Challenges at the Individual Level

AI has significantly impacted individuals' safety, privacy, autonomy, and human dignity. For example, autonomous vehicles and robots have occasionally caused accidents resulting in personal injuries. Privacy remains a critical concern, as AI systems often rely on vast amounts of user data to function effectively. This data collection raises serious privacy and data protection risks. Additionally, AI's influence on autonomy and dignity presents significant ethical challenges. Autonomy, the ability to think, decide, and act freely without external influence, may be undermined when AI-based decision-making becomes pervasive in daily life. Human dignity, a core human right that emphasizes respect and ethical treatment, must also be safeguarded in AI development. For instance, lethal autonomous weapon systems threaten to violate this principle, highlighting the importance of prioritizing dignity in AI technologies to protect individuals from harm.

12.7 AI Ethical Challenges at the Societal Level

At the societal level, ethical concerns center on the broad impacts of AI on communities, nations, and global well-being. Key issues include fairness and justice, responsibility and accountability, transparency, surveillance and datafication, AI controllability, democracy and civil rights, job displacement, and human relationships.

Bias and discrimination in AI pose significant challenges to fairness and justice, potentially exacerbating societal inequalities and harming vulnerable groups. For instance, AI algorithms used in the U.S. criminal justice system to assess crime risk have exhibited racial bias. Responsibility and accountability are also crucial, requiring clear assignment of responsibilities to those involved in algorithmic decision-making. Accountability ensures that those legally or politically responsible for damages provide justifications or compensation through established mechanisms.

Transparency, or understanding how AI systems operate, is vital to addressing AI's "black box" nature and ensuring accountability. Surveillance and datafication are growing concerns as AI increasingly collect user data through smart devices, contributing to mass surveillance. Safeguards must be implemented to ensure human control over AI systems.

Additional societal-level concerns include the impact of AI on democracy and civil rights, the displacement of jobs, and changes in human relationships, all of which require careful consideration and mitigation.

12.8 AI Ethical Challenges at the Environmental Level

AI's environmental implications focus on its effects on natural resources and the planet. While AI offers significant benefits, its widespread adoption entails environmental costs. The production of AI-related hardware such as chips, sensors, and storage devices consume substantial natural resources, including rare elements. The disposal of these devices at the end of their lifecycle contributes to environmental pollution.

Another critical issue is the high energy consumption required for AI's computational needs. To ensure long-term sustainability, AI must align with human development goals while preserving the planet's natural systems, which provide essential resources and ecosystem services. Key environmental concerns include resource consumption, pollution, energy costs, and the need for sustainable AI practices.

12.9 Stages of AI System's Lifecycle and Challenges

The typical system lifecycle or development process of an ML-based AI system involves the following stages: business analysis, data engineering, ML modeling, model deployment, and operation and monitoring (Nascimento et al., 2019). Each stage of the AI system development lifecycle can pose different ethical issues and challenges. Figure 12.3 shows the mapping of the key challenges associated with each stage of the AI system's lifecycle (Huang et al., 2022). The lifecycle usually begins with business analysis, which involves identifying and understanding the business problem to be solved and defining metrics for success. These metrics

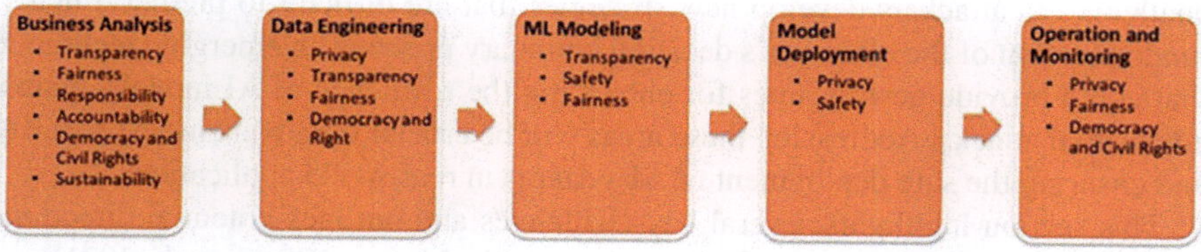

Fig. 12.3 Mapping of AI key ethical issues with each stage of the AI system's development lifecycle

should encompass both model performance metrics and key business performance indicators that the AI model is expected to improve.

The next stage, data engineering, focuses on activities such as data collection, labeling, cleaning, structuring, feature engineering, and other data-related operations. Following this, the process moves to the ML modeling stage, which generally involves an iterative process of algorithm selection or design, model training, and model evaluation. Once a satisfactory model is built, the process proceeds to the model deployment stage, where the ML model is integrated into organizational systems or made accessible via the web to receive data inputs and provide predictions. The operation and monitoring stage is the final stage that involves running the AI system which continuously evaluates its performance and impact.

Mapping ethical issues to the lifecycle stages of AI systems refers to identifying and addressing ethical concerns at each phase of an AI system's development, deployment, and use. This mapping indicates where ethical issues are most likely to arise or are predominantly caused by activities in each stage (Huang et al., 2022). Figure 12.3 depicts this mapping of the key ethical issues to specific stages of the AI lifecycle. This framework can guide the proactive identification and mitigation of ethical issues during the design and implementation of AI systems.

12.10 Future Research Directions

As AI systems continue to evolve, the landscape of adversarial machine learning presents numerous challenges that require further investigation. Future research directions in this field must address several critical areas to enhance the robustness and security of AI models. These include exploring the transferability of adversarial examples, which involves understanding how adversarial attacks can generalize across different models. Evaluating the robustness of defense methods remains essential to identify effective strategies against adversarial threats. Additionally, researchers need to focus on the difficulty in controlling the magnitude of adversarial perturbations, which can significantly impact the stability of AI systems. There is also a need for more attention to attacks beyond classification tasks, as current research has predominantly focused on classification models, leaving other applications vulnerable. The evolving threat of unknown unknowns poses a challenge, as attackers develop new strategies that are difficult to predict. Finally, randomization of the classifier's decision boundary presents an emerging technique that could provide new avenues for enhancing the resilience of AI models against adversarial attacks. Addressing these areas will be crucial for advancing AI security and ensuring the safe deployment of AI systems in real-world applications.

This section highlights several key challenges and outlines potential directions for future research aimed at addressing these critical issues (Oseni et al., 2021).

12.10.1 Transferability of Adversarial Examples

Adversarial examples in machine learning, particularly in deep neural networks, exhibit a phenomenon known as transferability (Wiyatno et al., 2019). This refers to the ability of adversarial examples crafted to deceive one model to also successfully mislead other models, even when the architectures, training datasets, or learning techniques differ. Transferability poses a significant security challenge, as adversarial examples generated for a specific model can exploit this property to attack another model without requiring access to its internal parameters, thereby enabling black-box attacks.

While empirical evidence strongly supports the existence of transferability, the underlying mechanisms driving this phenomenon remain inadequately understood. Notably, studies suggest that transferability might not be a universal property of all non-robust models, even in the presence of adversarial examples. In particular, the hypothesis regarding the ubiquity of transferability appears to be held inconsistently across different models and tasks.

In the case of deep neural networks, an intriguing future research direction lies in exploring the relationship between memorization in deep networks and the transferability property.

12.10.2 Evaluating the Robustness of Defense Methods

A significant challenge in the domain of adversarial machine learning is the lack of robust evaluation for existing defense mechanisms. The majority of existing defenses rely heavily on empirical evaluations, which often fail to provide robustness guarantees against unknown attacks (Wiyatno et al., 2019).

A promising future direction is to explore and develop theoretical frameworks that ensure provable robustness against adversarial attacks. The evaluation of defense methods against adversarial attacks remains an open research problem. Ensuring the robustness of these techniques requires the development of standardized evaluation protocols and more comprehensive metrics tailored to adaptive threat scenarios.

12.10.3 *Difficulty in Controlling the Magnitude of Adversarial Perturbations*

Adversarial example generation typically involves introducing small, imperceptible perturbations to input data with the aim of altering a neural network's predictions. However, determining the optimal magnitude of these perturbations presents a significant challenge. If the perturbations are too small, they may fail to produce effective adversarial examples, while excessively large perturbations become perceptible to humans, compromising their stealth and utility (Zhang & Li, 2020).

Striking the right balance between effectiveness and imperceptibility is critical yet complex, as it depends on various factors, including the architecture of the model, the characteristics of the input data, and the specific adversarial attack method employed. Consequently, developing methods that allow precise control over the magnitude of perturbations is an active area of research and a vital future research step toward understanding the adversarial vulnerabilities in neural networks.

12.10.4 *Lack of Research Focus on Attacks Beyond Classification Tasks*

Convolutional neural networks (CNNs) have achieved remarkable success in computer vision applications, driving a predominant focus on adversarial attacks targeting classification tasks such as image recognition and object detection (Moosavi-Dezfooli et al., 2016). While these applications are undeniably important, this narrow focus has led to a relative lack of research attention on adversarial attacks affecting other machine learning tasks. Although some studies have begun to investigate adversarial vulnerabilities in areas such as natural language processing, generative modeling, and reinforcement learning, these efforts remain disproportionately small compared to the extensive body of work addressing classification tasks. This research gap is concerning, as it is well-established in the literature that all machine learning models, including deep neural networks, are inherently susceptible to adversarial attacks.

Expanding research into adversarial threats against non-classification tasks, such as reinforcement learning, is essential. These tasks play a critical role in domains like autonomous systems, robotics, and game theory, where adversarial vulnerabilities could have severe real-world implications. A broader research focus will not only address these gaps but also contribute to the development of more robust and secure machine learning systems across a wider range of applications.

12.10.5 Evolving Threat of Unknown Unknowns

Unknown unknowns represent a significant threat to machine learning systems deployed in adversarial environments, akin to their critical role in cybersecurity challenges such as malware and intrusion detection (Biggio & Roli, 2018).

Unlike known unknowns, which are often modeled to simulate attacks in adversarial machine learning, unknown unknowns are unpredictable and can lead to high-confidence misclassifications. These arise when the inputs deviate substantially from the training data, revealing vulnerabilities in the model's ability to generalize. Addressing the threat posed by unknown unknowns requires machine learning systems to incorporate robust anomaly detection techniques capable of identifying and mitigating unforeseen inputs. However, the development of such capabilities remains in its infancy, and significant research efforts are needed to explore new pathways for detecting and responding to these elusive threats. Advancements in this area would not only enhance the security of machine learning systems but also improve their resilience in dynamic and adversarial environments.

12.10.6 Randomization of Classifier's Decision Boundary

Introducing randomization into the placement of a classifier's decision boundary has been proposed as a potential method for enhancing security against evasion attacks (Barreno et al., 2006). The idea is that randomization increases the effort required by adversaries to adaptively manipulate the decision boundary to achieve a targeted attack. Despite its promise, there have been relatively few studies investigating randomization as a viable defense strategy in literature. One key limitation of this approach is that randomization can also introduce a trade-off: while it may improve robustness against adversarial attacks, it can degrade the model's performance on clean data by increasing its initial error rate. This dual impact underscores the challenge of determining the optimal amount of randomization needed to strike a balance between robustness and accuracy.

The problem of identifying and implementing the right level of randomization to achieve robustness without significantly compromising classification performance remains an open research question, inviting further exploration in this area.

12.11 Conclusion

This chapter provides a comprehensive exploration of the multifaceted challenges and opportunities in securing AI systems. Beginning with a discussion of AI algorithmic, data, and application-specific challenges, we highlighted the vulnerabilities inherent in current AI systems, particularly in their reliance on vast datasets, complex algorithms, and diverse applications. These challenges were further categorized into key ethical concerns spanning individual, societal, and environmental levels, emphasizing the need to safeguard privacy, ensure fairness, and promote sustainability.

A detailed examination of the AI system lifecycle illustrated how challenges emerge at different stages, from data acquisition and model development to deployment and monitoring. We also delved into the growing complexity of adversarial attacks, discussing issues such as the transferability of adversarial examples, the difficulty in controlling perturbation magnitudes, and the evolving threat of "unknown unknowns." While evaluating the robustness of defense methods has made progress, there remains a significant research gap in addressing adversarial attacks beyond classification tasks.

Looking ahead, the future of AI security requires focused research on various open challenges. Notably, there is a need to understand the transferability of adversarial examples and improve the robustness of defense methods. The difficulty in controlling adversarial perturbations and the lack of research on attacks beyond classification tasks remain significant obstacles. The evolving threat landscape, characterized by unknown unknowns, requires adaptive strategies to address potential vulnerabilities. Additionally, randomization of classifier decision boundaries may offer a promising avenue for improving AI security. After reading this chapter, you should be able to answer the following questions:

- What are the AI security challenges and ethical issues?
- What are the main security challenges associated with AI algorithms, data, and applications?
- How do ethical challenges in AI manifest at the individual, societal, and environmental levels?
- What are the specific risks AI poses to privacy, autonomy, and human dignity?
- How does bias in AI systems impact fairness and justice?
- What environmental concerns arise from the widespread use of AI, and how can sustainability be integrated into AI systems?
- How do challenges emerge at various stages of the AI system lifecycle, and what impact do they have on system security?
- What are the potential future research directions in AI security?
- What are the implications of the transferability of adversarial examples on AI security?
- What challenges exist in controlling the magnitude of adversarial perturbations, and why is this significant?
- Why is there limited research on adversarial attacks beyond classification tasks, and which areas require further exploration?
- How does the randomization of classifier decision boundaries contribute to strengthening AI defense mechanisms against adversarial threats?

References

Barocas, S., Hardt, M., & Narayanan, A. (2023). *Fairness and machine learning: Limitations and opportunities*. MIT Press.

Barreno, M., Nelson, B., Sears, R., Joseph, A. D., & Tygar, J. D. (2006). Can machine learning be secure? In *2006 ACM symposium on information, computer and communications security (ASIACCS '06)* (pp. 16–25). Association for Computing Machinery.

Biggio, B., & Roli, F. (2018). Wild patterns: Ten years after the rise of adversarial machine learning. In *2018 ACM SIGSAC conference on computer and communications security (CCS '18)* (pp. 2154–2156). Association for Computing Machinery. https://doi.org/10.1145/3243734.3264418

Castelvecchi, D. (2016). Can we open the black box of AI? *Nature News, 20*.

Castelvecchi, D. (2019). AI pioneer: 'The dangers of abuse are very real. *Nature*.

CCPA. (2018). *California consumer privacy act (CCPA)*. State of California Department of Justice. Retrieved from https://www.oag.ca.gov/privacy/ccpa

Dilmaghani, S., Brust, M. R., Danoy, G., Cassagnes, N., Pecero, J., & Bouvry, P. (2019). Privacy and security of big data in AI systems: A research and standards perspective. In *IEEE international conference on big data (BigData)* (pp. 5737–5743). IEEE.

GDRP. (2024). *General Data Protection Regulation (GDPR)*. Retrieved April 2, 2024, from GENERAL DATA PROTECTION REGULATION (GDPR): https://gdpr-info.eu/

Huang, C., Zhang, Z., Mao, B., & Yao, X. (2022). An overview of artificial intelligence ethics. *IEEE Transactions on Artificial Intelligence*, 799–819.

Moosavi-Dezfooli, S.-M., Fawzi, A., & Frossard, P. (2016). DeepFool: A simple and accurate method to fool deep neural networks. In *2016 IEEE conference on computer vision and pattern recognition (CVPR)* (pp. 2574–2582). IEEE. https://doi.org/10.1109/CVPR.2016.282

Nascimento, E. D., Ahmed, I., Oliveira, E., Palheta, M. P., Steinmacher, I., & Conte, T. (2019). Understanding development process of machine learning systems: Challenges and solutions. In *2019 ACM/IEEE international symposium on empirical software engineering and measurement (ESEM)* (pp. 1–6). IEEE. https://doi.org/10.1109/ESEM.2019.887

Noble, S. U. (2018). *Algorithms of oppression: How search engines reinforce racism*. NYU Press. https://doi.org/10.2307/j.ctt1pwt9w5

Oseni, A., Moustafa, N., Janicke, H., Liu, P., Tari, Z., & Vasilakos, A. (2021). Security and privacy for artificial intelligence: Opportunities and challenges. *arXiv preprint* arXiv:2102.04661.

Roselli, D., Matthews, J., & Talagala, N. (2019). Managing bias in AI. In *The 2019 World Wide Web Conference (WWW '19)* (pp. 539–544). Association for Computing Machinery.

Wiyatno, R. R., Xu, A., Dia, O., & Berker, A. D. (2019). Adversarial examples in modern machine learning: A review. *arXiv preprint* arXiv:1911.05268.

Zhang, J., & Li, C. (2020). Adversarial examples: Opportunities and challenges. In *IEEE transactions on neural networks and learning systems* (pp. 2578–2593). https://doi.org/10.1109/TNNLS.2019.2933524

Chapter 13
Conclusion

The integration of artificial intelligence (AI) in cybersecurity has reshaped the landscape of digital defense, bringing new capabilities and challenges. As cyber threats evolve in complexity, AI provides a proactive mechanism to detect and mitigate attacks in real time. However, AI itself is susceptible to adversarial attacks, data manipulation, and biases, raising concerns about its security and trustworthiness. Understanding the interplay between AI and cybersecurity is essential for ensuring robust security frameworks while mitigating the risks associated with AI vulnerabilities. This book explores these dual aspects, presenting AI as both a tool for security and a target of cyber threats.

This book is structured into three key sections. The first section provides a foundational understanding of AI and its role in cybersecurity, covering topics such as cyber threat landscapes, AI applications in security, and fundamental machine learning models. The second section focuses on AI-driven security solutions, exploring how AI is used to protect networks, software, cloud environments, and IoT/OT systems from cyber threats. The final section examines securing AI itself, addressing adversarial attacks, privacy risks, ethical challenges, and frameworks for ensuring trustworthy and resilient AI models. For each topic in these sections, we created specific taxonomies to systematically classify techniques and models, explaining their mechanisms with detailed descriptions and supporting them with real-world examples to enhance clarity and applicability. By covering these critical aspects, this book offers a comprehensive guide for researchers, cybersecurity professionals, and AI practitioners seeking to harness AI's potential while safeguarding it against emerging threats.

The increasing reliance on AI in cybersecurity demands a deeper understanding of threat intelligence, attacker motivations, and predictive security mechanisms. AI-powered cybersecurity solutions enhance traditional approaches by detecting patterns of malicious behavior, identifying anomalies, and automating responses to cyber threats. However, AI-driven security is not without limitations. Adversaries continuously adapt, leveraging AI-powered attacks such as deepfake-based

D. P. Sharma et al., *Understanding AI in Cybersecurity and Secure AI*, Progress in IS, https://doi.org/10.1007/978-3-031-91524-6_13

impersonation, automated phishing campaigns, and adversarial perturbations that trick machine learning models. Addressing these challenges requires a comprehensive security framework that integrates AI-driven protection with ethical and regulatory considerations.

Machine learning (ML) and deep learning (DL) have become foundational in modern cybersecurity solutions, enabling systems to learn from vast amounts of data and improve their detection capabilities. Supervised, unsupervised, and reinforcement learning techniques contribute to security applications such as malware detection, fraud prevention, and behavioral analysis. Yet, as AI models become more advanced, they introduce new attack surfaces, including data poisoning, model inversion, and membership inference attacks. These vulnerabilities highlight the necessity of secure AI models that maintain robustness against adversarial manipulations while ensuring privacy-preserving mechanisms to protect sensitive information.

Cloud computing and the Internet of Things (IoT) present additional challenges in securing AI-driven environments. With the expansion of distributed AI architectures, securing data sovereignty, regulatory compliance, and data integrity across multiple jurisdictions has become a pressing concern. AI-based cloud security solutions leverage predictive analysis, automated threat response, and security orchestration, but misconfigurations, unauthorized access, and insider threats remain significant risks. Similarly, AI-driven IoT security must address device vulnerabilities, network-layer attacks, and firmware manipulation, ensuring the protection of smart environments, industrial IoT (IIoT), and operational technology (OT) networks.

MIX
Papier aus verantwortungsvollen Quellen
Paper from responsible sources
FSC® C105338

If you have any concerns about our products,
you can contact us on
ProductSafety@springernature.com

In case Publisher is established outside the EU,
the EU authorized representative is:
Springer Nature Customer Service Center GmbH
Europaplatz 3, 69115 Heidelberg, Germany

Printed by Libri Plureos GmbH
in Hamburg, Germany